David Ricardo. An Intellectual Biography

David Ricardo has been acclaimed – or vilified – for merits he would never have dreamt of, or sins for which he was entirely innocent. Entrenched mythology labels him as a utilitarian economist, an enemy of the working class, an impractical theorist, a scientist with 'no philosophy at all' and the author of a formalist methodological revolution. Exploring a middle ground between theory and biography, this book explores the formative intellectual encounters of a man who came to economic studies via other experiences, thus bridging the gap between the historical Ricardo and the economist's Ricardo.

The chapters undertake a thorough analysis of Ricardo's writings in their context, asking who was speaking, what audience was being addressed, with what communicative intentions, using what kind of lexicon and communicative conventions, and starting with what shared knowledge. The work opens in presenting the different religious communities with which Ricardo was in touch. It goes on to describe his education in the leading science of the time – geology – before he turned to the study of political economy. Another chapter discusses five 'philosophers' – students of logic, ethics and politics – with whom he was in touch. From correspondence, manuscripts and publications, the closing chapters reconstruct, firstly, Ricardo's ideas on scientific method, the limits of the 'abstract science' and its application, and, secondly, his ideas on ethics and politics and their impact on strategies for improving the condition of the working class.

This book sheds new light on Ricardian economics, providing an invaluable service to readers of economic methodology, philosophy of economics, the history of economic thought, political thought and philosophy.

Sergio Cremaschi is a former Reader of Moral Philosophy at the 'Amedeo Avogadro' University at Vercelli, Italy.

Routledge Studies in the History of Economics

John Locke and the Bank of England
Claude Roche

Poverty in Contemporary Economic Thought
Edited by Mats Lundahl, Daniel Rauhut and Neelambar Hatti

Thomas Aquinas and the Civil Economy Tradition
The Mediterranean Spirit of Capitalism
Paolo Santori

The Macroeconomics of Malthus
John Pullen

Competition, Value and Distribution in Classical Economics
Studies in Long-Period Analysis
Heinz D. Kurz and Neri Salvadori

David Ricardo. An Intellectual Biography
Sergio Cremaschi

Humanity and Nature in Economic Thought
Searching for the Organic Origins of the Economy
Edited by Gábor Bíró

European and Chinese Histories of Economic Thought
Theories and Images of Good Governance
Edited by Iwo Amelung and Bertram Schefold

For more information about this series, please visit www.routledge.com/series/SE0341

David Ricardo. An Intellectual Biography

Sergio Cremaschi

Routledge
Taylor & Francis Group

LONDON AND NEW YORK

First published 2022
by Routledge
2 Park Square, Milton Park, Abingdon, Oxon OX14 4RN

and by Routledge
605 Third Avenue, New York, NY 10158

Routledge is an imprint of the Taylor & Francis Group, an informa business

© 2022 Sergio Cremaschi

British Library Cataloguing-in-Publication Data
A catalogue record for this book is available from the British Library

Library of Congress Cataloging-in-Publication Data
Names: Cremaschi, Sergio, 1949- author.
Title: David Ricardo : an intellectual biography / Sergio Cremaschi.
Description: Abingdon, Oxon ; New York, NY : Routledge,
2022. | Series: Routledge studies in the history of economics |
Includes bibliographical references and index.
Subjects: LCSH: Ricardo, David, 1772-1823. | Economists—Great
Britain—Biography. | Economics—Philosophy. | Economics—
Moral and ethical aspects.
Classification: LCC HB103.R5 C74 2022 (print) | LCC HB103.R5
(ebook) | DDC 330.092 [B]—dc23
LC record available at https://lccn.loc.gov/2021024296
LC ebook record available at https://lccn.loc.gov/2021024297

ISBN: 978-0-367-75345-0 (hbk)
ISBN: 978-0-367-75347-4 (pbk)
ISBN: 978-1-003-16210-0 (ebk)

DOI: 10.4324/9781003162100

Typeset in Bembo
by codeMantra

Contents

About the author — ix

Preface: Science, logic, ethics and theology in Ricardo's intellectual biography — xi

1   Ricardo's *Sepharad* — 1
Twenty-one years in Ricardo's life 1
Anglo-Judaism from 1600 to 1793 3
Echoes from the Haskalah 5
Ricardo's education 5
Partial conclusions: the importance of being an outsider 13

2   Ricardo's encounter with the Quakers — 18
The Society of Friends 18
British Quakerism at the time of the French Revolution 20
The impossible marriage of a Jew with a Quaker 21
Ricardo's Quaker relations 25
Ricardo's involvement in a Quaker secession 26
Partial conclusions: the importance of being a husband 27

3   Ricardo's encounter with the Unitarians — 29
Scripture and reason 29
Ricardo's 'conversion' 31
Robert Aspland, the missionary to the Jews 33
Thomas Belsham, the Biblical scholar 34
James Lindsay, the campaigner for Toleration 38
John Bowring and Thomas Smith 40
Partial conclusions: the importance of being a Dissenter 41

4   Ricardo's encounter with geologists   46
   Ricardo's higher education 46
   The London Institution 50
   Chemistry after the phlogiston controversy 51
   Geology after the catastrophism-uniformitarianism controversy 52
   Richard Kirwan 53
   The Geological Society of London 56
   Controversies in geology: logic, definitions and causality 57
   From chemistry and geology to political economy 58
   Partial conclusions: the importance of a scientific education 62

5   Ricardo's encounter with philosophers and political economists   66
   Francis Horner and the Scottish philosophy 66
   Jeremy Bentham and the philosophic radicals 69
   James Mill, between Scottish philosophy and Benthamism 71
   Thomas Robert Malthus and the Cambridge philosophy 76
   Thomas Belsham and the Hartley-Priestley philosophy 79
   Jean-Baptiste Say and the idéologie *86*
   Partial conclusions: a high station among philosophers 88

6   Ricardo on logic and political economy   94
   Ricardian rhetoric 94
   Language and definitions 98
   Laws and causes 103
   Permanent causes and natural magnitudes 107
   Strong cases 109
   The redundancy of utility 112
   Ricardian logic and scientific practice 117
   Ricardian logic and policy advice 122
   Partial conclusions: a science without an art 124

7   Ricardo on ethics and political economy   130
   Moral impressions and the rational pursuit of happiness 130
   Just war 140
   Penal law and private morality 142
   Slavery 143
   Unlimited toleration 143
   Good government 146
   Ethics and the uses of political economy 152
   The miscarriage of all social theodicies 158
   Partial conclusions: neither a utilitarian nor theological optimist 166

Conclusions: a man from another planet 172

Appendix 175
The Christian Reformer: *text of the Christians' Petition 175*
The Christian Reformer & The Monthly Repository:
 presentation of the Christians' Petition in the House of Commons
 and the House of the Lords 178
The Sunday Times: *Daniel Whittle Harvey's obituary 179*
The Morning Chronicle: *Mill's Letter to the Editor 182*
The Monthly Repository: *obituary 184*
The Gentlemen's Magazine: *obituary 184*
The Penny Cyclopaedia: *George Porter's entry 186*
Index 189

About the author

Sergio Cremaschi (Bergamo 1949), 'Dottore in Filosofia' from the Catholic University, Milan, in 1971, after two years working in Somalia as a preparatory schoolteacher, was a research fellow at the Catholic University and Venice University and senior lecturer at the Catholic University. He was Reader of Philosophy of Religion at Ferrara University, then of Moral Philosophy at Turin University and the 'Amedeo Avogadro' University at Vercelli. He was a visiting fellow or lecturer at the New School for Social Research, New York, the Hebrew University, Jerusalem, Aarhus University, Denmark, Nuffield College, Oxford, and the University of Málaga. He has published on ethics and the history and philosophy of economics. He retired in 2014.

Preface

Science, logic, ethics and theology in Ricardo's intellectual biography

This book is a contextual reconstruction of an economist's intellectual biography. The purpose is to look where others did not, due to such factors as inapt modernisation, proneness to accept received views, constraints created by boundaries between disciplines and historiographic mythology.

The intent is to buy intellectual history, not in bulk but in retail. This implies looking at the co-text whenever the text is silent and at the context to make sense of what the text says or omits to say; it implies screening out what the text may not mean from what it may mean, reading utterances going beyond their literal meaning to seek out the speaker's communicative intentions, original audience and knowledge shared with that audience. Besides, it implies looking at the history of economic thought through spectacles different from the economist's, at the history of political ideas without reducing it programmatically to an appendix of the history of economic thought, at the history of ethics as the hotbed where the economic theory was sprouting and at the history of religion without secularist prejudice.

Sraffa's edition is still the starting point. He made an exceptionally meticulous job of it, despite not being a historian but rather an economist on loan to history. Yet, just like anyone else's, his personal history and theoretical approach carried a pre-comprehension that led to him emphasising some aspects and downplaying others. Thus a few chapters in the book try to cover blanks in Sraffa's reconstruction, including examples such as the story of the Italian liberal rabbi who, even before Ricardo was born, attempted to give a new start to London's Sephardic community; women intellectuals in the Delvalle-Ricardo family; the birth of the new magmatic science of geology; Unitarianism with its rationalist and socially committed message; and Ricardo's philosophical reading.

The reading of sources may be richer now than it was for our predecessors, but the merit is not ours. We are people of average stature standing precariously on the shoulders of giants. Dangerous though it may be for both our stability and the giants' backbones, coming after Schumpeter, Sraffa and Hollander gives us a broader perspective than any giant or person of above-average height could ever imagine. The attempt to detect real-world influences, sources, addressees and opponents may emancipate us from mental slavery to long-dead polemicists. It will certainly help to avoid mythological reconstructions such as Halévy's Benthamite Ricardo, Stigler's unphilosophical Ricardo and Hutchison's Millian Ricardo.

A century ago, under the sway of watered-down Hegelianism, intellectual historians used to believe that their work was done once they had detected one idea formulated by an author in another before him. It was a search for *causes* instead of *reasons,* or the construction of Biblical genealogies, like Bentham begot Mill and Mill begot Ricardo, Descartes begot the Physiocrats and the Physiocrats begot Ricardo or – proceeding in the opposite direction – the neoclassical begot modern economic science and Ricardo must have carried the genes of neoclassical theory. Intellectual history is not a quest for cause-effect relationships and Michelangelo's *Giudizio Universale* was no more an effect of the counter-Reformation than was Ricardo's economic theory an effect of the Industrial Revolution.

Besides, intellectual historians may dream that an author was influenced by another one merely because he was later raised to greater fame while being comparatively unknown at the time under discussion. Sometimes they read an implicit quote into a text because they forget that the same word has a different meaning in a different context. They may read documents in translation and forget that one word's shades of meaning in their own language are irrelevant when it stands for a Latin, Greek or Hebrew word. More often they may read documents in eighteenth-century English and take it for granted that words had the same shades of meaning or showed up in the same contexts as now. On other occasions, they may strive to stretch meanings of sentences to fit everything an author wrote to a system they assume he had in mind because they are prey to the myth of coherence: that whatever an author says reveals a system of ideas hidden in his mind. They often tend to read what an author said as being addressed to us with the intention of informing us of facts. However, when Ricardo complained about his neglected education to Mill, he was not informing us but expressing respect for Mill's education at a prestigious university and regret for having been excluded from such an opportunity himself. When he told Mary Edgeworth that he had been sent to Amsterdam to learn Dutch, French and Spanish but had hardly learnt anything he was not informing us, he was shielding himself from an Anglo-Irish aristocrat's prying curiosity vis-à-vis such an exotic bird as a Jew.

There are multiple reasons for the existence of opposing interpretations and misinterpretations in Ricardo scholarship. One is the comparative scarcity of documents, another is reticence by primary sources caused by a desire not to fuel English-chauvinist prejudice vis-à-vis a 'migrant', and a third one is the ballast of past attacks or hagiography. Layers of interpretations encrusted in the text may have done the rest, and the tendency to read sources naively and overlook contexts gives the coup de grace. Stories of 'influences' by Descartes, the Physiocrats, Bentham, Mill and – as if it were not enough – Dugald Stewart are part of the story together with the specular picture of the first *Metaphysikfrei* economist whose busy mind made no room for philosophy.

More than giving wrong answers, speculations about Ricardo's true philosophy, or lack of philosophy, answer the wrong kind of questions. The relationship between Ricardian economics and his intellectual outlook should be interpreted neither as the opposition of science to philosophy (Schumpeter, Hutchison and Stigler) nor as the dependence of science on one philosophy (Halévy). This relationship developed as a process through which distinct intellectual experiences equipped Ricardo with suggestions whereby he selected what he deemed useful to clarify his positive work or defend it from criticism. The owl of Minerva, as birdwatchers know, comes out at dusk. There was no Ricardian logic in 1811 to inspire his search for 'principles' that – as he wrote to Malthus on 17 April 1815 – could account 'for all the phenomena in an easy, natural manner' without getting lost in a 'labyrinth of difficulties' (*Works* 6, p. 214). Instead of schooling in one philosophy, Ricardo's equipment with logical, linguistic, epistemological, ethical and political ideas came from intellectual do-it-yourself. In order to respond to critics' objections he used material from several sources, a use that was not naive eclecticism but a search for arguments to fight what he felt to be delusory or ill-defined entities. His weapons came from an arsenal incompatible with epistemological realism, Cartesian rationalism or common-sense realism but bearing family resemblances with the Geological Society's legacy, Priestley and Belsham's epistemology and the post-scepticism of Adam Smith.

The author conducted part of the work during a stay at Nuffield College, Oxford in 2013, which was made possible by a Jemolo Fellowship. He is grateful to the Bodleian Library, the British Library, Harry Manchester College Library, the Fondazione Einaudi, Turin, and Milan Catholic University and State University libraries. He presented the first draft of a chapter at the 1999 ESHET Meeting in Valencia, others at the Conference of the International Society for Utilitarian Studies, Lisbon, 2003, the 2014 STOREP Conference in Bergamo, the 2018 ESHET Conference in Madrid, the International Conference on Economic Philosophy, Lyon, 2018, the 2018 STOREP Conference in Piacenza, the 2019 STOREP in Genova, the Conference on James Mill and John Stuart Mill/Classical Political Economy, Kyoto, 2019. The author is grateful to the discussants at these conferences, Nathalie Sigot, Andrea Salanti, Ghislain Deleplace, Yuji Sato. The author is also grateful to Maria Luisa Pesante, Salim Rashid, Antony Waterman, Arnold Heertje, Gilbert Faccarello, Heinz Kurz, Neri Salvadori, Richard Allen, Wilfried Parys, Emanuele Levi Mortera and Ryan Walter for sparing him mistakes. Finally, two friends played an essential role in the birth of this book: Marcelo Dascal, who worked with the present author on the controversy between Malthus and Ricardo, and Pier Luigi Porta, who introduced him to Ricardo scholarship.

Daphne Hughes has patiently eliminated from this book misprints, spelling mistakes and English usage infelicities. All that is left, of these and others blemishes, belongs to the author.

Chapter 7 contains materials from the following articles: 'Ricardo and the Utilitarians', *The European Journal of the History of Economic Thought*, vol. 11 (2004), no. 3 pp. 377–403. DOI: 10.1080/0967256042000246476; 'Theological themes in Ricardo's papers and correspondence', *The European Journal of the History of Economic Thought*, vol. 24 (2017), no. 4, pp. 784–808. DOI: 10.1080/09672567.2017.1315954.

Unless a translation appears in the bibliography, quotes from languages different from English are the author's translation.

Throughout the text and references, *Works* stands for Ricardo, D 1951–1973, *The Works and Correspondence of David Ricardo*, P Sraffa with the collaboration of MH Dobb (eds), Cambridge University Press, Cambridge. Published works, manuscript notes and speeches are listed in bibliographies. Reference to correspondence and evidence is made by citing volume and page of the Sraffa Edition. Thus, *Works* 6, p. 33 stands for *The Works and Correspondence of David Ricardo*, vol. 6, p. 33.

1 Ricardo's *Sepharad*

'Ricardo's father and family were of the Jewish persuasion; blameless according to the Decalogue, and uncommonly strict in all the peculiarities of the Mosaic ritual. In the same faith he was himself initiated' (*Sunday Times* 1823). This chapter attempts to reconstruct the first 21 years of Ricardo's life when he was first a child in a London Sephardi household and then, from the age of 13, a member of the Bevis Marks congregation. Primary sources are scarce, primarily because Ricardo's family did not like the idea 'that the public should be reminded of their Jewish and mercantile origin' (Mallet 1821–1822, 24 June 1830), but the chapter tries to add something to what is available on Ricardo's formative years (Sraffa 1955, pp. 16–43, Heertje 1970, 1975, 2015; Weatherall 1976, pp. 1–21; Henderson 1997, pp. 51–154).

Twenty-one years in Ricardo's life

The Memoir written by Ricardo's brother Moses is the most detailed report we have on his early life, albeit unfortunately less detailed than Moses would have liked to write. According to a contemporary, John Lewis Mallet,

> Mr Moses Ricardo, a brother of David Ricardo, and a man of information and intelligence who intended writing a Memoir of his brother, and was collecting materials for the purpose, has been prevailed upon by Ricardo's family to abandon the undertaking; and I understand from him that their real objection to it is, that as they are now people of fortune and of some consequence, and landed gentry, they do not like that the public should be reminded of their Jewish and mercantile origin.
>
> (Mallet 1821–182, 24 June 1830; cf. Sraffa 1955, p. 16)

Ricardo himself was far from enthusiastic about the idea of talking about his Jewish origins. The reasons were obvious. In Georgian England, Jews enjoyed a higher degree of integration than in any other European country, except for the Netherlands. Even so, there was a unique combination of comparatively liberal treatment at the legal and administrative level and 'genteel intolerance' through a perennial flood of 'casual garden-party anti-Semitism'

DOI: 10.4324/9781003162100-1

(Endelman 2002, p. 247). Anti-Jewish gossip was a temptation even for the author of *The Sunday Times* obituary, a liberal, a fellow-Unitarian and a close friend who did not, however, refrain from alluding to Jewish greed and sectarian spirit. The response to such subtle intolerance was assimilation. It was a step-by-step process passing through such stages as a mixed marriage and having the children christened, followed by adoption of the Christian mother's family name (Endelman 1999, pp. 257–258).

The tone of communication with non-Jewish partners was set by this climate, which 'encouraged them to mute their Jewishness, rather than accept it naturally or even reveal it' (Endelman 2002, p. 247; cf. Rubinstein 1996, pp. 60–66; Endelman 1999, pp. 86–117; Ruderman 2000, pp. 215–268) and encouraged the suppression of information about one's background, and the adoption of 'English' linguistic and cultural patterns. Modesty about one's skills was also advisable together with a constant attempt not to look too smart and, in case one could not help being so, not to show it around, for in England 'cleverness was bad form' (Ruderman 2000, p. 265). For these reasons we should read Ricardo's and his contemporaries' utterances in context, while bearing in mind not only contemporary and past events but also prevailing opinions. For example, when he complained that his education had been 'neglected' or that he 'learned nothing' during his stay in Amsterdam he was not addressing Sraffa, Weatherall, Heertje and Henderson but rather James Mill and Maria Edgeworth. When talking to the latter, the offspring of Anglo-Irish gentry, he may have been keen to avoid satisfying her curiosity vis-à-vis the exotic Judeo-Spanish world too much, a curiosity that was combined with a generous amount of sub-conscious prejudice, as revealed in the following comment in a letter to her mother:

> I have hitherto escaped saying anything about jews – nothing as rich as a jew has ever passed my lips but I live in fear that I shall not get out of the house without stumbling upon some thing belonging to jews.
>
> (Edgeworth 1971, p. 226)

The facts are that David was born in 1772 to Abigail Delvalle and Abraham Israel Ricardo, a wealthy Sephardi stockjobber born in Amsterdam in 1734, who had moved to London in 1760 and married the daughter of a respectable Sephardic family that had been living in England for three generations and had obtained British citizenship. Besides being an established businessman, the father became a *Parnas*, that is, an administrator of the Bevis Marks Synagogue (Hyamson 1951, pp. 437–439; Sraffa 1955, pp. 17–29). Abraham was a native speaker of Portuguese or Spanish (because of the family's stay in Leghorn and then in Amsterdam for several generations) and Dutch, and had learnt English as an adult. Abigail was a Spanish native speaker fluent in English. Until the early nineteenth century, the vehicular language in the schools affiliated with the Bevis Marks synagogue was Judeo-Spanish or Portuguese (Hyamson 1951, pp. 172–317; Mitchell 2000, pp. 101–104; Kerner 2018, pp. 239–248). We know that Spanish was still alive in 1803 when chief Rabbi

Isaac Mocatta, while stigmatising the congregation's state of spiritual decay, insisted that English should substitute Spanish as the language of sermons. However, a rule to this effect had to wait until 1840 (Gaster 1901, p. 154).

Anglo-Judaism from 1600 to 1793

After the expulsion of Jews from England in 1290 and attempts to set up tiny clandestine communities of Marrano immigrants in the sixteenth century, a flow of Iberian Marranos to London started between 1632 and 1655. Cromwell tried to secure legal status for Jews in England and, though his attempt failed, a situation of *de facto* toleration came into being allowing the establishment of a burial ground and a synagogue in Creechurch Lane in 1657. Throughout the eighteenth century, a steadily growing Sephardi community headed by an elite of brokers and merchants became a part of the London landscape. In 1697 twelve 'Jew Brokers' were admitted to the Royal Exchange. Besides the Sephardi community, an Ashkenazi congregation also came into being, in 1690, and kept steadily growing due to immigration from Poland via Germany and the Netherlands. Yet even though they had their magnates and managed to erect a new main synagogue in 1722, they remained for a long time a lower-class group (Roth et al. 2007, pp. 180–181).

Despite the growth and expansion of the Sephardi Congregation, latent centrifugal tendencies made themselves felt. One source was the appeal of Modern European philosophical and scientific culture to which the elite had enjoyed access during their phase as *Cristianos Nuevos* or *Christãos Novos* when a few of them had studied at Portuguese Universities. The authorities' temptation was to resort to disciplinary means to restore cohesion in a community made of members with varying degrees of orthodoxy. The Spinoza trial in Amsterdam was a symptom of a frenzy pushing authorities to the quite un-Jewish step of putting members' orthodoxy on trial, a duplication of the Spanish Inquisition's behaviour (Kaplan 2000, pp. 108–154). In London, sources of trouble were the same. The community came into being from an attempt to establish a foothold in London for the international Portuguese commercial network. It included people who felt themselves bound to this network by ethnic background and business partnerships but who had no intention of reverting to Judaism. It included others who resisted to the idea of abandoning their crypto-Jewish condition out of fear, habit or a desire to keep themselves free to return to Portugal. All this led to recurrent tension between the authorities and members or semi-members whose varying degrees of identification – or non-identification – went as far as stubborn resistance to circumcision (pp. 155–164). In a word,

> the centrifugal tendencies active within it from the first left their mark on its character and substance and drove many of its members from the centre to the periphery. The routes towards assimilation and integration into the surrounding community were traced upon it from its very first days.
>
> (p. 167)

Regulations of the London community established a duty to submit any-thing a member intended to publish in print – including calendars – to the authorities. Even staunch defence of Portuguese and Spanish was a side-effect of a policy of control over members and the erection of fences for pro-tection from the outside world (Kerner 2018, pp. 239–248). The Sephardi Synagogue appointed a succession of *Hahamim*, chief rabbis, often coming from places as distant as Smyrna and Oran. As Judeo-Spanish remained the community's main vernacular right up to the last decades of the eighteenth century, resettlement to London did not require of them a substantial ef-fort to adapt to a new milieu. Those who published on theological or legal subjects went on writing in Hebrew and Spanish, with the consequence of preserving the existing insulation from the Christian English-speaking outside world.

In 1701 the new Bevis Marks Synagogue was dedicated, an achievement marking the beginning of a new era, culminating in the three decades of David Nieto's magisterium (Roth et al. 2007, p. 180). Nieto, born in Ven-ice in 1654, had been a physician and preacher in Leghorn and was then appointed as *Haham* in 1702 (Gaster 1901, pp. 129–130; Katz 1994, pp. 196–201; Ruderman 1995, pp. 310–331; Karem 2004; Petuchowski 2007; Mimran 2012). He published *De la Divina Providencia*, that is, On God's Providence (Nieto 1704), a dialogue in good literary Spanish occasioned by the controversy aroused by a community member who had petitioned against him for professing Spinozism or Pantheism in his sermons. Another work, published in Hebrew and Spanish, was *Matteh Dan ve Kuzari Helehk Sheni*, or 'The Rod of Dan and Second Part of the book of Kuzari' (Nieto 1714) where he defends the Oral Law against the Karaites, an ancient Jewish sect whose doctrines, marked by rejection of the *Talmud*, was revived by former Marranos. A third work, also published in Hebrew and Spanish, is *Esh Dat, o sea Fuego Legal*, that is, 'Fire of the Law', which refuted Sabba-tianism, a Jewish sect founded by self-proclaimed Messiah Sabbatai Zevi from Smyrna who announced the abolition of the *Torah*, that is, the Biblical Law (Nieto 1715).

On balance, his work was a remarkable attempt to respond to the challenge coming from modern science and philosophy by resorting to philosophical arguments to defend rabbinic Judaism without indulging in traditionalist attitudes. For example, he goes so far as to adopt Sam-uel Clarke's denial of the distinction between miracles and natural events on the assumption that it is always God's will to determine the order of nature. Still, while doing so, he enlists on his side a Jewish authority such as Yehuda ha-Levi. What is more, he fights non-Jewish philosophers with their own weapons, discussing Aristotle's, Gassendi's, Descartes's and the chemical philosophers' conception of matter to show that, since their views are in conflict with one another, one 'cannot view any of them as certain but only as probable, plausible explanations of reality' (Ruderman 1995, p. 324; Kerner 2018, pp. 239–248).

Echoes from the *Haskalah*

Nieto's soon forgotten attempt took place half a century before Moses Mendelsohn's more successful one. Both tried to bring Judaism in touch with the eighteenth century while returning to its sources but

> Nieto's elaborated reconstruction of Judaism, like Mendelssohn's after him, could not withstand the mighty forces of Jewish social disintegration unleashed by the rapidly changing political and cultural ambiance of Enlightenment and revolutionary Europe.
>
> (Ruderman 1995, p. 331)

In the nineteenth century, when an echo of the reform movement launched by Mendelssohn first reached London, hardly anybody remembered Nieto's ideas. The Bevis Marks Synagogue had gone through 70 years of stagnation, not to say decay. At the beginning of the nineteenth century, when the community finally made a hesitant attempt to resist the tide, the dissolution of English Sephardi Judaism was already at an advanced stage.

In 1789 the great storm broke out, bringing promises of freedom, equality and brotherhood together with threats of war and – as happens in hard times – a revival of Millenarian movements among both Jews and English Dissenters, notably with the birth of Christian filo-Judaism. By this stage, the London Sephardi community had slipped into the afore-mentioned state of spiritual lethargy, and the spark of intellectual liveliness lit by Nieto had vanished. Such mental slumber contrasts strikingly with the swift transformation the community watched, without reacting, between the mid-century and the early decades of the next, by which time members had already integrated into all aspects of British social life (Katz 1994, pp. 254–259; Ruderman 2000, pp. 6–7, 215–216).

Ricardo's education

Primary education

In a letter to James Mill of 12 September 1817, Ricardo complained that his education had been 'neglected' (*Works* 7, p. 190) and he told Maria Edgeworth a few years later that his father had given him 'but little education', since he 'thought reading writing and arithmetic sufficient because he doomed [him] to be nothing but a man of business' (Edgeworth 1971, p. 226). What did he mean by such utterances? The former may be read as an expression of respect to James Mill, manifesting appreciation and envy for the higher education received at Edinburgh University under such a star as Dugald Stewart. In conversation with Maria Edgeworth, he was probably adopting the self-effacement tactic described by Endelman vis-à-vis a sympathetic Anglican counterpart whom he knew too well was soaked to the marrow of that kind of garden-party anti-Semitism he had sensed around him in the course of his life.

After a reasonable guess about what he may have meant, we can ask a different question, namely, what were the facts? What his brother Moses wrote about his education is remarkable for its self-censorship, owing to the abovementioned prejudice. Other sources are either as reticent or just ill-informed. The average message is that he received such an education as was customary for a boy destined for a commercial career. Once reticence is considered, and the word 'commercial' translated into 'Jewish', we may translate the above piece of information into something more explicit. David Ricardo, the son of a Sephardi stockjobber, could not attend a grammar school where he would have studied Latin, Greek, and Christian doctrine, but was sent to the school for boys associated with the Bevis Marks Synagogue, named *Sharei-Tikvah*, or Gates of Hope, where his father was an administrator. In 1664 the London Sephardi Congregation had set up a boys' school where

> instruction was given in Spanish, Portuguese and Ladino, although English was one of the secular subjects taught. A Talmudical college (*Beth hamedrash Heshaim*, 1664) was also sponsored by the Sephardim, and in 1730 the Villareal girl's school was founded to provide training in Judaism, languages, and domestic science.
>
> (Demsky et al. 2007, p. 204)

In more detail, the school for boys was re-organised first in 1735 and again in 1758 (Gaster 1901, pp. 35–36, 150–154; Hyamson 1951, pp. 94–95) with the result that, 'in addition to religious studies, the pupils were taught arithmetic and to read and write in English' (Black 1998, p. 14). Gaster (1901, p. 154) had dated the introduction of English as a subject 'as far back as the year 1772', but Roth (1964, p. 224) dates it back to 1735. Preparation for Bar Mitzvah at the age of 13 was a part of school education (Heertje 2015, pp. 219–221). A reasonable guess is that the education imparted included the prayers, reading in Hebrew, translating the Pentateuch into Spanish and, in the most advanced classes, reading bits of *Mishnah*, the first part of the *Talmud*, a collection of Rabbinic interpretations of Biblical commands drawn up at the beginning of the third century mostly in Hebrew (Wald 2007).

A comment on languages is in order here. In Amsterdam, the community languages were Spanish and Portuguese, and they remained so until Napoleonic times, when the elite 'adopted the Dutch language in their writings and speech' (Teensma 1993; Fuks-Mansfeld 2002, p. 165). The Spanish and Portuguese spoken in Amsterdam were no different from the language spoken in Spain and Portugal. Because of its wide use in the Sephardi diaspora, Spanish, 'became the main language of intellectual and literary creativity. Portuguese, by contrast, became the main language of the ordinances, and generally also the language of sermons in the synagogue' (Kaplan 2000, p. 144).

A similar co-existence of languages also persisted in the London community. Portuguese gradually lost weight as the flow of new Christians from Portugal ceased in the eighteenth century and, at the beginning of the nineteenth century, Portuguese was no longer understood and the question was whether to abandon Spanish as well. We will see that the study of Spanish, together with French and Dutch, featured in Ricardo's father's educational plans for his son. At the time the London school came into existence, it was a matter of course that the language for classwork was either Spanish (or Judeo-Spanish) or Portuguese, according to needs and possibilities. As already mentioned, from the mid-eighteenth century, the syllabus also came to include both English and arithmetic, but this does not imply that English was the language spoken in the classroom. It was not earlier than 1820 that English replaced Spanish entirely (Demsky et al. 2007, p. 214; cf. Mitchell 2000; Hyamson 1951, p. 312). Besides passages from the Hebrew Bible, it is also far from obvious what kind of written material was used for classwork. The renowned Amsterdam printers Menasseh ben Israel, Joseph Attias and David de Castro Tartas published literature in Spanish and Portuguese, as well as Hebrew, Yiddish, Latin and, exceptionally, Dutch and English (Wallet et al. 2007, p. 109). However, we do not know whether there were books for children.

A good number of David's brothers – it was a family of fifteen children – went into commercial professions. A notable exception was brother Moses, who became a surgeon, an option open to non-Anglicans since Medicine was a career accessible through apprenticeship without a University degree (Rubinstein 1996, p. 78) and cultivated scientific interests publishing papers in the *Annals of Philosophy* on properties of the distinct kinds of gas used for lighting (Ricardo, M 1821a, 1821b, 1821c, 1823a, 1823b; cf. Sraffa 1955, p. 56; Henderson 1997, pp. 138–139). Another exception was sister Sarah, who published a novel for children, arithmetic textbooks and essays on educational subjects (Cremaschi 2014). Less notable is the case for brother Samson, a member of the Stock Exchange, head of the British Iron Company and, in the 1850s, elected as Liberal MP, who published on currency defending his brother's project of a national bank (Ricardo, S 1837, 1838; cf. Sraffa 1955, pp. 60–61; 'Ricardo, Samson' 2011).

The most exceptional feature of David's education was a two-year stay at his uncle's home in Amsterdam. According to Sraffa, he may have attended the Amsterdam Jewish school (Sraffa 1955, p. 31), but this opinion rests on a cryptic sentence from the 'Memoir'. The education offered at Amsterdam's *Talmud Torah* at the end of the eighteenth century was a traditional programme of Jewish studies celebrated for its excellence in teaching and the width of its syllabus. According to the 1750 regulations, the age of compulsory education was from 5 to 14. In the lower classes, the emphasis was on correct reading in Hebrew, the study of the Pentateuch and its translation and commentary in Spanish. There was a senior branch called *Midrash Ets Hayim*, or Commentary of the Tree of Life, a name also adopted by the London parallel institution, offering three more years for the most gifted students with Hebrew as the language vehicle, the Talmud as the main subject and Hebrew grammar, rhetoric and poetry as minor subjects. Kaplan notes that 'one gains the impression that the social organisation and the curriculum of the *Ets Hayim* yeshiva in Amsterdam were quite like those of Jesuit schools and seminaries in Iberia at that time' (Kaplan 2000, p. 135). Rabbis appointed by Sephardi communities in Western Europe and the Mediterranean countries were among its former pupils. The lower classes, unlike the London 'Gates of Hope' still made no room for secular subjects and only in the last decades of the eighteenth century did the school 'modify its curriculum with the addition of French and Dutch' (Fuks-Mansfel 2002, p. 169).

In the Amsterdam archives there is no evidence of Ricardo's attendance at the school. In his first paper Heertje was favourable to Sraffa's hypothesis concerning the attendance at the Amsterdam *Talmud Torah* (Heertje 1970, p. 591) but he then shifted to the conjecture that young David 'received some education at the house on the Nieuwe Keizersgracht 70 in the form of reading, writing and arithmetic, French and Spanish from a private tutor' (Heertje 1975, p. 220).

Henderson objected that it is impossible to find any evidence of Ricardo's attendance at the Amsterdam school since there was no official registration but only private agreements with a teacher (Henderson 1997, pp. 147–153). However, his conclusion that 'there is no evidence that he received any particular Jewish education' (Heertje 2015, p. 220) is incompatible with his own opinion that the study of the *Talmud* did contribute decisively in moulding Ricardo's cast of mind' (p. 224).

Weatherall endorses the secular education hypothesis. He conjectures that Ricardo received the same kind of education as two other children of financiers – Isaac D'Israeli, six years older than Ricardo, who also stayed in Amsterdam for a few years, and Lyon Goldsmit, six years younger, who received a secular education at a public school (Weatherall 1976, p. 13). However, his argument relies on inaccurate information. D'Israeli's education, both in London and in Amsterdam, had always been under private tutors. His father enjoyed higher socio-economic status but a more marginal stance in the Community than Ricardo did and could thus opt for private tutors without facing too many drawbacks. Besides, the D'Israeli family had only recently arrived from Italy, and learning Spanish – the language spoken in the classroom – might have been considered too demanding for a boy who already had to learn English. In Goldsmit's case, he did attend an English school in London, something that in the 1780s still required extraordinary arrangements since all schools were still religious institutions. The reasons why Goldsmit's father had to resort to such an uncommon decision were related to the different situation of the Ashkenazi community, whose recently established school was a charity set up where no Ashkenazi magnate would have sent his son.

The 'Memoir', in its reticent style, declares that the father,

> who had designed him to follow the same business in which he was
> engaged, and whose transactions lay chiefly in that country, sent him
> thither not only *with a view* to his becoming acquainted with it, but also
> that he *might be placed* at a school of which he entertained a very high
> opinion.
>
> (Ricardo, M 1824, p. 3, emphasis added)

The phrasing adopted might suggest that the father had *considered* the possibility of enrolment at the Amsterdam *Talmud Torah* and, though he had
toyed with the idea, in the end young David could *not* be enrolled at this
school. The reason was certainly not the language, since the language spoken in the classroom in both London and Amsterdam was still Spanish. One
reason may have been that the level of education in Jewish subjects David
had reached might have been lower than the one expected for his age at the
Amsterdam school. As a consequence, his uncle may have resorted to a less
ambitious plan, namely tuition in Dutch, French and Spanish accompanied
by the preparation for Bar Mitzvah, perhaps under a teacher from the *Talmud
Torah*. Ricardo's already mentioned recollections reported by Maria Edgeworth describe his Amsterdam stay as an educational disaster. He mentions
the fact that his father had sent him 'at eleven to Amsterdam to learn Dutch,
French Spanish' but, he adds, 'I was so unhappy at being separated from my
brothers and sisters and family that I learned nothing in two years but Dutch
which I could not help learning' (Edgeworth 1971, p. 266).

So far, there is little we may safely conclude about the Amsterdam stay.
Nonetheless, an overlooked implication is that the very circumstance that his
father had *thought of* sending him to the Amsterdam *Talmud Torah* is a proof to
the fact that the 'common school' he attended in London was *not* a 'secular'
school.

George Porter, Ricardo's brother-in-law, also inspired by mandatory reticence, gave origin to the myth of a phantom Dutch commercial school while
writing that the father, being a member of the Stock Exchange, and

> designing his third son, David, for the same occupation, gave him a good
> but plain commercial education. For this purpose he was sent, when
> eleven years of age, to a school in Holland, where he remained for about
> two years.
>
> (*Penny Cyclopaedia* 1841)

Also, McCulloch wrote that Ricardo received 'such an education as is usually given to young men intended for the mercantile profession' (McCulloch
1846, p. xv). The French editor of Ricardo's writings mused that he attended
'a school in Holland, where they taught him the soundest theories of exchange and the art of the perfect businessman' dropping a casual remark

about 'the financial instinct that used to distinguish his race [...] since the famous days of the golden calf' (Fontayraud 1847, p. xvii).

A reasonable argument may be that Ricardo was neither educated under private tutors nor did he attend a non-existing 'secular' school. Admission of a Jewish boy to an English (Christian) school was an unusual business and, since Ricardo's father was a *Parnas*, sending his son to a Christian school would have been disgraceful enough. The father *considered* sending him to the Amsterdam Jewish school, and this implies previous attendance at the London Jewish school. The (conjectural but feasible) conclusion is that Ricardo received an education (in Spanish) where, besides English and arithmetic, he must have learnt Hebrew, prayers, the Pentateuch and – particularly if between the ages of 14 and 17 he had attended some night-classes at the *Ets Hayim* school – a smattering of *Mishnah*. According to this reconstruction, he did – as he once complained to Mill – lack the benefits of a 'classical education' but had nonetheless enjoyed those of an education that was just as demanding.

Further education

There is a blank concerning the private tuition Ricardo received after 'his father began to employ him in the Stock Exchange' (Ricardo, M 1824, p. 4). The 'Memoir' tells us that, during 'his intervals of leisure he was allowed any *masters for private instruction* whom he chose to have' (p. 3). It adds that 'in early life', besides his remarkable 'solidity and steadiness of character' (p. 4), he acquired 'those *habits of deep thinking*, which in the end enabled him to develop the most abstruse and intricate subjects [...] instead of receiving passively the ideas of others' (p. 4), thus showing '*a taste for abstract and general reasoning*' (p. 4). Later, 'at the age of nineteen and twenty, *works of that description which occasionally occupied his attention afforded him amusement and cause for reflection*' (pp. 4–5, emphasis added). Let us try decoding the above statements. We know that primary education at the *Sharei-Tikvà* school lasted until the age of fourteen. The *Ets Hayim* school offered three years further education to the most gifted students, among whom there had been David's maternal great grandfather. It is worth noting that it was a widespread custom, and somewhere an established rule – for example, in the 1690 regulations of the Metz community in Germany – that 'those aged 14–18 who did not continue attendance in a yeshivah were required to study at least one hour daily' (Demsky et al. 2007, p. 177). In Ricardo's father's expectations, one may easily imagine that private instruction would have meant attending a night-class at the *Ets Hayim* school. We may add that Ricardo was fourteen in 1787 when he started his further education and was sixteen in 1789 when the French Revolution began. It is not by chance that, four years later, David's avatar in correspondence with Priscilla was Osman, a character from Voltaire's *Zaïre*. The Memoir goes on to report that he

> never yielded his assent on any important subject, until after he had thoroughly investigated it. It was perhaps in opposing these strong prejudices,

that he was first led to that *freedom and independence of thought* for which he was so remarkable, and which has indeed extended itself *to the other branches of his family.*

(p. 5, emphasis added)

We can decrypt this statement more quickly than previous ones. It amounts to saying that Ricardo came to adopt Enlightenment ideas. These, in turn, might have sounded to his ear like a more radicalised version of Nieto's lesson, namely that the essence of religion is to love one's neighbour and the essence of the cult is to venerate the Deity, with varying external forms and bonds of universal brotherhood to connect humankind. The implication may have been that when religious rules clash with such a virtuous passion as sincere love for a woman, this should come first and the rules should give way. Led by such considerations – we may conjecture – David took the path of a mixed marriage, a path along which Moses, Sarah and other siblings followed him. It thus appears plausible to conclude that Ricardo's education was less 'neglected' than reports tend to suggest.

Intellectuals in the family network

Additional light may be shed by evidence of intellectual interests in the family network. The Ricardo family's Dutch branch was more than a family of merchants. A well-known figure is Immanuel Capadose, a medical doctor and man of letters (Ricardo 1891, p. 210) who left a doctoral dissertation in Latin (Capadose 1767). His nephew and adoptive son Abraham Capadose also became a physician, as well as a Christian convert who joined the *Réveil*, the Pietist Dutch movement fighting revolutionary and liberal ideas (Capadose 1843a, 1843b, 1851). Ricardo describes Isaac da Costa, the son of Ricardo's Dutch cousin Rebecca Ricardo, a doctor in Law and Philosophy and a poet (da Costa 1821–22, 1823, 1848–49) as 'one of the best poets in Holland' and 'a metaphysician' (Ricardo 1891, p. 207). With his wife Hannah Belmonte, he also converted to Christianity.

Coming to the English branch, the Delvalle had been a family of tobacco merchants. Ricardo's great grandfather Isaac was a member of the rabbinic tribunal, implying that he was a Talmudic scholar. He was among the pupils of the *Ets Hayim* at the time David Nieto was teaching in 1725. Sraffa (1955, p. 27) reports an incident, offhandedly defining it as a 'curious theological dispute'.

In fact, rather than curious, the dispute reveals a tendency to heterodoxy in Sephardi communities where neo-Karaitism and Sabbatianism exerted a certain fascination for former Marranos. A certain Isaac Barrientes, entering a class while Nieto was commenting on the burning-bush story from *Genesis*, interrupted the lesson claiming that Moses had learnt his philosophy from the Egyptians and adding that the very idea of the creation of the world by God was an Egyptian legacy. As to the episode of the burning bush, Moses had just dreamt it. The intruder also argued that God does not speak because he has neither mouth nor any other human organ. In the end, under pressure from outraged pupils, he proclaimed that salvation depends on compliance with divine law while orthodoxy is irrelevant (Gaster 1901, pp. 128–129). Note that the dissident's words resonate enough of neo-Karaitism (probably not Sabbatianism because of the role he assigns to divine law) and also smell of Masonic doctrines – the secret tradition of Egyptian wisdom to be found profusely in Voltaire's writings – while making room for the Enlightenment claim of a moral essence of religion.

Rebecca Delvalle, one of Ricardo's aunts, married a Christian engraver specialising in scientific publications (Sraffa 1955, p. 29) and she herself cultivated scientific interests that will deserve more detailed discussion in another chapter.

The advantages of a classical education

In 1823, after Ricardo's death, James Mill wrote in *The Morning Chronicle* that 'Mr Ricardo had everything to do for himself and he did everything [...] he had his mind to form, even his education to commence and to conduct' (*Morning Chronicle* 1823). Probably in reaction to Mill's exaggerations, Moses's Memoir declares that it is not true 'as has been insinuated, that Mr Ricardo was of a very low origin, and that he had been wholly denied the advantages of education' (Ricardo, M 1824, p. 4). As a matter of fact, there is almost no reference in Ricardo's correspondence to his Jewish education and, while he mentions his knowledge of Dutch, he mentions French and Spanish just as languages his father wanted him to learn, implying that what he learnt amounted to nothing. However, Ricardo also conveyed such information through speech acts addressing specific hearers, and we should keep in mind not just his modesty and taste for understatement but also his communicative intentions in the given context. He may have avoided boosting his cultural diversity for the same reasons as any other Jew of the time would have done, and may have felt it was better not to mention that, while the gentry's offspring enjoyed the opportunity of studying one modern and two classical languages, he had enjoyed the delights of one dead language and three living ones. He never mentioned Hebrew – the knowledge of which, at least at a minimal level, was a prerequisite for bar-Mitzvah – nor did he ever give any proof of acquaintance with Biblical or Talmudic subjects, but this silence hardly amounts to evidence of his receiving a 'secular' education. The above-mentioned self-effacement strategy may account for such silence in terms of communicative strategies vis-à-vis rooted prejudice.

At any rate, the little we know about Ricardo's education highlights more exciting aspects than 'neglect'. The circumstances described seem to imply that the education he received was neither enough to make a scholar nor was the 'practical' education current among the English lower middle class. Everything considered we could say that, not unlike other religious outsiders such as Isaac Watts and Joseph Priestley who were denied access to Oxford or Cambridge, he received a kind of education that enabled him to achieve equally remarkable results. Even Mill, in a letter of 19 October 1817, admitted that this might have been an asset, insofar as it left him free from 'prejudices' created by current education (*Works* 7, p. 196).

Thus, even though young Ricardo did not enjoy the advantages of a 'classical education', this would only imply that his mind missed the opportunity of being shaped by Latin and Greek grammar – the joys of Aorist! – but at least had the opportunity, together with Dutch, French and Spanish, of exerting itself with the simple and logical structure of Hebrew, which was no less formative than the somewhat cumbersome grammar of Latin and Greek (Henderson 1997, pp. 142–143). Furthermore, the study of three modern languages on top of an ancient one beat by four to three the standard fare of the gentry's offspring, consisting as it did of Latin, Greek and French. Nonetheless, for lack of practice, as an adult he may have virtually forgotten any Hebrew and even Spanish, but was still fluent in Dutch and had a working knowledge of French. Sraffa wrote that he 'could understand French but spoke too little of it to keep up a conversation' (Ricardo 1891, p. 178). In fact, at the beginning of his grand tour on the continent, he wrote from France that his 'imperfect knowledge of the language' (Ricardo 1891, p. 181) prevented him from asking local people precise enough questions on the places they were visiting. In a letter to Mill from Koblenz of 4 August 1822, he writes:

> I converse with very few. I do not know enough of French to keep up a conversation in that language, but I do very well when I can find any one who can speak French, and understand English. I met one or two in Holland [...] and I had pleasure in speaking to them.
>
> (*Works* 9, pp. 212–213)

Once in Germany, the problem had become that of finding local people who could speak French. He once reports, yet, of 'a vehement dispute in French' with somebody trying to cheat him where Swiss currency was concerned (Ricardo 1891, p. 224). In Geneva he reports having had a hard time when thrown into the middle of a conversation in French, but having a sense of relief when he could talk in English with Sismondi (p. 271) and, once in Italy, he reports having made an effort on several occasions to find somebody who could speak French (p. 330). What is more, he read Say's *Traité*, Dumont's compilations from Bentham's manuscripts and Pierre Bayle's *Dictionnaire*.

Partial conclusions: the importance of being an outsider

1. Ricardo was born a member of the London Sephardi Community, a distinct group with its own religious, legal, educational and charitable institutions whose everyday language was a mix of Judeo-Spanish and

Portuguese while educated adult males could read Hebrew. He received a far from ordinary school education from the ages of 5 to 14, followed by part-time education for another three more years, which was not as bad as he and contemporary sources tended to represent it. If by chance he had received some minimal Talmudic instruction, he may have drawn from that the intellectual practice of asking questions and looking for logical contradictions.

2. No break with his religious community took place before the age of 21. He was simply cast out for marrying a non-Jew, which severed family relations but involved no official act implying loss of personal status as a Jew.

3. Marshall's jibe about Ricardo's 'Semitic' mind (Marshall 1885, p. 12) is just one example of chauvinism combined with a due amount of pseudo-scientific racial theories. 'Semitic' is an adjective denoting a linguistic group, not a population, and the Sephardi Jews had some degree of in-marriage for centuries but had not so much to share, qua population, with the Ashkenazi.

4. His biography was that of a Sephardi Jew, the son of a Portuguese-Italian-Dutch immigrant and a third-generation descendant of Spanish immigrants who grew up in a religious, cultural and linguistic minority receiving a non-standard education which opened up for him the Hebrew language, the Bible, the Mishnah, and in a milieu where intellectual excellence was highly valued. Such a biography made him an intellectual outsider, and his intellectual and moral assets came primarily from the circumstance of being a citizen of two worlds.

References

Unpublished

Mallet, JL 1821–1825, *Manuscript Diary*, Bodleian Libraries MSS, Oxford, Facs. d. 145–146.

Published

Black, G 1998, *JFS. A History of the Jews' Free School, London since 1732*, Tumseden Publishing, London.

Capadose, I 1767, *Dissertatio Medica Inauguralis de Mensium Tardatione* [Inaugural Medical Dissertation on the Cycle's Delay], apud Theodorum Haak, Lugduni Batavorum.

Capadose, A 1843a, *Aan mijne geloofsgenooten in de Nederlandsche Hervormde Gemeente te 'sGravenhage* [To my fellow believers in the Dutch Reformed Congregation in 'sGravenhage], no publisher details, Den Haag.

Capadose, A 1843b, *Overdenkingen over Israëls Roeping en Toekomst* [Reflections on Israel's Vocation and Future], Amsterdam.

Capadose, A 1851, *Rome en Jerusalem* [Rome and Jerusalem], Utrecht.

Cremaschi, S 2014, 'Sarah Ricardo's Tale of Wealth and Virtue', *History of Economics Review*, vol. 60, no. 2, pp. 30–49. DOI: 10.1080/18386318.2014.11681263.

da Costa, I 1821–1822, *Poëzy* [Poems], 2nd edn, Kruzeman, Haarlem.

da Costa, I 1823, *Bezwaren tegen den geest der eeuw* [Objections to the Spirit of the Century], Herdingh, Leyden.

da Costa, I 1848–1849, *Israël en de Volken; een overzicht van de geschiedenis der Joden tot op onzen tijd*, 2nd edn, Bohn, Harleem; Engl. transl. 1850, *Israel and the Gentiles: Contributions to the History of the Jews. From the Earliest Times to the Present Day*, Nisbet, London.

Demsky, A; Moriel, Y; Bortniker, E; Graff, G; Pilch, J; Shachar, B & Abramovitch, S 2007, 'Education, Jewish', in F Skolnik (ed.), *Encyclopaedia Judaica*, vol. 6, Thomson Gale, Detroit, MI, pp. 159–214.

Edgeworth, M 1971, *Letters from England 1813–1844*, C Colvin (ed.), Clarendon Press, Oxford.

Endelman, TM 1999, *The Jews of Georgian England, 1714–1830. Tradition and Change in a Liberal Society*, University of Michigan Press, Ann Arbour, MI. DOI: 10.3998/mpub.7895.

Endelman, TM 2002, *The Jews of Britain, 1656 to 2000*. University of California Press, Berkeley. DOI: 10.1525/9780520935662.

Fontayraud, A 1847, 'Notice sur la vie et les écrits de David Ricardo', in *Œuvres complètes de David Ricardo*, Guillamin, Paris.

Fuks-Mansfeld, RG 2002, 'Enlightenment and Emancipation, from c.1750 to 1814', in J Blom, RG Fuks-Mansfeld & I Schoeffer (eds), *The History of the Jews in the Netherlands*, Littman Library, Oxford, pp. 164–191.

Gaster, M 1901, *History of the Ancient Synagogue of the Spanish and Portuguese Jews*, Printed for private circulation, London.

Heertje, A 1970, 'Enkels Opmerkingen Over Het Leven van David Ricardo' [A Few Remarks on the Life of David Ricardo], *De Economist*, vol. 118, no. 6, pp. 588–597.

Heertje, A 1975, 'On David Ricardo (1772–1823)', *The Jewish Historical Society of England. Transactions. Sessions 1970–73*, vol. 24, pp. 73–81.

Heertje, A 2015, 'Jewish Background', in H Kurz & N Salvadori (eds), *The Elgar Companion to David Ricardo*, Elgar, Aldershot, pp. 216–224. DOI:10.4337/9781784715489.

Henderson, JP 1997, *The Life and Economics of David Ricardo. With Additional Chapters by J.B. Davis*, WJ Samuels & GB Davis (eds), Kluwer, Dordrecht.

Hyamson, AM 1951, *The Sephardim of England. A History of the Spanish and Portuguese Jewish Community, 1492–1951*, Methuen, London.

Kaplan, Y 2000, *An Alternative Path to Modernity. The Sephardi Diaspora in Western Europe*, Brill, Leiden.

Karem, Y 2004, 'Nieto, David (1654–1728)', in HCG Matthew & B Harrison (eds), *Oxford Dictionary of National Biography*, vol. 40, Oxford University Press, Oxford, pp. 898–899.

Katz, D 1994, *The Jews in the History of England, 1485–1850*, Clarendon Press, Oxford.

Kerner, A 2018, *Lost in Translation, Found in Transliteration: Books, Censorship, and the Evolution of the Spanish and Portuguese Jews' Congregation of London as a Linguistic Community, 1663–1810*, Brill, Leiden.

Marshall, A 1885, *The Present Position of Economics*, Macmillan, London.

McCulloch, JMR 1846, 'Sketch of the Life and Writings of Mr. Ricardo', in *The Works of David Ricardo*, JMR McCulloch (ed.), edn used: Murray, London, 1888, pp. xv–xxxiii.

Mimran, S 2012, 'Une minorité et son guide spirituel: la communauté séfarade de Londres et le rabbin David Nieto (1701–1728)' [A Minority Group and Its

Intellectual Leader: The London Sephardi Community and Rabbi David Nieto (1701–1728)], *Revue française de civilisation britannique*, vol. 17, no. 2, pp. 37–60. DOI: 10.4000/rfcb.671.

Mitchell, B 2000, 'Language Usage in Anglo-Sephardi Jewry', *European Judaism*, vol. 33, no. 1, pp. 99–108. DOI: 10.3167/ej.2000.330113.

Morning Chronicle 1823, 'Mr. Ricardo', *The Morning Chronicle*, Monday September 15, p. 1 (Reprinted in the Appendix of this book).

Nieto, D 1704, *De la Divina Providencia o sea Naturaleza Universal o Natura Naturante, Tratado Theologico* [Of Divine Providence, That Is, Universal Nature or *Natura Naturans*], in M Artigas (ed.), *Segunda antología sefaradí: continuidad cultural (1600–1730)*, Editorial Verbum, Madrid, 2013, pp. 209–226.

Nieto, D 1714, *Mateh Dan y segunda parte del Cuzari* [Dan's Rod and Second Part of the Letter to the Kuzars' King], in M Artigas (ed.), *Segunda antología sefaradí: continuidad cultural (1600–1730)*, Editorial Verbum, Madrid, 2013, pp. 237–265.

Nieto, D 1715, *Esh Dat ò Fuego Legal* [The Law's Fire], in M Artigas (ed.), *Segunda antología sefaradí: Continuidad cultural (1600–1730)*, Editorial Verbum, Madrid, 2013, pp. 266–278.

Penny Cyclopaedia 1841, 'Ricardo, David', in *The Penny Cyclopaedia*, vol. 19, pp. 507–508, Knight, London (Reprinted in the Appendix of this book).

Petuchowski, J 2007, 'Nieto, David (1654–1728)', in F Skolnik (ed.), *Encyclopaedia Judaica*, vol. 15, Thomson Gale, Detroit, MI, p. 261.

Ricardo, D 1891, *Journal of a Tour on the Continent*, in *Works* 5, pp. 177–352.

Ricardo, M 1821a, 'On the Comparative Advantage of Illumination by Gas Produced from Oil and from Coal', *Annals of Philosophy*. New Series, vol. 1, no. 3, pp. 209–215.

Ricardo, M 1821b, 'Further Observations on Oil and Coal Gas', *Annals of Philosophy*. New Series, vol. 1, no. 4, pp. 383–385.

Ricardo, M 1821c, 'Reply to Mr. Low on Oil and Coal Gas', *Annals of Philosophy*. New Series, vol. 2, no. 1, pp. 44–47.

Ricardo, M 1823a, 'On the Advantages of Oil Gas Establishments', *Annals of Philosophy*. New Series, vol. 5, no. 3, pp. 218–222.

Ricardo, M 1823b, 'Observations on Sir W. Congreve's Report on Gas Light Establishments', *Annals of Philosophy*. New Series, vol. 6, no. 1, pp. 1–12.

Ricardo, M 1824, 'A Memoir of David Ricardo', in *Works* 10, pp. 3–15.

Ricardo, S 1837, *Observations on the Recent Pamphlet of J. Horsley Palmer, Esq. on the Causes and Consequences of the Pressure on the Money Market*, Knight, London.

Ricardo, S 1838, *A National Bank the Remedy for the Evils Attendant upon our Present System of Paper Currency*, Richardson, London.

'Ricardo, Samson' 2011, in WD Rubinstein, M Jolles & HL Rubinstein (eds), *The Palgrave Dictionary of Anglo-Jewish History*, Palgrave Macmillan, Houndsmill, p. 799. DOI: 10.1057/9780230304666.

Roth, C 1964, *A History of the Jews in England*, 3rd edn, Clarendon Press, Oxford.

Roth, C; Krausz, E & Kershen, AJ 2007 'London', in F Skolnik (ed.), *Encyclopaedia Judaica*, vol. 13, Thomson Gale, Detroit, MI, pp. 179–184.

Rubinstein, WD 1996, *A History of the Jews in the English-Speaking World: Great Britain*, MacMillan, Houndsmill.

Ruderman, DB 1995, *Jewish Thought and Scientific Discovery in Early Modern Europe*, Yale University Press, New Haven, CO.

Ruderman, DB 2000, *Jewish Enlightenment in an English Key. Anglo-Jewry's Construction of Modern Jewish Thought*, Princeton University Press, Princeton, NJ.

Sraffa, P 1955, 'Addenda to the Memoir', in *Works* 10, pp. 16–106.

Sunday Times 1823, 'David Ricardo', *The Sunday Times* September 14, 3rd edn, p. 1 (reprinted in the Appendix of this book).

Teensma, BN 1993, 'The suffocation of Spanish and Portuguese among Amsterdam Sephardi Jews', in J Michman (ed.), *Dutch Jewish History* III, Hebrew University of Jerusalem, the Institute for Research on Dutch Jewry, Jerusalem & van Gorcum, Assen, pp. 137–177.

Wald, SG 2007, 'Mishnah', in F Skolnik (ed.), *Encyclopaedia Judaica*, vol. 14, Thomson Gale, Detroit, MI, pp. 319–331.

Wallet, B; Michman, J; van Bekkum, W; Braesz, C & Adler, I 2007, 'Amsterdam', in F Skolnik (ed.), *Encyclopaedia Judaica*, vol. 2, Thomson Gale, Detroit, MI, pp. 108–110.

Weatherall, D 1976, *David Ricardo. A Biography*, Nijhoff, The Hague.

2 Ricardo's encounter with the Quakers

Abraham Ricardo's family lived

> not far from that of an eminent surgeon of the name of Wilkinson. Ricardo formed an honourable attachment to one of the daughters of this gentleman; she was beautiful, accomplished, and amiable; but she was not of the seed of Jacob.
>
> (*Sunday Times* 1823)

This chapter reconstructs the circumstances of Ricardo's marriage with a Quaker and its consequences on his life, intellectual interests, and moral and political commitments, arguing that contacts with Quaker milieus contributed to shaping his interests in natural science and his philanthropic and political commitments.

The Society of Friends

More than a dissenting sect

As a consequence of his marriage, Ricardo was left from 1794 to 1808 in a religious no man's land. The Society of Friends, his wife's religious community, was more than a dissenting sect. In the beginning, it looked like a movement of spiritual renewal with the ambition of addressing the whole of British Society. At the time of Cromwell's Commonwealth, its founder George Fox was the most influential among preachers of spiritual renewal from an inner experience of 'illumination'. Their message was the existence of an Inner Light whose authority was superior to any other, including the Scriptures. They added that 'forms' and 'opinions', that is, preaching, sacraments and theological doctrines might be set aside as useless. The still preserved public worship amounted to silent prayer meetings. From the very beginning, they suffered harsh repression. After 1660, with the restoration of the Monarchy, the Quakers became the first target to hit, before other dissenters, since their refusal of such practices as oaths made them look like dangerous revolutionaries. Their courage in facing martyrdom contributed to spreading their

DOI: 10.4324/9781003162100-2

message and their numbers at the end of century reached about 20,000 (Frost 1986, pp. 2085–2090).

Quaker anti-theology

At first, Quaker preachers hardly thought of formulating a doctrine. They accepted the main doctrinal articles of early Christianity, no less than the contents of the Scriptures. Nevertheless, more than doctrinal formulas, they considered them to be the expression of an inner revelation. They rejected the pillars of Calvinist theology, from justice as justification, to the corruption of human nature and the Socinian doctrines, the specular opposite of Calvinist theology. Their novel claims were the existence of an Inner Light, a gift granted to everybody, and its effect in uplifting to full perfection the individual who has been 'convinced' by such immediate revelation.

Implications for everyday life were, first, faith in radical equality between human beings; second, simplicity in one's lifestyle, including dress, nourishment and diversions; third, the refusal of any human hierarchy; fourth, a duty of truthfulness, the implication of which was the refusal to take oaths. Besides, Quakers promoted religious freedom, attacked established Churches and refused to pay tithes. Reasons alleged for refusal were that the Civil Government should not interfere in matters of religion and private conscience and that compulsory support of the ministers of any Church is both incompatible with the liberty which the Gospel confers on the children of God and a violation of 'common justice' (Jones 1921, pp. 148–153). A strict application of the Evangelical precept of love for our neighbours carried with it refusal of war and resistance to conscription.

In the last quarter of the seventeenth century, some organisation was set up, with weekly prayer meetings and monthly and annual business meetings to make decisions on all sorts of practical matters. Typically, the first written texts produced were not theological writings but so-called 'Disciplines', that is, sets of practical rules. After the first decades, when Quaker preachers lost hope of converting the whole of Christianity, not to say humankind, to the authentic original preaching of Christ, they gradually adopted a different view of the Society of Friends as a 'rest' – a Biblical concept – called to profess testimony of the true spirit of Christ.

After the 1689 Edict of Toleration, the Society evolved into one more dissenting sect, ruled according to a growing body of rules and moral precepts, both enforced with increasing rigour (Frost 1986, pp. 2690–2692). Robert Barclay produced the first theological formulation of the Inner-Light doctrine. In his Latin *Apologia* of 1676, also published in English in 1678, he presented this doctrine as the third way between Calvinism and Socinianism. His theological theses on the 'true foundation of knowledge' declare that the highest happiness consists in the real knowledge of God coming from 'Divine revelation and inward illumination', 'which is evident, and clear of itself' (Barclay 1678, p. 3) independent of the 'Test, either of the outward testimony of the Scripture, or the natural reason of Man' and is 'the only sure and certain way to attain the true and saving knowledge of God' (p. 8).

The rise of a Quaker middle class

One striking example of the unintended-results principle is the Quakers's rise on the social ladder. In a single century they in fact changed from a scattered flock of peasants to a lively urban middle-class group, including a commercial elite gradually taking hold of vital sectors of the economy: in the eighteenth century the banking system, in the nineteenth century the iron industry, textiles and the railways. Barclays British bank still bears the name of the Quaker merchant James Barclay, the first of its founding partners. One reason for such social climbing was a tendency to shift from agriculture to commerce so as to avoid paying tithes to the established Church. Another reason was an ascetic lifestyle fostering industry and parsimony. A third one was their growing reputation for honesty that secured customers. Forced emigration to America also turned into a blessing, yielding the advantages granted by belonging to a network stretching across the Atlantic, giving near-monopoly over Atlantic trade (Freeman 2015). Every blessing brings a price to pay; in this case, the prevalence of newly established Quaker 'forms' over the original Quaker spirit (Sykes 1958; Davies 2000). In a word, the Quakers 'found themselves to be both losers and winners at the beginning of the modern era', and their story was 'the tragedy of a failed nonviolent revolutionary initiative, which came at a key moment of transition into the capitalist world order we have inherited' (Gwyn 1995, p. x).

Another side of the same freezing of a revolutionary movement was an increasingly mystical spirituality, classified by most historians as 'Quietism', analogous to contemporary Catholic Quietism recommending a state of psychological passivity to keep ready to hear the divine calling. It consisted of simplicity and humility, refusal of theological speculation, a feeling that reason is no use as a guide in one's life, and a sense of one's indignity, strangely contrasting with the Quaker belief in a personal call from God. Such mysticism without theology was an unstable compound that could precipitate into either liberal theology or moralistic traditionalism. In fact, in the last decade of the eighteenth century, two distinct currents crystallised: the Orthodox Evangelicals and the Rationalist Liberals (Frost 1986, pp. 2692–2694). It was at this time that Ricardo came to be in touch with the Quakers.

British Quakerism at the time of the French Revolution

The crisis started with the Irish secession. In 1797, Irish Quaker Abraham Shackleton started a controversy with his Meeting's Elders about the 'Hebrew wars'. He refused to believe that Biblical passages enjoining war and massacre of the Canaanites were the words of God, on their incompatibility with the precept to love one's enemies. The National Yearly Meeting of Ireland for

1798 took sides with the Elders, decreeing that 'a standard should be lifted up against the spirit of speculation and unbelief' and that Friends should be 'disowned' who 'persist in maintaining such sentiments and doctrines' (Jones 1921, p. 295). The result was that influential Irish Friends sided with Shackleton giving birth to the 'Irish movement'. This movement was

> primarily an intellectual awakening. It was directed against crude views, against the excessive application of discipline, especially in matters pertaining to marriage regulations, against invasion of personal liberty of thought, against the tendency to adopt evangelical phraseology and habits of mind.
>
> (p. 298)

Hannah Barnard's case provided the occasion for expansion of the secession to England. She was an American Quaker Minister, an extraordinarily gifted woman who had become renowned for her inspired and edifying preaching. No one ever raised doubts about her faithfulness to the best of Quaker tradition until 1797, when the Hudson monthly Meeting gave her permission to travel to Europe 'on a religious concern'. In Ireland, she preached everywhere with the local Societies' satisfaction until she discussed with Shackleton's supporters the issue of the 'Hebrew wars', manifesting identical opinions. As a result, the Meeting refused to issue a certificate authorising her to travel on the Continent as a preacher on her 'erroneous views about war' and refusal to accept a literal reading of scriptural passages (Jones 1921, pp. 299–307). After American members accused her of faithlessness, Deism and Atheism, the Hudson Monthly Meeting disowned her in June 1802. The case polarised two opposed camps of orthodox-evangelicals and liberal-rationalists.

The impossible marriage of a Jew with a Quaker

Refusal of marriage celebrated by a priest meant refusal of one of those 'forms' which Fox had declared unnecessary because the Meeting's members were just witnesses, the spouses were the only ministers in marriage, and its substance lay in the expression of the spouses' will. In point of doctrine, this was hardly revolutionary since even the Roman Catholic Church taught the same. The difference was in practice. As the Friends crystallised into one more sect, their revolutionary calls to universality turned into the opposite, that is, a sectarian exclusionary rule. The prohibition against celebrating marriage by the rite of the established Church became the prohibition to marry any non-member, no matter if according to Quaker ritual (Jones 1921, pp. 189–190; Davies 2000, p. 197) and, unsurprisingly, this was one more point criticised by the liberal alignment. In the first half of the nineteenth century, the fact of sticking to this rule carried a demographic catastrophe for the British Quakers, with a dramatic fall in numbers resulting from the exclusion of 5,000 members who had entered into mixed marriages. In mid-century, the point was finally re-examined, and the regulations modified in 1859 (Jones 1921, p. 951).

At about the age of 20, in the early 1890s, Ricardo started a romance with Priscilla, one of Quaker surgeon Josiah Wilkinson's daughters. The love story met with disapproval by both families but with graver consequences on Ricardo's side. His marriage meant an interruption of relations with his family and de facto exclusion from the Sephardi Synagogue. The reason was non-recognition of his marriage as valid even though it applied to the act as such, without affecting his legal status as a Jew (Rosenthal et al. 2007, p. 376). This story is what we might read, through the smokescreen of reticent language, in a letter from Maria Edgeworth to her mother on 14 November 1821. She writes:

> When Mr Ricardo Senr. was paying his court to Mrs Ricardo *some of their friends* not approving of their attachment they corresponded for some time under the feigned names of Osman and Jesse and they afterwards agreed that they would call their eldest son *Osman*.
> (Edgeworth 1971, p. 264, emphasis added)

Edgeworth gives us a clue about the climate in which the wedding took place. The fact that David adopted the name Osman as a pseudonym is revealing. It is a name he had found in *Zaïre*, a piece by Voltaire, the eighteenth-century apostle of toleration, written in 1732 and translated in 1736 being then repeatedly performed in London's theatres (Voltaire 1736). Orosmane, or Osman in English versions, is a Sultan who loved a Christian woman named Zaïre (Weatherall 1976, p. 25; Henderson 1997, pp. 180–182). The source of Priscilla's *nom de plume*, instead, is unclear. Weatherall fancies that it could have been Jessie instead of Jesse, and thus a Scottish name reflecting the popularity of Scottish ballads at the time (Weatherall 1976, p. 26). Edgeworth's editor makes a more sensible suggestion, namely that it alludes to Jessica, the daughter in Shakespeare's *Merchant of Venice* who falls in love with a Christian against her father's will (Colvin 1971, pp. xxiii–xxiv). One more is that Jesse, or Yishai, is the name of King David's father. No less reticent than Edgeworth's report is the Memoir when declaring that Ricardo's father

> was a man of good intellect, but uncultivated. His prejudices were exceedingly strong; and they induced him to take the opinions of his forefathers *in points of religion*, politics, education &c., *upon faith, and without investigation*. Not only did he adopt this rule for himself, but he insisted on its being followed by his children; his son, however, never yielded his assent on any important subject, until after he had thoroughly investigated it. It was perhaps *in opposing these strong prejudices*, that he was first led to *that freedom and independence of thought* for which he was so remarkable, and which *has indeed extended itself to the other branches of his family*.

Soon after he had attained the age of twenty-one, Mr Ricardo *married*; and this threw him upon his resources, as he *quitted his father* at the same time.

(Ricardo, M 1824, p. 5, emphasis added)

Whittle Harvey, the already mentioned *The Sunday Times* editor, had been, so to say, more outspoken when writing that

Ricardo's father and family were of the Jewish persuasion; blameless according to the Decalogue, and uncommonly strict in all *the peculiarities of the Mosaic ritual*. In the same faith he was himself initiated [...] The father's residence was at Bow, not far from that of an eminent surgeon of the name of Wilkison [sic]. Ricardo formed an honourable attachment to one of the daughters of this gentleman; she was beautiful, accomplished, and amiable; but she was not of the seed of Jacob, and perhaps *had not the inheritance of Rachel*. The old man forbade his son's union with a Christian; and upon his persevering, deprived him of his share of the business. Ricardo was, however, firm in his attachment, which the event proves to have been made with that judgment which was the leading feature of his character; and so he married the lady, and became a Christian, attaching himself to the Unitarian Chapel, in Essex-street, where he and his family have regularly attended the instructions of Mr Belsham.

(*Sunday Times* 1823; emphasis added)

The reticence of the two former accounts contrasts with the generous concessions to prejudice in the last one, but these are two faces of a coin, that is, we may better understand reticence when reminded of ubiquitous prejudice.

Priscilla and David married in December 1794 with an Anglican priest acting as a civil servant who officiated the marriage (Sraffa 1955, p. 38; Henderson 1997, pp. 165–166). This procedure responded to legislation from 1753 establishing that, apart from Jewish and Quaker marriages, a Church of England Minister should officiate at all other marriages, an odd enough arrangement but one providing at least a context where marriage between a Jew and a Quaker became possible (Weatherall 1776, p. 25; Sraffa 1955, p. 38). Thus, it was love what led Ricardo to a break with his family and congregation.

Henderson (1997, p. 163) fancies his abandonment of religious practice before marriage but on no better evidence than the average behaviour of twentieth-century American teenagers. At the time, such a dropping out of religious practice by a teenager living in a Jewish household was almost inconceivable. The mentioned break with Ricardo's parents lasted till the father surrendered to the force of things and sought reconciliation some time after the mother's death and shortly before his own in 1812 (Weatherall 1976, pp. 26–28). We cannot say whether the mother was more of a hardliner, or whether it was just time to cause the surviving parent's surrender. In the already quoted words from the 'Memoir', David's 'freedom and independence of thought [...] extended itself to the other branches of his family' (Ricardo 1824, p. 5). Once reticent phrasing is uncoded, this means that the majority of the Ricardo siblings also became Christians by marriage (Weatherall 1776, p. 27; Sraffa 1955, pp. 54–61). This was just a symptom of the mentioned massive phenomenon of assimilation that had begun, to a vast extent through mixed marriages (Endelman 1999, pp. 248–271). After the shock of a break with his parents, David gradually recovered his relationship with brothers and sisters, and most of them followed his example in matters of marriage and religion. Moses married his brother's sister-in-law Fanny, and Sarah married George Porter, notably a political economist to whom her older brother may have introduced her. Introducing prospective spouses to his brothers and sisters seems to have been among David and Priscilla's most successful activities. In fact, besides Moses and Sarah, Esther married William Wilkinson, one of Priscilla's nephews who, after Esther's death, married her older sister Rachel (Sraffa 1955, p. 44).

For Priscilla, the story told above about Quaker Discipline of marriage carried lighter consequences. The Ratcliffe Meeting sanctioned the marriage by 'disownment', a sanction that implied loss of full-member status but not exclusion from prayer meetings and Priscilla went on attending prayer meetings up to 2008. Besides, it was possible to register at the Meeting the birth of non-members' children, which happened for all Ricardo's children. There was an annotation, 'Parents not Members of our Society', added to the first three certificates issued (those of Henrietta, Priscilla and Fanny, born in 1796, 1797 and 1800) but not to the later ones (Ricardo Papers; Sraffa 1955, pp. 41–42). It is improbable that Priscilla had been re-admitted, something that implied an apology in writing for having married outside the Society, and there is no evidence that this ever happened. A more plausible account may be that in 1802, eight years after their marriage and before their fourth child's birth, there was a minor change in the rules, making the annotation unnecessary. The Meeting had specified in its *Discipline* that

> where any marry by a priest, or in any other manner contrary to the established rules of the Society, they shall be dealt with in a spirit of Christian love and tenderness, agreeably to our own Discipline; and that after the commission of such offence, *their collection shall not be received*, nor shall they be *relieved in the manner of poor Friend*, nor *admitted to sit in Meeting of Discipline* until they *be restored into unity* with the Monthly Meeting to which they belong.
>
> (Jones 1921, p. 189)

In a word, the penalty for what Priscilla Wilkinson had done was exclusion from the condition of a full member, which implied taking part in decision making, contributing to the Society and being entitled to benefits in case of need, but not from prayer meetings, which were on principle open to everybody.

Marriage with Priscilla left David without a place where to go within English Judaism and, albeit without any official act, he found himself cast off from the Bevis Mark Synagogue (Henderson 1997, pp. 166–167). The first reformed Synagogue was to make its appearance in London half a century after and thus no alternative within Judaism was available at the time. The one offered by the spirit of the time was, yet, conforming to the idea that religion is necessary and permanent, but religions are contingent and changing. What Voltaire calls 'universal religion' and Adam Smith 'pure and rational religion' may manifest itself in various shapes. This idea provided the roadmap for Ricardo's religious peregrinations.

As regards family ties, Ricardo reacted positively to their abrupt severing. A few years after he had become, in a sense, the new head of the family (Henderson 1997, pp. 167–175). One might read the story in terms of symbolic parricide and subsequent appropriation of the father's role. Alternatively, we might read it in terms of David's Biblical story, the winner in a duel with a giant and a feud with a king. By converse, the name Abraham could be the mark of the destiny for somebody who believed he was obliged to sacrifice his son but repented in the end. Among factors accounting for prestige won among brothers and sisters was David's professional success. At the time of his marriage, he had worked as his father's clerk for seven years, but he had started by then doing business on his own. *The Sunday Times* report tells that one of the London private banks, Forster, Lubbocks, & Clarke, offered him support and this made it possible for him to go on doing business on a broader scale. In a couple of years, he had made giant strides on the stock market. In 1796, Abraham and David Ricardo were both among loan-contractors in the so-called Loyalty-Loan indicted by William Pitt, a loan meant to support Britain's war with France. While the father participated with three thousand pounds, the son invested one thousand, which can give a measure of the weight of David's financial activities after just a couple of years in business (Sraffa 1955, pp. 43–57; Weatherall 1976, pp. 30–31; Henderson 1997, pp. 197–8; Heertje 2015, p. 266).

Ricardo's Quaker relations

The Sunday Times reports that Ricardo attended Thomas Belsham's services at Essex Street Chapel. However, as illustrated in next chapter, between 1808 and 1812 he had been attending Robert Aspland's services at Gravel Hill Chapel, and it is unclear what kind of religious practices he followed between 1794 and 1808, respectively, the year of his marriage and the year when a dissenting Quaker introduced Priscilla and David to Robert Aspland.

Disownment by the Society of Friends, as mentioned, did not prevent Priscilla from attending the Meeting House with her children. Sraffa reports Elizabeth Allen's recollections about Priscilla, who continued for many years 'to attend the Friends' Meeting at Ratcliff, and how much she was admired as she swept grandly and proudly up the meeting, followed by her fine, elegant daughters' (Sraffa 1955, pp. 45–46). There is no evidence that Ricardo ever attended the prayer meeting though the latter was open to everybody and we cannot rule out that he may have attended occasionally. In the meantime, he may well have still considering himself a Jew, albeit a marginal one.

Regarding Priscilla's family, even though relationships with her father were disappointing, there is no evidence of total break of relations with the family. In the first years after marriage, before relationships were re-established with David's sibling and with his father, there were more contacts with the Wilkinsons. Ricardo also set up durable connections to discuss in another chapter, with Quakers with whom he shared scientific interests.

One more question to ask is what kind of ideas he may have come in contact with through the Quaker connection. He found a milieu of middle-class professionals without a 'classical education' who, besides their profession, were interested in working in the most innovative areas of natural science of the time, chemistry, mineralogy and geology, subjects far enough from the Anglican elite's intellectual hunting reserve made of classical studies, law, and Newtonian natural philosophy (Cantor 2015). He would have hardly met with any philosophical culture since the Quakers still mistrusted further education but neither would have he met with any theology, and he would have heard just arguments against theological speculation with which a Jewish mind could have been sympathetic. Had he ventured – but there is no evidence that he ever did – into Barclay's *Apology*, he would have found the idea of an essential role for intuitive knowledge. After having absorbed traditional Jewish predilection for the *way of wisdom* as opposed to *speculation*, he might have found additional reasons to deem theology an elusive and inconclusive task. While waiting to see what he did surely hear from Unitarian ministers, we already have reasons to avoid taking Ricardo's later expressions of mistrust in theology for a profession of Atheism.

Ricardo's involvement in a Quaker secession

Thomas Foster, a London Quaker, became the unwitting leader of an episode of secession that echoed the Irish Movement. The issues at the root of the dispute concerned the use of authority and Biblical literalism. Foster published between 1801 and 1808 under a pseudonym – it was current custom – a few pamphlets challenging what he saw as an increasingly authoritarian attitude by Elders and Ministers. He expressed the feeling that such an attitude implied betrayal of Fox's preaching. He also defended Hannah Barnard and the Irish Quakers, who questioned the divine inspiration of Biblical text enjoining wars and massacres on Israel. His priorities were: first, to defend the doctrine of 'strict Unity and natural placability of God [...] in opposition to the Trinitarian and Calvinistic tenets'; second, to recommend 'more just and reasonable ideas on the doctrine of divine influence on the human mind'; third, to 'excite an increased attention to the Scriptures'; fourth, to insist on the 'obligation to regard the simplicity of the apostolic faith' (Foster 1813,

p. xvi). Disciplinary action was taken against him by the London Quaker Meeting in 1813, indeed on vague allegations, namely, publishing anonymous pamphlets, challenging official Quaker documents and joining the Unitarian Book Society. All this amounted to an indictment conducted more on doctrinal heterodoxy than improper conduct, something hardly compatible with the original Quaker spirit. The outcome was Foster's expulsion from the Society (Sraffa 1955, p. 41).

The Foster case was a landmark in Ricardo's religious peregrinations. Robert Aspland wrote in his diary for 29 December 1809: 'I was introduced at Mr Foster's, Bromley Hall, to my new hearer, Mr David Ricardo and his lady. He is sensible, she is pleasant' (Aspland 1850, p. 234). The report implies that Aspland first met Ricardo with his wife at Thomas Foster's home and that shortly after the meeting – as we know from other sources – they had become regular attendants at his services. There are other implications to draw from this episode. One is that, between 1794 and 1809, Ricardo had not yet been attending Unitarian services. This fact suggests that he may have either still seen himself as an Israelite albeit a not very observant one, or that he instead defined himself as a friend of the Friends. As mentioned, there is no evidence of his attendance at the Quaker meeting, but we do have evidence that his introduction to Unitarianism took place via the Society of Friends. One more implication – or better, a fact proved by the circumstance of his membership in the London Geological Society – is that he was in touch with people from both milieus who had an interest in natural science.

Partial conclusions: the importance of being a husband

1. Ricardo's marriage was a turning point in his life, with more importance than marriage used to have for males in his time and place; it left him in a religious no man's land; it marked a break with his family; it occasioned severing ties with a religious, ethnic and linguistic community; and it occasioned new ties within a new and lively milieu.
2. In the years before his marriage he had already absorbed some of the Enlightenment ideas, namely that religion is primarily a moral message, unsurprisingly consisting of justice and mercy, that particular cult institutions are transient and not essential, and love between a man and a woman comes before religious affiliations. These ideas are *not* tantamount to Atheism but are the message shared by all European *Aufklärer*, whether theists or professed believers in the Jewish and Christian God.
3. Such travel into a no man's land was not so exceptional in his time and place when an increasingly significant part of Sephardi new generations severed ties with their community mostly through mixed marriages.
4. Both Priscilla's influence and his acquaintance with other Quakers arguably played their part in shaping Ricardo's moral and political attitudes and intellectual interests, encouraging him to engage first in natural science and then in political economy.

References

Unpublished

Ricardo Correspondence and Papers. Miscellaneous Private, Cambridge University Library. GB 12 MS.ADD.7510

Published

Aspland, RB 1850, *Memoir of the Life, Works and Correspondence of the Rev. Robert Aspland of Hackney*, Whitfield, London.

Barclay, R 1678, *Apology for the True Christian Divinity*, Forbes, Aberdeen.

Cantor, G 2015, 'Quakers and Science', in SW Angell & P Dandelion (eds), *The Oxford Handbook of Quaker Studies*, Oxford University Press, Oxford, pp. 520–534. DOI: 10.1093/oxfordhb/9780199608676.001.0001.

Colvin, C 1971, 'Introduction', in M Edgeworth, *Letters from England 1813–1844*, C Colvin (ed.), Clarendon Press, Oxford, pp. iii–xlii.

Davies, A 2000, *The Quakers in English Society: 1655–1725*, Clarendon Press, Oxford. DOI: 10.1093/acprof:oso/9780198208204.001.0001.

Edgeworth, M 1971, *Letters from England 1813–1844*, C Colvin (ed.), Clarendon Press, Oxford.

Endelman, TM 1999, *The Jews of Georgian England, 1714–1830. Tradition and Change in a Liberal Society*, University of Michigan Press, Ann Arbor. DOI: 10.3998/mpub.7895.

Foster, T 1813, *A Narrative of the Proceedings of the Society Called Quakers, within the Quarterly Meeting for London and Middlesex: Against Thomas Foster, for Openly Professing their Primitive Doctrines Concerning the Unity of God*, Stowe, London.

Freeman, M 2015, 'Quakers, Business and Philanthropy', in SW Angell & P Dandelion (eds), *The Oxford Handbook of Quaker Studies*, Oxford University Press, Oxford, pp. 420–433. DOI: 10.1093/oxfordhb/9780199608676.001.0001.

Frost, F 1986, 'Quakers (Quakérisme)', in M Viller et al. (eds), *Dictionnaire de spiritualité*, vol. 12, Beauchêne, Paris, pp. 2684–2702.

Gwyn, D 1995, *The Covenant Crucified: Quakers and the Rise of Capitalism*, Pendle Hill Pubns, Wallingford.

Heertje, A 2015, 'Jewish Background', in H Kurz & N Salvadori (eds), *The Elgar Companion to David Ricardo*, Elgar, Aldershot, pp. 216–224. DOI: 10.4337/9781784715489.

Henderson, JP 1997, *The Life and Economics of David Ricardo. With Additional Chapters by J.B. Davis*, WJ Samuels & GB Davis (eds), Kluwer, Dordrecht.

Jones, RM 1921, *Later Periods of Quakerism*, Macmillan, London.

Ricardo, M 1824, 'A Memoir of David Ricardo', in *Works* 10, pp. 3–15.

Rosenthal, E; Scereschewsky, B; Verbit, MF & Della Pergola, S 2007, 'Mixed Marriage', in F Skolnik (ed.), *Encyclopaedia Judaica*, vol. 14, Thomson Gale, Detroit, MI, pp. 373–385.

Sraffa, P 1955, 'Addenda to the Memoir', in *Works* 10, pp. 18–64.

Sunday Times 1823, 'David Ricardo', *The Sunday Times*, September 14, 3rd edn, p. 1 (Reprinted in the Appendix of this book).

Sykes, J 1958, *The Quakers. A New Look at their Place in Society*, Lippincott, Philadelphia, PE.

Voltaire, 1736, *The Tragedy of Zara: As it is Acted at the Theatre-Royal, in Drury-Lane, by His Majesty's Servants*, J. Watts, London.

Weatherall, D 1976, *David Ricardo. A Biography*, Nijhoff, The Hague.

3 Ricardo's encounter with the Unitarians

Scripture and reason

Ricardo 'became a Christian, attaching himself to the Unitarian Chapel, in Essex-street, where he and his family have regularly attended the instructions of Mr. Belsham' (*Sunday Times* 1823). Unitarianism was a Dissenting current that coagulated into a self-standing body when, in 1774, former Anglican minister Theophilus Lindsey founded a Unitarian chapel in Essex Street, London. Joseph Priestley, coming from the Independents, founded another in Bristol, followed by others coming from the Presbyterians. Their unifying traits – rejection of the Trinitarian dogma, Jesus's divine nature, original sin, eternal punishment, and vicarious atonement – were justified on both Scriptural and philosophical grounds.

Among the first grounds was the need for a correct historical and linguistic approach to the Bible, avoiding inaccurate translations from ancient languages and naïve readings of figurative expressions. Philosophical grounds, instead, inspired the elimination of doctrines 'contrary to reason', like the ones that could be found in dogmas from the Councils of Nicaea and Chalcedon, which were a mix of Platonic concepts and Biblical terminology.

Extremely influential among the founders of Unitarianism was David Hartley. Priestley was a direct follower of Hartley in philosophy and thus, 'so close became the relationship between Hartleyan philosophy and Unitarianism at this time that acceptance of the former was often a prime factor in leading to conversion to the latter' (Watts 1998, p. 41).

On balance, Unitarian theology was an attempt to respond to the Enlightenment challenge from within Christianity, not unlike Kant's religion within the bounds of pure reason. The problem with such theology was the lack of a critical hermeneutics such as that launched by Tubingen scholars. This deficiency left it exposed to the constant temptation to tailor Biblical texts according to need or read into them a very eighteenth-century worldview. Unitarian divines were increasingly tempted to cut passages as 'interpolated' whenever they seemed incompatible with a preconceived theology (Canovan 1980). Harriet Martineau, born into the sect, sourly noted that once Unitarian divines had 'begun to cut away and alter, there was no reason for

DOI: 10.4324/9781003162100-3

stopping' (Martineau 1855, p. 38) and described the set of beliefs that was left: first, God, albeit with a milder image than that of the orthodox; second, no devil; third, a hope for rewards but no fear of punishment; fourth, Christ as the purest of all beings; fifth, the Holy Ghost as mere fiction; sixth, all miracles as facts; seventh, a future life as a continuation of the present and not a new form of existence; eighth, the resurrection of the flesh (pp. 40–41).

Unitarian services gave pride of place to the 'instructions' leaving scant room for the expression of sentiments, music or the figurative arts. The result for upper-class congregations was a sober Anglican liturgy purified from Trinitarian doctrines and, for the lower classes, Dissenter style preaching. Besides services, the Unitarian Chapel was the venue for lecture courses. Belsham mentions in his memoirs for 1797 his 'private seminary' and his 'course of lectures'.

Unitarians stressed the humanitarian and civic character of Christian commitment and were in the forefront among radicals and reformers during the years of the French Revolution, becoming targets for persecution as alleged traitors (Dickinson 1977; Hone 1982; Stuart 2003, pp. 149–157). A good example is Gilbert Wakefield, Malthus's Cambridge tutor, who served a two-year prison term because of a harmless pamphlet. After 1800, Unitarians had to redefine their political orientation and, besides a commitment to religious freedom, they adopted a more or less marked attitude in favour of 'Reform', the catchword denoting the extension of the franchise and separation of Church and State (Stromberg 1954, pp. 156–163; Watts 1998, pp. 14–32, 109–112; Davie 1978, pp. 55–72). They had the same reasons as the Quakers for favouring Toleration. They were, however, in a more awkward situation than the Quakers who, albeit devoid of full civil and political rights, by now enjoyed a recognised legal status. Their predicament was that the profession of anti-Trinitarianism remained a criminal offence until 1813 (Davie 1978, pp. 65–68). More than for *toleration* as defined by Locke, excluding Atheists and Roman Catholics from its benefits, they campaigned for *unlimited religious freedom*.

One of the battles fought by the Unitarians was the advancement of women. Rejection of original sin and human depravity prompted optimism about human nature and, by implication, female nature, just as the rejection of Biblical literalism dismantled Scripture-based arguments for female inferiority. Besides, the philosophical doctrine of associationism prompted the conviction that human intellect was the same in both genders so that education could elicit the best intellectual qualities from women too. As a result, young women from Unitarian families enjoyed better than average education, and Unitarian women such as Anna Barbauld (Watts 1998, pp. 77–95, 152–161; McCarthy 2004) ran schools and published on educational subjects.

In conformity with the teaching that cultivation of the intellect is a divine precept, the Unitarians advocated education for the lower classes, established schools and supported plans for a system of general education. Moreover, being excluded from Universities, they founded their own colleges. Belsham was among the founders of Hackney College, which was intended, among other things, to educate future generations of Unitarian Ministers but was discontinued due to financial reasons. A Unitarian Academy founded by Aspland in 1813 also failed, and for the same reasons. As a result, Manchester College was the sect's only school to survive (Aspland 1850, p. 317; McLachlan 1931, pp. 94–97; Smith 1954, pp. 149–152; Watts 1998, pp. 56–69, 144–149) and scarcity of institutions providing for the education of future ministers contributed to the decline of Unitarianism in England, as described by Harriet Martineau (1855, p. 58) with a bleak portrait of the ministers of her time.

The Unitarian intellect concentrated on experimental science and technology (Watts 1998, pp. 33–53), and the next chapter will describe how the London Geological Society's founders were mostly Quakers or Unitarians. Eminent personalities in various scientific fields belonged to the sect, including Charles Darwin and Stanley Jevons, an economist of the generation following that of Ricardo and Malthus. Unitarians such as Florence Nightingale were on the front line in humanitarian campaigns. Elizabeth Gaskell was a remarkable writer in the 'social novel' genre. On balance, the Unitarians,

> in proportion to their numbers and their relatively brief history, made a greater contribution to English culture than all the other dissenting sects put together [...] overwhelmingly in speculative thought, in ideas rather than images, arguments rather than fictions, chains of reasoning rather than artefacts.
>
> (Davie 1978, p. 67)

Ricardo's 'conversion'

Towards the end of 1809, Ricardo became one of Aspland's 'hearers' at New Gravel Pit Chapel, Hackney. In Aspland and Belsham's usage, a 'hearer' was just a regular attender at the Unitarian services. Baptism did not supply a standard of membership since its practice was a matter of disagreement, with Priestley and Belsham among those in favour of infant baptism, others against it – and with Aspland among those who were against both infant and adult baptism. A corollary of this situation is that the question of whether Ricardo ever received Baptism is unimportant.

Note that Ricardo's Unitarianism is mentioned in *The Sunday Times* obituary but omitted in the 'Memoir'. As a result, Gorton (1851) writes without any reference to sources that Ricardo privately professed Unitarian doctrines while still adhering to the Church of England. Other nineteenth-century commentators ignore the issue and even Sraffa (1955a, pp. 39–40), who rediscovered the forgotten *The Sunday Times* obituary, could hardly be said to have been enthusiastic about the discovery. For example, among 'oddments' in Ricardo's library, he mentions 'two Unitarian sermons' (Sraffa 1955b, p. 402) with no further details and refers to Belsham's *Memoir* simply on the connection between Ricardo and Thomas Smith (*Works* 7, p. 171; 8, p. 75) without mentioning Belsham's comments on Ricardian political economy. Later commentators hardly added anything to the topic. Henderson writes that Ricardo 'relinquished all ties with the Jewish religion' while speculating that, 'if not an atheist, an agnostic be the direction which probably best describes David Ricardo's eventual resolution of the religious issue' (Henderson 1997, p. 163). On the same page he slips in the information that in 'later years, he attended the lectures' (pp. 163) of Thomas Belsham and Robert Aspland, with a Freudian slip that turns an *instruction*, that is, a *sermon*, into a harmless *lecture*. Milgate and Stimson (1991, pp. 78–87) discuss Ricardo's Speech in support of a petition for religious freedom duly reporting that MP Joseph Hume introduced it (p. 85) but, with another Freudian slip, omitting that what he supported was the 'Christians' petition against the prosecution of infidels' whose 'prime mover' was Robert Aspland (*Christian Reformer* 1823; *Monthly Repository* 1823a; *Works* 5, pp. 324–331). Depoortère (2002, pp. 500–501) adds the conclusion that Ricardo's Unitarianism was 'the best method of hiding his atheism'.

Attending Gravel Pit Chapel implied acquaintance with Aspland, who held the morning service but maybe with Belsham as well, since the latter, though already in charge of Essex Street Chapel, still lived at Gravel Pit until he moved to Essex Street in 1812, the same year that Ricardo moved 'to the western side of London' (Aspland 1850, p. 251 fn.). From 1814 to 1823, when Ricardo used to spend half the year at Gatcomb, he went on attending services at Essex Street Chapel when in London or, at least, this is implied by the information that 'he and his family have regularly attended the instructions of Mr. Belsham' (*Sunday Times* 1823).

No evidence suggests Ricardo's desertion from Unitarianism at any stage of his life. On his nomination as a High Sheriff of Gloucestershire in 1817 as well as when entering Parliament, he obtained exemption from receiving Holy Communion according to the rites of the established Church (Sraffa 1955a, p. 42). During his tour on the Continent, on 30 July 1822, he attended Sunday service at the 'English church' in Amsterdam – that is, the *Engelse Kerk*, an English-language Presbyterian Chapel – where he 'heard a tolerably good sermon by a man whom some of us thought was an English man' (Ricardo 1891, p. 210). He regularly subscribed to New Gravel Pit Chapel from 1809 to 1812 and still sent donations to his old Chapel several years after he had shifted to Essex Street Chapel (*Works*, vol. 10, p. 40). Note that, due to accidents concerning the Essex Street archives during the Second World War (Godfrey 1999; Godfrey & Ditchfield 2001) we have no access to documents testifying contributions to this Chapel.

The official Unitarian Magazine reported the parliamentary discussion about the petition for Toleration mentioned above with its vigorous defence by Ricardo (*Monthly Repository* 1823a) and, at his death, published an obituary highly appreciative of both his intellectual merits and the spirit of independence shown in the debate about Toleration (*Monthly Repository* 1823b).

Nonetheless, we should deal with two pieces of counterevidence. The first is an entry from the *Imperial Dictionary,* which declares that, although he adhered to the principles of Unitarianism, yet 'he usually attended the service of the established church' (Gorton 1851). This sentence contradicts *The Sunday Times* obituary but, *if correct,* might describe Ricardo's attendance of Sunday services during his stays at Gatcomb, which was possibly acceptable behaviour where a nearby Unitarian Chapel was lacking. The other is a report of his funeral service. His burial place is at Hardenhuish, whose Anglican church and graveyard were located on the estate of his son-in-law Thomas Clutterbuck, near Chippenham and less than one mile away from Gatcomb (*Works*, vol. 10, p. 12; Weatherall 1976, pp. 190–191). A relevant detail is that the grave of his Unitarian friend Thomas Smith was in a Unitarian graveyard at Cirencester, ten miles from Gatcomb (Weatherall 1976, p. 66). Nonetheless, Anglican graveyards used to host both Dissenters and Roman Catholics wherever a dedicated graveyard was lacking and, since Hardenhuish belonged to the family's estates and was the place chosen by Priscilla as her residence after Ricardo's death (p. 188) she may have decided that the family's funeral chapel could not be elsewhere.

Robert Aspland, the missionary to the Jews

Ricardo's Minister between 1809 and 1823 was former Baptist Robert Aspland (1750–1829) who oversaw the New Gravel Pit Unitarian Chapel at Hackney (Webb 2004a). In 1806 he founded the *Monthly Repository* and in 1815 the *Christian Reformer.* According to his son's report, he succeeded in interesting 'more than one Jewish family in the truths of Christianity' (Aspland 1850, p. 10 fn.), and his sermon on the death of Theophilus Lindsey (Aspland 1808), had 'a considerable circulation amongst intelligent members of the Hebrew faith' (Aspland 1850, p. 10 fn). In his journal for 29 December 1809, he mentions Ricardo as his 'new hearer', and an endnote adds that the latter 'continued to attend at the Gravel Pit until his removal to the western side of London' (Aspland 1850, p. 251; Sraffa 1955a, p. 40). For 4 January 1810 Aspland writes that he 'walked to Mile-end Road to dine, for the first time, with my new hearer, Mr. David Ricardo. Dr. Lindsay of the party [...] we had a long debate on the natural evidences of a future state' (Aspland 1850, p. 251). Lindsay's arguments on the topic are presented in one of his sermons. The first is man's intellectual perfectibility (Lindsay 1818a, p. 10); the second his moral perfectibility (pp. 11–12); the third is the implausibility of the idea that God will annihilate a human being when he has reached the apex of his moral and intellectual growth (p. 17).

Aspland campaigned for Toleration, extended to a point Locke would never have dreamt of, namely including atheists, and promoted the abovementioned 'Christians' Petition against the Prosecution of Unbelievers'. In a sermon he notes that 'our Lord and the apostles' never endorsed the idea that religion should be placed 'under the patronage of the state' (Aspland 1812,

p. 9), arguing that the magistrate cannot repress error since he is 'equally liable, with others, to prejudice and error' (p. 9), and adds that the civil power cannot repress immorality since 'in the present imperfect state of society, there is much misconduct that must be referred to the righteous judgment of God, much licentiousness growing up along with liberty' (p. 11). He then notes that no religion professedly sanctions vice and contends that competition among religions may help to improve each of them. He concludes that 'an unbeliever is as much entitled by natural rights, and also on Christian principles, to attack Christianity as I am to defend it' (p. 22).

Thomas Belsham, the Biblical scholar

Thomas Belsham (1750–1829), the son of an Independent Minister, was educated at the dissenting Daventry Academy. He became a minister like his father and taught divinity there until he felt unable to profess Trinitarian doctrines and resigned in 1789. He was a lecturer at Hackney Unitarian College, where Priestley also lectured before emigrating to America (Williams 1833, p. 441), and in 1794 accepted the pulpit of New Gravel Pit Chapel, Hackney and in 1805 that of Essex Street Chapel, where he moved to live in 1812 (Webb 2004b). Besides services, in 1797 he mentions his own 'private seminary' consisting of Saturday-evening lectures and Sunday-morning lectures (Williams 1833, p. 482), in 1800 a series of 'lectures upon Christian doctrine' attended by 100 hearers (p. 503), in 1806 'a course of lectures, after the morning service, upon the Evidences of the Christian Religion' (p. 568). He contributed to a revised version of the New Testament (Belsham 1808) and authored exegetic and theological works, including a defence of Christian revelation (Belsham 1807) and an essay arguing the absence of Jesus's divine nature from early Christian preaching (Belsham 1817).

A few topics recurrent in his sermons are worth mentioning. The first is the duty to search for truth and awareness of limits to our knowledge. His farewell letter to students at Daventry Academy recommends: 'Seek for truth with impartiality. Follow evidence wherever it leads [...] Always be willing to receive information, and maintain a due sense of human fallibility' (Williams 1833, p. 398). In his journal, he writes that

> the scepticism of serious and inquisitive persons seems to me to arise principally from a desire of mathematical precision and certainty in the evidences of revelation, without sufficiently adverting to the consideration, that in all great practical questions, and in this amongst the rest, is our duty to regulate our conduct by probability. Often, while we are seeking after certainty, the time of action is lost.
>
> (Williams 1833, p. 467)

He insists that 'human knowledge is limited, both in its extent and in its degree' (Belsham 1826, p. 2), for example, if 'we know little of the properties of things, how much less can we understand of the essences, and internal constitution of substances themselves' (pp. 7–8), and even less can we know of God; we may just infer his existence

> from the works of nature, from our own existence, from the marks of contrivance in the universe, from the exquisite adaptation of means to ends, from the obvious preponderance of good over evil, and from the powerful, irresistible tendencies of things to a better and a happier state [...] But here our knowledge stops'.
>
> (pp. 4–5)

Belsham preached that we should develop God's most precious gift, that is, our intellect. We should 'pay a general attention to every branch of learning, but to select and pursue with particular assiduity two or three branches of science only' (Williams 1833, p. 398), not those 'without the grasp of the human mind' as the study of 'substances, and essences, the nature of matter and spirit, the mode of the divine existence' (Belsham 1827, p. 55), but those which may be 'useful'. These are, first, astronomy which – he writes – is useful in so far as it prompts reverence to God's wisdom, second, the study of 'the powers of nature in order to improve the arts of life', third, the study of 'the principles of the social compact, and the laws of civil society' (p. 56).

The second topic is the nature of faith. It consists, more than in assent to theoretical claims, in a *practical* attitude. Inquiry into subjects the human mind is unable to grasp is useless. Also in such useful subject as the study of human society the evidence of principles we can establish 'seldom amounts to more than to a high degree of probability' (Belsham 1801, p. 110), and in everyday life we rely on no more than probability 'in the choice of connections, professions, and situations' (p. 110). Thus, 'even the most important doctrines of natural and revealed religion are more properly the object of rational belief than of certain knowledge' (p. 110 fn.).

The third topic is the duty to pursue virtue. While in the physical world, in Bacon's phrase, Knowledge is power, 'in the moral world knowledge is virtue' (Belsham 1807, p. 182). The 'creatures of God are made for happiness' (Belsham 1827, pp. 118–119). Virtue,

> is the same as wisdom; it is the best means of attaining the best ends to ourselves and others. And vice is *folly*; it is the pursuit of happiness by means which are subversive of it, and which lead to misery.
>
> (p. 119)

Virtue is productive of happiness, for the 'true reward of virtue is peace of mind' (p. 105) and this holds true even for those who do not expect a better state of existence to succeed the present, for 'self-government, and active benevolence, would generally lead to the highest satisfaction which the condition of human nature in this transitory and precarious state would allow'

(p. 122). Its merit does not lie 'in its laying the Supreme Being under any obligation to reward it' but in its 'natural and necessary tendency to produce individual and social happiness' (p. 128).

The fourth topic is the existence of a future state. Note that this is the topic discussed by Aspland on his first visit to Ricardo's home. Belsham contends that there are purely rational, albeit not conclusive, arguments independent of the Scriptures in favour of the existence of such a state (Belsham 1826, pp. 439–461). The Christian religion promises a reward to virtue in another life and – he argues, unwittingly echoing Kant's third postulate of practical reason – we should assume its existence since it would allow for endless growth of virtue and a state of unlimited happiness (Belsham 1827, pp. 122–123). Our thirst for knowledge adds more evidence since it sounds implausible that 'the acquisition of intellectual treasure' should be 'interrupted by death, often at a time when success appears to at hand' (p. 59).

However, since divine revelation never says anything contrary to reason, we should seriously consider also 'presumptions from natural appearances against the doctrine of future life'. Rational arguments in favour of future life cannot consist in weak analogies such as the seed coming back to life in spring (Belsham 1826, p. 450) or the argument from the distinction of the soul from matter, which – unsurprisingly for a follower of David Hartley – he believes to be 'fallacious in the extreme' (p. 452). The decisive point is that, even though we ignore what happens with the 'principle of thought' after death, yet 'our ignorance does not prove that' the latter 'may not exist under the protecting care of omnipotence, and, that it may not again, when united to an organised substance, be restored to the full exercise of all its powers' (p. 454). Our knowledge yet is quite limited, we cannot answer the question of how this power can exist without a substance in which it may inhere, and the 'decay of the faculties in age appears almost an unsurmountable objection against the doctrine of a future life' (Williams 1833, p. 520).

The fourth topic is the compatibility of moral agency with divine fore-knowledge. Following Priestley, Belsham adhered to necessitarianism (Williams 1833, p. 426). He writes that experience suggests that 'the world is governed by general laws' (Belsham 1827, p. 154; cf. p. 42) and we should avoid concluding that still unexplained phenomena are supernatural. Meteorology is an excellent example of the limits of human knowledge. Nobody 'can foretell today, with precision, what the weather will be to-morrow' (p. 338) but the conclusion 'that the causes of the winds are not subject to general laws' is hardly proof of 'philosophy and good sense'. We may assume that the plan of Providence is conducted 'by general laws, without occasional deviations' (p. 145). It is more honourable to the 'divine character and government' that God's purposes should be accomplished 'by the operation of laws originally constructed with exquisite wisdom and foresight, and as adapted to every possible occurrences, rather than by frequent interruptions' (p. 152) of the regular action of the laws of nature. Philosophical necessitarianism does not detract from the duty of 'exertion' (p. 142) for a moral agent is somebody capable of virtue and vice and should be assumed 'to be rewarded for his virtue, and to be punished in exact proportion to his offences' (p. 118).

The fifth topic is theodicy, that is, to answer the question of the origins of evil. Priestley had tried in the wake of Leibniz and forerunning Paley (1802) to solve the problem of evil writing that, since 'all evils and inconveniences have final causes', once the final cause has ceased to exist, 'evils tend to be eliminated by themselves' (Priestley 1762, p. 250), and

> everything painful and disagreeable in the world appears to a philosopher [...] to be excellently provided as a remedy of some greater inconvenience, or a necessary means of a much greater happiness; so that, from this elevated point of view, he sees all temporary evils and inconveniencies to vanish, in the glorious prospect of the greater good to which they are subservient.
>
> (Priestley 1767, p. xvii)

Belsham writes too that philosophical necessitarianism is an appealing doctrine because 'it demonstrates the inseparable connexion between moral and natural evil, and proves that by the established course of nature every vice shall be followed by adequate punishment' (Belsham 1801, p. 310). This doctrine also proves that 'the preponderance of happiness' is 'very considerably on the side of virtue' and 'every purpose of substantial justice is answered independent of a future state' (p. 351) and is 'inseparably connected with that of optimism' since it shows that all events are 'necessary parts of a great system, which shall eventually produce the greatest possible sum of happiness and virtue, both to the universe and to individuals' (p. 313; cf. Belsham 1814, p. 30).

Nonetheless, he admits our inability to account for its existence in an entirely satisfactory way for the reason why some particular evil is necessary 'is something we simply do not know' (Belsham 1795, p. 13). He writes that the world is governed by the Providence of God acting through general laws and aiming at the greatest good. We see enough in the world as a whole, 'to be satisfied' that there is 'a great preponderance of good'. Nonetheless, 'when we consider the divine dispensations in detail, we shall immediately discover that they are far beyond the reach of human sagacity' (Belsham 1827, pp. 36–37) and the existence of evil in a universe where 'there is but one governing will, and [...] all the inferior and subordinate wills are made subservient' to the former's designs is a genuine problem. The conjecture that 'evil, as well as good, proceeds immediately from God [...] permitted by his wisdom, limited by his power, and overruled by his providence for the production of good' (p. 172) is a preliminary answer to the question. However, to prove in particular cases how the present evil is the best way to future good is 'far beyond the reach of human sagacity [...] That *evil*, *natural* and *moral*, is unavoidable in the works of God, is a problem of very difficult solution' (p. 37).

The seventh topic is Toleration. John Locke had started with a distinction between the goals pursued by religious communities and the more limited ones of the civil magistrate but then had introduced two exceptions, for Roman Catholics, who paid loyalty to a foreign ruler, and for Atheists, who cannot be trusted since they cannot utter an oath. Belsham had it clear in mind, instead, that morality is independent of religion, and therefore identification of Atheism with immorality is unjustified. While attacking William Wilberforce, the spokesman of Anglican Evangelicalism, he writes that 'the chief doctrine of Christ and his apostles is, that the virtuous shall rise to happiness, and the vicious to suffering, how little soever their conduct may be governed by a regard to these important principles' (Belsham 1798, p. 24). He declares that 'the general conduct of a man will be nearly the same, whether the doctrine of a future life be admitted or not' (Belsham 1795, p. 15). In a letter, he adds:

> I have known so many intelligent and virtuous men who have of late become unbelievers, that I am far from regarding the relinquishment of the Christian religion as necessarily impeaching either the understanding or the morals, and I am much hurt when I hear any insinuation of this kind thrown out by others.
>
> (Williams 1833, p. 466)

Belsham may have first met Ricardo in 1810 after the latter joined the Gravel Pit Chapel where the former was in residence albeit in charge of Essex Street Chapel. He then became his Minister when the latter moved to West London in 1812 and began attending services at Essex Street Chapel (Cremaschi 2015). He was aware of Ricardo's political ideas, albeit reluctant to follow him in what he felt to be too radical a programme (Williams 1833, pp. 701–702). Ricardo wrote to Mill on 6 September 1819, after the Peterloo Massacre, that Belsham was a lukewarm reformer, and indeed they 'had many political discussions, without the least loss of friendship' (*Works* 8, p. 56) but at least he speaks too 'with great indignation [...] against the conduct of the Manchester Magistrates' (p. 56).

As mentioned, Belsham was also a lecturer in philosophy, first at Daventry Academy and then at the Unitarian Hackney College. He was the author of a treatise on the philosophy of mind. In this capacity, he is the subject of another chapter, together with other contemporary philosophers with whom Ricardo was acquainted.

James Lindsay, the campaigner for Toleration

James Lindsay, a Scot, was the Minister of a chapel at Monkswell Street affiliated to the Unitarian branch of Presbyterianism. He was on friendly terms and shared enthusiasm for Reform with James Mill, another Scot living in London. As mentioned, Ricardo was acquainted with him. Indeed, one of the two unidentified Unitarian sermons listed by Sraffa is his 'Sermon on the Death of the Rev. Hugh Worthington' which attacks the 'metaphysical subtleties' in theological discussion, the 'unmeaning distinctions' and the 'pestiferous art' of 'system-making' while recommending to abandon those subjects 'which in their very nature are beyond the grasp of human comprehension' (Lindsay 1813a, p. 4) and vindicating the 'beautiful simplicity of Christ's religion' (p. 29).

In another sermon, 'On the spirit of a man compared with the spirit of a beast', he manifests mistrust in metaphysical speculations about matter and spirit arguing that, since even 'of matter, though it lies open to our sense we know nothing but a few properties' (Lindsay 1818a, p. 3), *a fortiori* we cannot pretend to know anything of spirit. Besides, he declares that the assumptions at the root of these disputes are plagued by logical inconsistencies, for example, the idea that spirit is immortal by its nature is absurd since no created thing can be eternal by itself (p. 3). Echoing Scottish philosophy, he then argues that the human mind is superior to animals because it is capable of 'moral perception', it soon acquires the ability to distinguish actions, not just as pleasant or painful, but also 'as being in themselves either good or evil', it has 'a taste for moral, as for natural beauty', 'perceives the excellence of virtue and the turpitude of vice' and has 'desires which coincide with his perceptions' (p. 11). In the same sermon, he comments on the elusive character of happiness suggesting that human imagination 'constantly anticipates a happiness, which is for ever eluding his grasp' (p. 20) and the possession of 'present good' is 'precarious and transient' (p. 21).

In a third sermon, 'On the superiority of religion over infidelity' he argues that 'a cold-blooded virtue which has nothing to touch the heart' and offers but 'cooler satisfactions' (Lindsay 1818b, p. 74) is not a sufficient motive for action. Instead, 'that higher wisdom, which consists in the knowledge of God and of ourselves' highlights 'the connexion between duty and happiness' (p. 70) thus arousing 'the active joys of piety and hope' (p. 76), sentiments without which we would lack a motive for moral action. His argument in favour of faith against infidelity is that belief offers advantages in terms of happiness over unbelief. Even though we admitted that the belief that God exists and will judge us with justice rests on less convincing evidence than is the case, it would not be *wise* to forfeit this belief for 'any hope is better than none' (p. 84). The decisive argument is that renouncing belief in the existence of God, should this belief be true, would be a mistake without any remedy. 'Other errors may be rectified' (p. 86) but anybody who intends

> he who affects to deny his God, and to renounce his hopes of futurity, ought to be well satisfied in his own mind that he stands upon safe ground. For if he err, he errs in a point, in which but one experiment can be made.
>
> (p. 86)

Thus, to opt for unbelief, we would need an infinite amount of evidence. On the contrary, the slightest evidence would be enough to opt for faith. Note that this argument echoes Blaise Pascal's argument according to which, *whatever* the probability for God's existence is, if one is not *absolutely sure* of his non-existence he should, in terms of rational-choice theory, place a bet on God's existence, and in the meanwhile turns Hume's argument against belief in miracles upside down, two arguments based on the calculus of probabilities albeit going in opposite directions.

In a fourth sermon, 'On the Influence of Religious Knowledge as tending to produce a gradual improvement in the social state', Lindsay argues that 'uncorrupted Christianity' tends to 'enlarge the mind by the most important discoveries; to purify the heart from evil affections; and to exalt and bless social life, by making man faithful, gentle, and benevolent' (Lindsay 1813b, p. 18). He welcomes the fact that progress of knowledge carried by post-Reformation controversies, has brought about the existence of advocates

> not only for Toleration, but for that unbounded freedom of opinion, to which alone genuine Christianity must owe its future prevalence, and its permanent influence.
>
> (p. 22)

Note that Ricardo repeats the phrase 'not only Toleration, but unbounded freedom of opinion' in a letter to Mill of 9 September 1821 naming it 'Dr Lindsay's Principle' (*Works* 9, p. 60).

John Bowring and Thomas Smith

John Bowring, the editor of a collection of Bentham's works published in 1834 (Stone 2004), and one of the handful of Unitarians who joined the Benthamite coterie, mentions Ricardo in his memoirs (Bowring 1877, pp. 58, 68).

A more significant relationship was the one with Thomas Smith, a lawyer who had retired to his Easton Grey estate, 10 miles away from Gatcomb. He had been Belsham's pupil at Daventry Academy (Williams 1833, p. 743) and, as testified by his correspondence with the senior civil servant John Whishaw (*Gentleman's Magazine* 1822; Whishaw 1907) was an alert spectator of British intellectual life. Ricardo wrote to Malthus on 4 September 1817 that 'Mr. Smith's house is the centre of attraction for all his able London friends and he is kind enough to allow me to participate in the pleasures which their company affords his' (*Works* 7, p. 187). Maria Edgeworth, in a letter of 10 November 1821, comments that Ricardo and Smith 'suit each other delightfully' (Edgeworth 1971, p. 261). The Ricardo Papers include 21 letters from Smith, three from his widow and a response from Ricardo himself. Smith's letter of 13 February 1818, the only one published by Sraffa, reports an anecdote concerning money offered to a fund for charitable purposes by a Theatre Manager and the indignant reactions to money flowing from so impure a source (*Works* 7, p. 389), a story expressing contempt by a 'rational believer' vis-à-vis moralism ad hypocrisy. An unpublished letter of 1 May

1820 confesses his coming closer to Ricardo's more radical political views, professing to be 'a complete convert to the necessity of reform' and to believe it to be 'essential to the salvation of the Country', from the opposite dangers of 'the establishment of a military despotism' and of 'a democratic revolution'. In another of 6 June 1820 Smith goes one step further, writing that he is 'in fair way to join the radical party' (Ricardo Papers). Ricardo's letter to Smith, also omitted in Sraffa's edition, endorsed a claim from Adam Smith, namely that human beings sympathise more with unhappiness than happiness, commenting that people 'do not speak much of their happiness, but they proclaim their misery in a loud voice' (Heertje & Weatherall 1978, p. 570).

Partial conclusions: the importance of being a Dissenter

1. The first question to answer, or rather, get rid of, is the true nature of Ricardo's beliefs. John Stuart Mill, in a letter to John Lalor of 3 July 1852, wrote: 'A. Smith, Turgot, Say, Ricardo & my father not one of whom was a believer in Christianity' (Mill 1972, p. 93). However, how could he have known unless by recourse to necromancy? Historians should keep in mind that an author's 'religious beliefs or unbeliefs are seldom stable or coherent, seldom completely understood by that person or others, and never reliably signified by documentary evidence alone' (Waterman 2004, p. 89) and there is nothing to suggest Ricardo's hidden Atheism. The facts are that he was just one more Jewish convert to Christianity, and adhered to Unitarianism, the most consistent kind of 'rational religion' available and a step involving a less traumatic break with Judaism in terms of doctrine than those that would have been involved by adhesion to the established Church or other congregations.

2. Another issue is the relationship between Ricardo's religious affiliation and his views on Toleration. He defended 'Dr. Lindsay's principle', which was more radical than Locke's. However, 'unfettered freedom of opinion' – far from being the mark of an Atheist – was the very motto of Unitarianism. Ricardo had it clearly in mind that freedom of opinion is freedom for those who have opinions different from our own.

3. One more question is the influence of Unitarian theological doctrines on Ricardo's intellectual itinerary. The Unitarian divines used to preach a duty to develop our intellectual faculties as a fundamental duty, and Ricardo might have learnt something from Lindsay and Belsham on both theological doctrines and logic, ethics, and political theory. A point discussed in another chapter is the influence of theodicy on political economy.

4. Another is the question of the *purely philosophical* doctrines, on principle independent of Unitarian theology, to which Ricardo may have been exposed through Unitarian connections. The ones Ricardo may have heard about were: limited scepticism; a eudemonist ethical theory admitting of morality independent of religion; a normative ethic stressing

benevolence and the development of our mental faculties; the tendency to produce general happiness as the criterion for assessing the moral goodness of actions. It is as well to insist that these were *not* theological doctrines but just ideas from a philosophical school, that religions are not philosophies even though religious circles may, for contingent reasons, provide occasions for getting acquainted with particular philosophical doctrines.

5. An inescapable question is whether Ricardo's religious affiliation had any bearing on his philanthropic activity and commitment to bettering the condition of the working classes. James Mill's comment is well-known on Ricardo's devotion to 'the cause of mankind' in a letter to John Mc-Culloch of 19 September 1823 (*Works*, 9, p. 390). Ricardo contributed to many beneficent initiatives and actively engaged in a couple of them. Besides, as discussed in another chapter, as a politician, he adopted what looked to his contemporaries as a pro-poor attitude.

6. The last question concerns the sources of Ricardo's peculiarities when compared with Malthus, Mill and other political economists. Commentators from the past two centuries sometimes came up with strange ideas, including a 'Semitic' character for Ricardian economic theory. Instead, Ricardian economics was no more Jewish or Unitarian than Schumpeter's was Catholic or Gide's Huguenot. Because of his personal story, including shifting religious affiliations, Ricardo was an outsider in his time and place, and this contributed to the moulding of his distinct 'cast of mind'. This circumstance was grasped reasonably enough by his brother Moses when he wrote that it was 'perhaps in opposing' their father's 'strong prejudices, that he was first led to that freedom and independence of thought for which he was so remarkable' (Ricardo, M 1824, p. 5). James Mill got it right – at least once – when writing that Ricardo had enjoyed the asset of freedom from those 'prejudices which were the bequest of current education' (*Works* 7, p. 196) while Henry Brougham hit the target in describing him as 'a man from another planet' (*Works* 5, p. 56).

References

Unpublished

Ricardo Correspondence and Papers. Miscellaneous Private, Cambridge University Library. GB 12 MS.ADD.7510.

Published

Aspland, R 1808, *A Sermon on Occasion of the Death of the Rev. Theophilus Lindsey*, Longman, London.
Aspland, R 1812, *A Vindication of Religious Liberty*, Stower, Hackney.

Aspland, RB 1850, *Memoir of the Life, Works and Correspondence of the Rev. Robert Aspland of Hackney*, Whitfield, London.

Belsham, T 1795, *Knowledge the Foundation of Virtue. A Sermon*, Johnson, London.

Belsham, T 1798, *A Review of Mr. Wilberforce's Treatise Entitled a Practical View of the Prevailing Religious System of Professed Christians*, Johnson, London.

Belsham, T 1801, *Elements of the Philosophy of the Mind, and of Moral Philosophy. To Which Is Prefixed a Compendium of Logic*, Johnson, London.

Belsham, T 1807, *A Summary View of the Evidence and Practical Importance of the Christian Religion in a Series of Discourses Addressed to Young Persons*, Johnson, London.

Belsham, T 1814, *The Progress of Intellectual, Moral, and Religious Improvement during the Present Reign*, Johnson & Eaton, London.

Belsham, T 1817, *A Calm Inquiry into the Scripture Doctrine concerning the Person of Christ*, 2nd edn., The Unitarian Society, London.

Belsham, T 1826 *Discourses, Doctrinal and Practical*, vol. 1, Hunter, London.

Belsham, T 1827, *Discourses, Doctrinal and Practical*, vol. 2, Hunter, London.

Belsham, T et al. 1808, *The New Testament. An Improved Version*, Taylor, London.

Bowring, J 1877, *Autobiographical Recollections of Sir John Bowring, with a Brief Memoir by Lewin B. Bowring*, King, London.

Canovan, M 1980, 'The Irony of History: Priestley's Rational Theology', *The Price-Priestley Newsletter*, no. 4, pp. 16–25.

Christian Reformer 1823, 'Intelligence. The Christians' Petition to Parliament against the Prosecution of Unbelievers', *The Christian Reformer, or, New Evangelical Miscellany*, vol. 9, no. 202, June, pp. 221–224 (Reprinted in the Appendix of this book).

Cremaschi, S 2015, 'Belsham, Thomas and Ricardo', in H Kurz & N Salvadori (eds), *The Elgar Companion to David Ricardo*, Elgar, Aldershot, pp. 14–17. DOI: 10.4337/9781784715489.

Davie, D 1978, *A Gathered Church. The Literature of the English Dissenting Interest, 1700–1930*, Routledge, London.

Depoortère, C 2002, 'On Ricardo's Method: The Unitarian Influence Examined', *History of Political Economy*, vol. 34, no. 2, pp. 499–503. DOI: 10.1215/00182702-34-2-499.

Dickinson, HT 1977, *Liberty and Property. Political Ideology in Eighteenth-Century Britain*, Weidenfeld & Nicholson, London.

Edgeworth, M 1971, *Letters from England 1813–1844*, C Colvin (ed.), Clarendon Press, Oxford.

Gentleman's Magazine 1822, 'Smith, Thomas', *The Gentleman's Magazine*, no. 91, July, p. 91.

Godfrey, P 1999, 'Records Held at Essex Hall'. *Transactions of the Unitarian Historical Society*, vol. 22, no. 1, pp. 76–78.

Godfrey, P & Ditchfield, G 2001, 'The Unitarian Archives at Essex Hall', *Archives. The Journal of the British Records Association*, vol. 26, no. 104, pp. 58–70.

Gorton, JG 1851, *A General Biographical Dictionary*, 3rd edn., Whittaker, London, entry: 'Ricardo, David', vol. 3, p. 747.

Heertje, A & Weatherall, D 1978, 'An Unpublished Letter by Ricardo', *The Economic Journal*, vol. 88, no. 351, pp. 569–571. DOI: 10.2307/2232055.

Henderson, JP 1997, *The Life and Economics of David Ricardo. With Additional Chapters by J.B. Davis*, WJ Samuels & GB Davis (eds), Kluwer, Dordrecht.

Hone, JA 1982, *For the Cause of Truth. Radicalism in London 1796–1821*, Clarendon Press, Oxford.

Lindsay, J 1813a, *A Sermon on the Death of the Rev. Hugh Worthington*, Johnson, London.

Lindsay, J 1813b, *A Sermon on the Influence of Religious Knowledge*, Johnson, London.

Lindsay, J (ed.) 1818a, 'Of the Spirit of Man Compared with the Spirit of Beasts', in *Sermons on Various Subjects*, Hunter, London, pp. 1–28.

Lindsay, J 1818b, 'On the Superiority of Religion Over Infidelity'. In J Lindsay, *Sermons on Various Subjects*, Hunter, London, pp. 69–86.

Martineau, H 1855, *Autobiography*, edn used: L Peterson (ed.), Broadview Press, Peterborough, ONT, 2007.

McCarthy, W 2004, 'Barbauld, Anna Letitia (1743–1825)', in HCG Matthew & B Harrison (eds), *Oxford Dictionary of National Biography*, vol. 3, Oxford University Press, Oxford, pp. 736–738.

McLachlan, H 1931, *The Unitarian Movement in the Religious Life of England*, Allen & Unwin, London.

Milgate, M & Stimson, SC, 1992, *Ricardian Politics*, Princeton University Press, Princeton, NJ.

Mill, JS 1972, *The Later Letters of John Stuart Mill, 1849–1873, 1, FE Mineka & DN Lindley (eds), The Collected Works of John Stuart Mill 14, University of Toronto Press, Toronto.

Monthly Repository 1823a, 'Parliamentary. Christians' Petition against the Prosecution of Unbelievers', *The Monthly Repository*, vol. 18, no. 212, August, pp. 485–494 (Reprinted in the Appendix of this book).

Monthly Repository 1823b, 'David Ricardo', *The Monthly Repository*, vol. 18, no. 213, September, p. 551 (Reprinted in the Appendix of this book).

Paley, W 1802, *Natural Theology*, edn used: Gregg, Westmead, 1970.

Penny Cyclopaedia 1841, 'Ricardo, David', in *The Penny Cyclopaedia*, vol. 19, Knight, London, pp. 507–508 (Reprinted in the Appendix of this book).

Priestley, J 1762, *A Course of Lectures in the Theory of Language and Universal Grammar*, in *The Theological and Miscellaneous Works*, vol. 23. J Towill Rutt (ed.), Kraus reprint, New York, 1972.

Priestley, J 1767, *The History and Present State of Electricity with Original Experiments*, 2nd ed., Bathurst, London.

Ricardo, D 1891, *Journal of a Tour on the Continent*, in *Works* 10, pp. 177–352.

Ricardo, M 1824, *A Memoir of David Ricardo*, in *Works* 10, pp. 3–13.

Smith, JWA 1954, *The Birth of Modern Education. The Contribution of the Dissenting Academies 1660–1800*, Independent Press, London.

Sraffa, P 1955a, 'Addenda to the Memoir', in *Works* 10, pp. 16–64.

Sraffa 1955b, 'Appendix (D) Ricardo's Library', in *Works* 10, pp. 389–402.

Stone, G 2004, 'Bowring, Sir John' (1792–1872)', in HCG Matthew & B Harrison (eds), *Oxford Dictionary of National Biography*, vol. 6, Oxford University Press, Oxford, pp. 987–990.

Stromberg, RN 1954, *Religious Liberalism in Eighteenth-Century England*, Oxford University Press, Oxford.

Stuart, A 2003, *Unitarian Radicalism, Political Rhetoric, 1770–1814*, Palgrave MacMillan, New York.

Sunday Times 1823, 'David Ricardo', *The Sunday Times*, 14 September, 3rd edn., p. 1 (Reprint in the Appendix of this book).

Waterman, AMC 2004, *Political Economy and Christian Theology since the Enlightenment*, Palgrave MacMillan, Basingstoke.

Watts, R 1998, *Gender, Power and the Unitarians in England 1760–1860*, Longmans, London.

Weatherall, D 1976, *David Ricardo. A Biography*, Nijhoff, The Hague.

Webb R K 2004a, 'Aspland, Robert (1782–1845)', in HCG Matthew & B Harrison (eds), *Oxford Dictionary of National Biography*, vol. 2, Oxford University Press, Oxford, pp. 726–728.

Webb, R K 2004b, 'Belsham, Thomas (1850–1829)', in HCG Matthew & B Harrison (eds), *Oxford Dictionary of National Biography*, vol. 5, Oxford University Press, Oxford, pp. 45–46.

Whishaw, J 1906, *The 'Pope' of Holland House: Selections from the Correspondence of John Whishaw and His Friends, 1813–1840*, EM Seymour (ed.), Fisher Unwin, London.

Williams, J 1833, *Memoirs of the late Reverend Thomas Belsham*, Printed for the Author, London.

4 Ricardo's encounter with geologists

'Glassmakers and dyers are not necessarily chemists, because the principles of chemistry are intimately connected with their trade' (Ricardo 1810, p. 147). This incidental remark shows up in 'On Mr Randle Jackson's Speech', one of Ricardo's pamphlets from the bullion controversy, within the context of an attack on 'practical men', the 'merchants' who do not deserve, in the name of an experience confined to their trade, the title of 'political economist'. However, what was the reason for taking chemistry as an example? It is hardly a novelty that Ricardo's early interest in the natural sciences was influential in moulding his cast of mind. Sraffa conjectured that it had a 'more decisive influence on Ricardo's characteristic cast of mind than the teaching of his later mentors, James Mill and Bentham' (Sraffa 1955, p. 35), but he did not explore the issue more in depth. This chapter illustrates what evidence would have been available to Sraffa if he had been interested in doing so.

Ricardo's higher education

An earlier chapter discusses Ricardo's education and reconstructs his family network. It was a commercial environment that nevertheless had some intellectual figures. Such primary socialisation could have left a gifted young man with an acute feeling of discrepancy between the kind of education he had received and the one others in his milieu had an opportunity to enjoy. The Memoir says that, from the age of 14, he was employed by his father in the Stock Exchange but, during 'his intervals of leisure he was allowed any masters for private instruction whom he chose to have' (Ricardo, M 1824, p. 3). Although he did not enjoy the advantages 'of what is called a classical education' – the Memoir adds –

> it is doubtful whether it would have been a benefit to him, or whether it might not have led his mind to a course of study, in early life, foreign to those habits of deep thinking, which in the end enabled him to develope the most abstruse and intricate subjects, and to be the author of important discoveries, instead of receiving passively the ideas of others.

(p. 4)

DOI: 10.4324/9781003162100-4

It is hard to say whether Moses Ricardo was pointing directly at James Mill as a negative example, but the tone of the passage is ironic. He adds that young David

> showed a taste for abstract and general reasoning; and though he was without any inducement to its cultivation, or rather lay under positive discouragement, yet at the age of nineteen and twenty, works of that description which occasionally occupied his attention afforded him amusement and cause for reflection.
>
> (pp. 4–5)

The Memoir adds that at the age of 21 he began to do business on his own and soon became one of the most respected men in his trade mainly because of his extraordinary quickness in perceiving stock market trends. Ricardo believed he had not learnt very much from his experience in the world of finance and, in a letter to John Sinclair of 31 October 1814, writes that most members of the Stock Exchange 'consider more, the immediate effect of passing events, rather than their distant consequences' (*Works* 6, pp. 150–151). The Memoir also tells us that, as soon as his improved economic conditions allowed him some leisure, he began to consecrate his spare time to mathematics and natural science. His brother-in-law George Porter writes that, while he

> was most actively engaged in business, he continued to devote much time to study and to scientific pursuits. He was of the original promoters of the Geological Society of London, and for some years a member of its council; he also acquired a considerable knowledge of chemistry, as well as an acquaintance with mathematics.
>
> (*Penny Cyclopaedia* 1841, p. 507)

The Memoir adds that 'he was drawn to the study of mathematics, chemistry, geology, and mineralogy by the example and instigation of a friend with whom he was then very intimate' (Ricardo, M 1824, p. 6). About the anonymous friend's identity, neither William Frend nor Joshua Basevi sound like plausible names, each suggested by Sraffa. The former was indeed a mathematician but never devoted his interests to chemistry, mineralogy or geology, and there is no proof that he ever met Ricardo before 1807 (Sraffa 1955, p. 34), that is, ten years after Ricardo's awakening to scientific interests. The latter, though a member of the Geological Society, was not a scientist and there is no evidence to suggest that he might have exerted an intellectual influence on Ricardo (pp. 34–35).

A solution might be to cut the knot instead of untying it. Perhaps the unnamed friend never existed or perhaps, not informed enough about the early years of his brother's independent life since relationships with his siblings were not restored until later, brother Moses may have backdated James Mill's influence on David's career by a few years. Alternatively, somebody else could have acted as a source of 'example and instigation' and a link with the Geological Society.

Wilson Lowry was a famous engraver who had married Ricardo's aunt, Rebecca Delvalle, three years after David's marriage and one year before he started cultivating scientific interests. An obituary reports that

> in the year 1812 Mr. Lowry was elected a fellow of the Royal Society; of the Geological Society he was a member from the time of its establishment. In both these societies he was beloved and respected, and was frequently consulted on occasions interesting to the progress of science.
> (*Annual Biography* 1825, pp. 101–102)

Note that, first of all, since Lowry was a Christian, Aunt Rebecca had the same reasons as David for being cast out of the family and this circumstance may have contributed to making Lowry 'very intimate' with him. Probably brother Moses had to leave Lowry nameless, using the anodyne phrase 'a friend' because of his relationship with the Delvalle family, that is, those Jewish and mercantile relatives that the Ricardo family did not like to hear mentioned. Recourse to the expression 'a friend' in order to avoid naming a relative was not too abnormal. An example can be found in Malthus's preface to the first *Essay* in which, to respect his father's wish not to be mentioned, he writes that the pamphlet originated from a 'discussion with a friend' (Malthus 1798, p. i).

An engraver specialising in drawings for scientific publications such as Alexander Tilloch's *Philosophical Magazine*, the *Journal of the Society of Arts*, Abraham Rees's *Cyclopaedia*, and Jeremiah Joyce's *Scientific Dialogues,* Lowry was drawn by his professional frequentations to acquire competences in scientific fields (Guyatt 2004). The obituary – in the same periodical that published Ricardo's 'Memoir' – declares that 'it is regrettable that posterity will know little more of him than that he was an inimitable engraver' (*Annual Biography* 1825, p. 101). It mentions his remarkable 'mathematical knowledge', his acquaintance with anatomy, medicine, chemistry and the facts that Lowry was a 'skilful engineer' and 'was deeply learned' in mineralogy and geology (p. 101). It also mentions his 'intellectual power with which few even of his scientific or professional friends were acquainted [...] his extraordinary talent in discussing the most abstruse metaphysical questions' (p. 102) adding that the 'first philosophers of the age, with whom he was very intimate, can attest that he held a distinguished rank among them' (p. 101). The obituary also regrets that 'Mr. Lowry had neither the leisure nor the inclination to publish anything of his own' (p. 104). However, at least he wrote many 'small articles' for Ree's *Cyclopedia*, 'two or three little essays which appeared many years ago in Tilloch's *Philosophical Magazine*' (p. 104) and a letter on the subject of the Mosaic Deluge published in the *Imperial Magazine* for January 1820 where he defends recent theories on the history of the Earth from the widespread accusation of 'impiety' (p. 104). Lowry had a clear stance in the geological debate, 'neither a complete Wernerian, nor a complete Huttonian' (p. 103). He believed that 'it was not fair or reasonable to expect that the Bible should contain an accurate philosophical system; that infidels should not attack the Scripture, because it did contain such a system' (p. 103) for the language of the Scripture is not unlike 'the highly figurative and hyperbolical language of all the eastern nations' (p. 104). On free will, Lowry was 'a rigid necessitarian' (p. 102). On the nature of matter, rather than the more extreme doctrine of George Berkeley, he followed that of Roger Boscovich, according to which matter is just 'the effect of a certain ever-acting, unknown power' (p. 103). In politics 'he preferred the theory of the republican, and the practice of the aristocracy' (p. 104) while, in political economy, his opinions 'coincided with those of Ricardo and Malthus' (p. 104).

Rebecca Eliza Delvalle Lowry was encouraged by her husband to become one of the first women scientists. At her death, she was 'celebrated for her acquirements in the sciences, but more especially mineralogy' (*Gentleman's Magazine* 1849; Henderson 1997, p. 29). In 1817, *The Philosophical Magazine* announced that 'Mrs Lowry would recommence her instructions directly after Christmas, at her house, 57, Great-Titchfield street' (*Philosophical Magazine* 1817, p. 465). William Phillips, a Geological Society's founder member, while listing opportunities of instruction in mineralogy either at Universities or through private instruction, recommends Mrs Lowry, 'whose fine collection of minerals, models, and instruments used in the mineralogical and geological researches, cannot fail, under her instruction, of being advantageous to her pupils' (Phillips 1816, pp. vi–vii).

Rebecca's daughter and Ricardo's cousin Delvalle Lowry wrote, at the age of 22, *Conversations on Mineralogy* (1822) illustrating it in collaboration with her father. At a later age, pressed by need, she returned to writing publishing the *Engineer's Manual of Mineralogy and Geology* (Lowry Varley 1846) and *Rudimentary Geology* (Lowry Varley 1848). *Conversations on Mineralogy* is an introductory book for children written on the model of Mrs. Jane Haldimand Marcet's *Conversations on Chemistry* (Haldimand Marcet 1808). The book recommends for private instruction the author's mother,

> Mrs. Lowry, (at her house in Titchfield Street,) who has for several years devoted a great part of her time to the collection of a very extensive and valuable collection of Minerals'.
>
> (Lowry Varley 1822, p. ix)

Like Marcet's books, Delvalle's *Conversations* consist of a dialogue between a tutor, in this case, 'Mrs L.' – an obvious allusion to her mother – and two children. After Marcet's chemistry and political economy, the book addresses one more highly disputed subject: mineralogy (Larsen 2017, pp. 107–112). Two points deserve mention. One is that the work is 'uncharacteristically lacking in religious references' (p. 112) with which all popularisations of geology abounded – but note that the book did not go beyond mineralogy.

The second is its illustration of the relationship of chemistry, mineralogy and geology. Mrs L. says that it

> is chemistry which teaches us the *essential difference* between one mineral and another [...] and without it, mineralogy would be *a catalogue of names*; the same denomination might be given to two or more minerals very different in their nature, if they resemble each other in *appearance*.
>
> (Lowry Varley 1822, p. 7; my emphasis)

In turn, mineralogy relates to geology, for 'the consideration of the different ages of minerals, belongs to geology' (p. 248).

To such, not completely 'unlettered', context also brother Moses belongs. He became a medical doctor and published papers on lighting gas. The youngest sister Sarah, in turn, was the author of a novel for children, textbooks of arithmetic and essays on educational subjects.

As within the family network, Ricardo also met middle-class professionals without a University education among Quakers and Unitarians who, besides their professional activity or as an extension to it, were cultivating the new frontline disciplines: chemistry, mineralogy and geology. Mill's condescending comment that Ricardo at the age of 40 still had 'even his education to commence' (*Morning Chronicle* 1823), betrays Mill's pride and prejudice more than any biographical detail.

After successful speculations, Ricardo retired from business, invested his fortune in landed property, and decided to devote his energies to intellectual pursuits (Sraffa 1955, pp. 67–94).

The London Institution

Sraffa lists the 'London Institution for the Advancement of Literature and the Diffusion of Useful Knowledge' among the societies to which Ricardo belonged, adding that he 'was a life-subscriber member since its foundation' (Sraffa 1955, p. 49). It was founded in October 1805 to provide a Westminster alternative to the Royal Institution, which had, in turn, been founded in the City in 1799. The founders were a few leading men of science, among them Henry Thornton, an Evangelical banker, a reformer and MP and the author of *An Enquiry into the Nature and Effects of the Paper Credit of Great Britain* (Thornton 1802), a work opening that discussion on monetary policies to which Ricardo himself contributed. The Institution's project was to provide a place with a vast reference library for members and course participants and a venue where distinguished men of science could deliver lecture courses. The programme aimed to diffuse the knowledge of useful mechanical inventions and science applied to everyday purposes.

The Institution was first established in Old Jewry whence it was moved to King's Arms Yard in 1811. Finally, in 1819, a mansion was opened in Finsbury Circus, built to host the Institution. Before that, an extensive collection of books had been acquired (Cutler 1976, pp. 53–73 and 86–95). In the new building, provided with a lecture-theatre, courses of lectures were held on various subjects, with pride of place reserved for chemistry because of the high standing of such lecturers as Humphry David (Woodward 1908, p. 271; Cutler 1976, pp. 125–128). A vital contribution to the foundation came from Richard Sharp, a wealthy merchant of Dissenting origins who became a Whig politician and an anti-slave-trade activist and was in close contact with Joseph Priestley (Knapman 2004). Members included one of Ricardo's colleagues at the Stock exchange, the already mentioned Henry Thornton, who shared his interest in political economy. Ricardo seems to have used the library but could not benefit decisively from the lecture courses since these started when he was already concentrating his interests on political economy.

Chemistry after the phlogiston controversy

A short illustration of state of the art in chemistry at the turn of the century is in order here. Robert Boyle (1627–1691) is the 'father' of modern chemistry. To him is ascribed the so-called Boyle's law which establishes for any gas an inversely proportional relationship between pressure and volume. In *The Sceptical Chymist* (1661) he attacks alchemists and vindicates an 'experimental' approach inspired by Francis Bacon, contending that assertions should only be accepted if corroborated by experiment. He attacks both the Aristotelian and the Paracelsian theory of the elements, defending as an alternative the 'corpuscular philosophy', a combination of Gassendi's and Descartes's natural philosophies that makes every natural phenomenon result from a collision between particles.

Joseph Priestley (1733–1804) was, among other things, a chemist and a controversial figure because of his defence of phlogiston, a fire-like element contained within combustible bodies. In 1697 Georg Ernst Stahl had earlier redefined such an element, introduced by Johann Joachim Becher under the name *terra pinguis*, naming it *phlogiston*, a substance that bodies were supposed to release in combustion. Priestley both defended and modified this theory. He was the first to isolate 'dephlogisticated air', that is, oxygen, but resisted Lavoisier's new oxygen theory (Schofield 1975). The main trouble with phlogiston theory was that experimental results were incompatible with the assumption that substances were losing mass during combustion because metals, on the contrary, turned out to become heavier. Nonetheless, despite his opposition to Lavoisier, Priestley stimulated the latter to introduce intellectual clarifications in his theory (Barrotta 2000).

Antoine-Laurent de Lavoisier (1743–1794), born in Paris and educated to be a lawyer, became a high-ranking public servant but concentrated his intellectual energies on geology and chemistry and was elected in 1768 to the Académie Royale des Sciences. He gave a decisive contribution to the scientific revolution in chemistry. There had been a long step-by-step march away from the Aristotelian doctrine of the four elements, and two of them, namely air and fire, had been the focus of natural philosophers in the eighteenth century. Lavoisier concentrated on combustion, performing experiments on the calcination of metals, which yielded the conclusion that metals acquire weight during calcination, a conclusion incompatible with the phlogiston theory. While Priestley introduced the term 'dephlogisticated air' as a tag for the new element that both had succeeded in isolating – a specially 'good' part of the air that made combustion possible – Lavoisier gave it a new name: oxygen. It was a detail of terminology, but a detail on which many consequences depended. Lavoisier's choice carried such implications as the fact that air was a compound of different chemical substances at the vaporous state and that combustion consisted, rather than in separation of phlogiston from fuel, in combining one chemical element with oxygen. In his *Traité élémentaire de chimie* [A Basic Treatise on Chemistry], he presented a new nomenclature of substances with the oxygen theory as its basis (Guerlac 1980). After Lavoisier, the last proponents of phlogiston theory tried for a short time to fight the oxygen theory by adding additional assumptions, thus making their theory more and more complicated.

The moral of the controversy is that it was not a matter of empirical verification or falsification, but one of internal consistency, simplicity and economy, and definitions were more than purely verbal issues (Partington & MacKie 1981).

Geology after the catastrophism-uniformitarianism controversy

That a famous economist had been a member of a Geological Society may sound less astonishing if we bear in mind that he was not yet an 'economist'. Both geology and political economy were sciences in their infancy, attracting enormous interest among the educated public and were both at the crossroads between religion and science.

James Hutton (1726–1797), a Scottish physician, gave a new impulse to the British controversy about geo-history by introducing the uniformitarian hypothesis, opposed to the catastrophist hypothesis until then prevalent. He claimed that the formation of rocks was the result of a constant process, the centre of the Earth was hot, and the history of the Earth involved an enormously long timespan. These claims implied that the received account of the origins of fossils according to which they were traces of living beings that had perished in the Universal Flood was mistaken, which implied a denial of the Biblical narrative's historical truth. Besides, the kind of inner teleology assumed to lead earth history had allegedly Deistic implications making our planet an 'eternal earth machine' and denying the Creator's role (Rudwick 2005, pp. 158–171). Richard Kirwan, the father of the London Geological Society, attacked the uniformitarian hypothesis and the Society's orientation always remained anti-Huttonian.

As mentioned, the popularity of the new science depended on broader implications that it appeared to carry. Controversies were fuelled by

> constant attack from those who interpreted the Bible literally and objected to the introduction of a purely secular viewpoint into both scientific and social issues. One by one, geology began to cast suspicion on all cherished aspects of the Old Testament account; first the Mosaic account of the Flood, then the antiquity of the Earth, and finally both the origins of man and the action of Providence in sustaining him.
>
> (Rashid 1981, p. 731)

These reasons for popularity were not far different from those by which political economy had become the battleground of unending controversy between a traditional worldview where such topics as family, procreation, poverty and charity belonged to a consecrated domain of values that needed defence from impious attacks, and the new scientific outlook. Nonetheless, the birth of a new paradigm in geo-history turned out to be a more complex and subtler process than the coming of science and the waning of superstition. For example, the image of time implied by developments in geology was closer to the Biblical view than to the eternity of the world cherished by eighteenth-century deists (Rudwick 2005, pp. 158–171).

Richard Kirwan

Some information pertaining to the intellectual career of the London Geological Society's father may serve to complete the picture. Richard Kirwan (1733–1812), the offspring of Irish gentry, studied at the University of Poitiers in France, then entered a Jesuit novitiate but left it at his brother's death in order to succeed him as the owner of the family estates. He then entered a barrister's career but soon left it in favour of scientific pursuits and moved to London in 1768, where his house became the meeting point for practitioners of the natural sciences, and he was elected a fellow of the Royal Society in 1780. Notably, under Priestley's influence, he became a Unitarian after three decades as a nominal Anglican (Scott 1973).

Kirwan was among the last supporters of phlogiston theory with his *Essay on Phlogiston and the Constitution of Acids* (Kirwan 1787). The work was translated into French with critical notes by Lavoisier and some of his associates, whose arguments Kirwan tried to refute, though admitting at last that their arguments were too strong (Akeyrod 2003).

The subjects of Kirwan's controversy with James Hutton were the primitive state of the globe and the consequences of the Universal Flood. He discusses the Huttonian theory at length in his *Geological Essays* (Kirwan 1799, pp. 54–86, 433–499). The point he attacks is a lack of consistency in the account of the present world's origins. Hutton had assumed that it consisted of the remains of a previous one, a conjecture suffering – Kirwan writes – from 'inconsistency with actual appearances' (p. 433) and ending in vicious circularity in that it assumes that rocks were composed of shells before the existence of a 'sea' when defined as a liquid mass limited by rocks at its bottom and borders. Infinite regress implied by Hutton's view of the present world as consisting of relics of a previous one also evoked the 'Deistic' idea of an eternal world. Kirwan's alternative is that the superficial part of the globe was initially 'in a soft or liquid state' (p. 7), a solution of minerals and water, the latter in higher quantity than the present one subsequently flowed partially into 'empty cavities' (p. 47). This hypothesis, justified 'on merely philosophical grounds and abstracting from all theological considerations' (p. 54) allegedly enjoyed the additional asset of compatibility with the account of the Creation reported in the Genesis (pp. 46–56).

The Kirwan-Hutton controversy, no less than any other controversy in science, arose from multiple and complex reasons. Hutton had launched the discussion about the philosophical and theological implications of geology while sharing the anti-dogmatic but moderate attitude of the Scottish Enlightenment. His work in geology, aimed at framing a set of hypotheses accounting for such phenomena as the existence of fossils, strata and various kinds of minerals, was conducted precisely in a secularising but not anti-religious spirit. Although Kirwan disliked the possible anti-religious implications of Hutton's hypothesis, he formulated his objections in purely scientific terms. He shared Hutton's assumption that a scientific account of the Earth's history need not take the Biblical narrative into account as the Bible had no intention of teaching us science. Nonetheless, he attacked Hutton's hypothesis as being unnecessary to account for phenomena for which he could work out a simpler one (p. 54).

In the preface to the second edition of his *Elements of Mineralogy*, while commenting on recent progress in the science, he writes that knowledge:

> has been still farther extended; (i) precise lines of discrimination have been traced even in the minutest sub-divisions of the science, (ii) the gross indications of the unassisted sense, freed from their attendant fallacies, have been pressed into its service; (iii) the more refined chemical tests still further perfected, have been rendered more conclusive, (iv) many new species brought to light, (v) the catalogue of the supposed elementary substances nearly completed, (vi) and the great art of analysis, extended far beyond its former limits, now nearly reaches the precision of an algebraic formula.
>
> (Kirwan 1810, pp. v–vi)

A sharp distinction he insists on is that between art and science. He writes that

> Mineralogy, though tolerably understood by many as an art, could scarce be deemed a science, being, for want of precise definitions of its objects,

incapable of communication: the *same* substance, from some slight variation of appearance, was often denoted by different names, and *different* substances by the same name; its descriptive language was, for the most part, arbitrary, vague, and ambiguous.

(p. xi)

Note that such complaints about confusion carried by lack of explicit definitions will be echoed more than once in Ricardo's comments on Malthus. Kirwan adds that what had made the transition from art to science possible was the fact that

descriptive language was at last reduced to as much precision as it was capable of receiving [...] and by the union of external characters thus described, with the results of chemical analyses, the denominations of most of the earths and stony substances then known, were finally settled.

(p. xi)

In the *Geological Essays*, he acknowledges

the practical skill which several miners are known to possess in many parts of the world. Uncombined, however, with any general theory, the knowledge thus attained is generally imperfect being circumscribed [and] frequently darkened and perplexed with notions either falsely assumed, or erroneously generalized.

(Kirwan 1799, p. iv)

Kirwan also published a *Logick* where he parts ways with Lockean tradition (Kirwan 1807, p. iii) and defines the discipline as the science studying relations of terms and propositions and the art that teaches how to develop correct arguments, which is, albeit 'dry and abstract', useful 'in discussing any subject, whether, moral, political theological, metaphysical [...], or economical' (p. ii). The work includes chapters on Syllogism, Fallacious Proofs, Probable Proofs, Sophisms. Another work is *Metaphysical Essays*. It vindicates the utility of authentic metaphysics in fighting superstition notwithstanding discredit thrown on it by confused and intricate notions in past times associated with the subject and welcomes innovations introduced by Locke, Berkeley, Condillac and Dugald Stewart (Kirwan 1809, pp. i–viii).

Kirwan's contributions to mineralogy and geology were the starting point for the Geological Society, whose library still possesses the *Geological Essays* and the *Elements of Mineralogy* (Geological Society Library Catalogue). We may assume that Ricardo knew their contents since they treated the very topics discussed at the Society's meeting. There are family resemblances, again, between some themes in Kirwan's philosophical works, for example, his treatment of false forms of reasoning and Ricardo's taste for *reductio ad absurdum*, his choice as an example of an illogical principle in the *Logick* of the claim that sovereigns should force subjects to adhere to the true religion and Ricardo's analogous argument in his parliamentary speech on toleration, and his negative judgement on Locke's logic and Ricardo's less than enthusiastic comments on Locke's *Essay.*

The Geological Society of London

In England, the landscape of scientific research was different from France, Prussia and other European countries. The first difference was the lack of one central official institution since the Royal Society and the Linnean Society were independent associations. The second was that the Linnean Society concentrated on the classification of living species, and the Royal Society had a broader scope but excluded what is now called humanities and social sciences. This circumstance is one of the reasons for the birth of specialised learned societies. The Askesian Society, whose curious name originated from the Greek word for 'effort', was founded in London in 1796 as a debating club for learned men interested in chemistry, the earth sciences and meteorology. The founder was William Allen, a Quaker philanthropist and anti-slavery campaigner who owned the Plough Court pharmaceutical company founded by Quaker apothecary Silvanus Bevan (Jones 1921, pp. 337–338), whose laboratory he put at the Society's disposal. Other founding members were Richard Phillips and William Pepys, also Quakers. Also, a British Mineralogical Society composed of people with more considerable business interests, had existed from 1799 to 1806 (Weindling 1983).

The Geological Society of London was founded in 1807 by members of the Askesian Society and others from the British Mineralogical Society. The choice of name was far from obvious. *Geologie* was a word used in French to denote theories about the history of the Earth such as Hutton's, but its adoption as a name for the new society implied a shift in meaning. Under George Bellas Greenough's influence, the new society's line was anti-Huttonian (Rudwick 2005, p. 465). At the time, the accepted map of knowledge still divided it into two fields: theology (in turn, natural or revealed), and secular studies, in turn, literary and 'philosophical'. The latter were subdivided into natural history, supposedly descriptive of phenomena, and natural philosophy or physics supposedly exploring the causes of phenomena, so that 'the sciences of the earth, like other kinds of natural knowledge, were spread across this mental map in ways that are unfamiliar to modern eyes' (p. 640). Natural history included mineralogy, which made room for the collection and classification of fossils, and physical geography; natural philosophy included geognosy (the study of rock strata in mines) and earth physics but geo-history could not be identified prima facie with any of these subdisciplines. Thus, the

> early years of the new century saw a final transformation in the meaning of 'geology', from denoting the avowedly speculative project of geotheory

[...] to its consolidation as a useful label covering all the sciences of the Earth except that increasingly questionable genre.

(p. 468)

The Geological Society's founder members were William Babington, James Parkinson, Humphry Davy, George Bellas Greenough, Arthur Aikin, William Allen, Richard Knight, James Laird, James Franck, William Haseldine Pepys, Richard and William Phillips, and Jacques Louis Comte de Bournon. Half of them were also members of the Royal Society, and the majority were either Quakers or Unitarians (Torrens 2009). In a short time, the society reached a membership of 80 paying members, plus about 100 honorary members' resident out of London and exempted from paying fees while encouraged to contribute reports of their observations on the field to be processed by the paying members.

Ricardo became a member in 1808 and in April 1810 joined the board of permanent trustees, which had seven members, besides the newly established council, which numbered 21, where he served from 1810 to 1811 and again from 1815 to 1816 (Woodward 1908, pp. 32–33, 37, 306; Sraffa 1955, pp. 49–50; Henderson 1997, p. 241). The Society published *Transactions* where almost all early members published at least once. Ricardo, though an active member and more than once elected to offices, never contributed. We cannot go beyond guesswork about scientific literature he may have read and intellectual influences fellow members may have exerted. Nevertheless, it is guesswork based on robust evidence about ideas circulating in the Society.

Controversies in geology: logic, definitions and causality

One of the concerns pressed by members was *explicit definitions*, a familiar idea for Ricardo scholars. George Bellas Greenough (Wyatt 2004), the Society's first chairman, insisted on such a necessity declaring that the source of scientific controversies is the absence of well-defined terminology. He takes the word stratum as an example. Albeit 'so familiar to us', this word is used in a sense 'very far from being precise' (Greenough 1819, p. 1) and, while discussing geological strata, everybody 'uses the word stratum, no one enquires its meaning' (p. 9). The term stratification – he goes on –

is by no means unconnected with theory [...] it is obvious that as long as the propriety of using the term depends on the idea we entertain of the manner in which strata were formed, unity of opinion can alone preclude confusion of language.

(p. 29)

Another controversial topic is *multi-causality*. Greenough is, on the one hand, in favour of simple causal explanations. Commenting on authors conjecturing several partial deluges as an alternative to the universal deluge, he rebukes their 'defiance of the recommendation of Newton, not to multiply causes unnecessarily' (p. 152). He lists at least six kinds of causes, besides deposition, that may have contributed to determining the formation of the parallel planes exhibited by the surface of different beds (pp. 28–35). Besides, he lists four causes of inequalities on Earth's surface at work before diluvian action, namely, crystallisation, partial deposition, subsidence, volcanoes, and earthquakes (pp. 204–210).

One more concern is to avoid *confusion of effects with causes*. Greenough writes that 'at great depths, where there is no motion there can be no abrasion' and thus 'submarine valleys existed before the existence of the ocean', currents 'were rather *the effect* of these valleys than *the cause* of them' (p. 141). Since the Huttonian account of the rocks' curvature assumes 'that all the rocks have been forced up once from the bottom of the sea, and primitive rocks twice', it seems to assume that 'the primitive rocks have acquired their vertical or inclined posture in consequence of this violent elevation, the secondary in spite of it' (p. 57 fn.), thus formulating an illogical explanation where '*the effect preceded the cause*' (p. 71).

Another preoccupation is the *distinction between permanent and transitory causes*. For example, Greenough accepts the idea that there may have been a deluge but, while trying to identify possible causes for such an event, he first rules out a universal flood caused by a growth in the quantity of water on Earth and then discusses possible causes of the movement of masses of water to cover different parts of the Earth at different moments. He argues that we should rule out *permanent causes* for this event on the ground of its character of a unique event and single out some *transitory cause*, for example, the transit of a celestial body, 'a cause foreign to our globe [...] which, having acted its part once, may not have occasion to repeat it in the long period of five thousand years' (p. 196).

From chemistry and geology to political economy

A scientific education

Sraffa is as accurate as usual concerning the London Institution and the Geological Society of London. Weatherall (1976, p. 49) speculates about Ricardo's intellectual awakening between 1805 and 1812, suggesting that the London Institution's intellectual atmosphere 'clearly appealed to David Ricardo, since he rose steadily in its hierarchy, becoming a Visitor in 1815 and a manager in 1823'. Henderson ignores Ricardo's scientific interests, going no further than the Geological Society's mention as the setting of Ricardo's encounter with Horner (Henderson 1997, p. 241). King briefly repeats information obtained from Sraffa, namely that he 'also belonged to the London Institution, using its large reference library' (King 2013, p. 8). Heertje (2015) ignores his scientific interests. The facts described here suggest that Sraffa was both right and wrong.

Attendance at the London Institution provided Ricardo with a proxy for higher education. Since Ricardo met with the requirements for admission to the Geological Society, his previous self-taught education should have been not too shaky. Moreover, it is also Sraffa's opinion that he hardly needed schooling in Benthamite philosophy to be in a position to work out original contributions to economic theory. On the other hand, at the London Institution and the Geological Society Ricardo learnt something different from what Sraffa was unconsciously looking for, namely *natural science* as a robust alternative to the vagaries of Marginalist *subjectivism*. It was not the steel and crystal building of Science but a science involved in endless controversies and striving for identity.

Besides, as a result of the above reconstruction, a few details may be assumed to be established that may add something to the picture of Ricardo's intellectual career. These are that, at the age of 25, he undertook a remarkable experiment in self-taught education, specialising in scientific subjects and achieving some acquaintance with *mathematics* and more serious competence in *chemistry*.

Note that the path he took was by no means an eccentric choice, being a typical one for urban middle class with significant proportions of Quakers, Unitarians and Jews. As mentioned, non-Anglicans could not apply for admission to Oxford and Cambridge. Indeed, such intellectual figures as Joseph Priestley and Isaac Watts completed their education at Dissenting Academies, non-Anglican educational institutions that in the eighteenth century had raised their standards to the point of competing with the two Universities. Towards the end of the century, while making a living by trade or one of those liberal professions to which access was possible, several such outsiders dedicated their efforts to 'useful' knowledge, one that would yield practical applications besides dispelling prejudice.

Ricardo was admitted as a member of the Geological Society one year after its foundation. Requirements for admission included residence in London, paying considerable fees, enjoying a gentleman's status, and being judged competent in the relevant fields. This circumstance implies that somebody who knew him well and had acknowledged authority should have vouched for his competence. As mentioned, one such person could have been his acquired relative Wilson Lowry, a middle-class Anglican who had undertaken the same self-taught education as Ricardo.

Chemistry, geology and experimental farming

One indirect link connecting chemistry, mineralogy, geology and Ricardian political economy is experimental farming. At the Geological Society Ricardo came in touch with two members who had advanced knowledge of chemistry and carried out experiments in its application to agriculture.

The first was Humphry Davy (1778–1829). After a self-taught education, he had published on chemical subjects following Lavoisier in general but rejecting his theory of caloric. In 1802 he became a Professor of Chemistry at the Royal Institution, where he had young Michel Faraday as an assistant, and in 1803 a fellow of the Royal Society. He isolated several elements, such as potassium, sodium and magnesium. From 1803 to 1812, he delivered an annual lecture course on experimental agriculture established by the Board of Agriculture (Knight 1980; 2004).

The other member was Smithson Tennant (1761–1815) who studied chemistry under Joseph Black in Edinburgh and then obtained a Doctor of Medicine degree from Cambridge University. From 1788 he was resident in London where he became a member of the Askesian and then of the Geological Society, and in 1813 Professor of Chemistry at Cambridge. He proved the identity of coal and diamond and discovered iridium and osmium (Goodman 1991; Usselman 2004). Like Francis Horner and David Ricardo, he was a member of the King of Clubs where he heard discussions on topics of political economy (Usselman 2005, pp. 129–131). A remarkable circumstance is that he conducted experiments in agricultural chemistry on an estate he had acquired in Somerset.

There is no evidence that Ricardo attended Davy's lectures on agriculture, but he could not have ignored their existence (Morgan 2012, pp. 54–55). Besides, his meetings with Tennant may have offered the occasion for conversations on agricultural subjects (to Malthus 22 March 1813; 16 September 1814; Whishaw to Ricardo 8 August 1815, in *Works* 6, pp. 90, 135, 244).

How cognisant was Ricardo on agriculture at the time he moved to Gatcomb? At this time, John Sinclair, an acquaintance of Ricardo offered to 'give any information you may wish for, on the subject of agriculture, the doctrines of which are now so much simplified, that in a few months you may acquire all the information necessary to become a good farmer' (Sinclair to Ricardo, 29 October 1814, in *Works* 6, p. 150). Ricardo's reply is:

> I am not yet become a farmer. I leave the management of them wholly to others, and hardly take sufficient interest in what is going on, to make it probable that I shall ever be conversant with agricultural subjects.
> (to Sinclair 31 October 1814, in *Works* 6, p. 150)

A literal reading would suggest that Ricardo was utterly uninformed about agriculture at this stage and acquired more competence only later when he was required to acquire it in his capacity as a Member of Parliament. A more careful reading might suggest, first, that he was also following the general rule 'Try not being smart, and in case you cannot help it, at least do not show it around', second, that he was also politely inviting Sinclair to keep away. The reasons may be that, though Sinclair was undoubtedly an authority in the field, a member and sometime president of the Royal Highland and Agricultural Society of Scotland and, besides, a corresponding member of several European agricultural societies, he was also a former supporter of the Pitt government, that is, not precisely a fellow-traveller in politics.

The facts are that, besides information on 'chemical agriculture' obtained from colleagues at the Geological Society, Ricardo followed the discussion on agricultural matters in relation to the Corn Laws, of which he was a strenuous opponent (Morgan 2012, pp. 50–51). After he acquired his Gatcomb estates, the letters by Edward Wakefield, Ricardo's land agent, kept him informed 'of his duties as a good landlord, his tenant farmers' problems, the difficulty of finding reliable new tenants, the state of the market for land, and the prices of produce' (Morgan 2012, p. 51). In Parliament, he was appointed a member of the Select Committee on the Causes of Agricultural Distress in 1821 and 1822. Thus, it is possible that his contacts at the Geological Society may have contributed to awaken his interest in experimental agriculture.

Ricardo's first meeting with a political economist

The Horner brothers, both members of the Geological Society, happened to be the authors of Ricardo's introduction to the circle of political economists. Leonard Horner (1785–1864), the son of a Scottish linen merchant, moved to London in 1804 as a partner in his father's firm after studying chemistry, mineralogy and geology at Edinburgh University. He became a member of the Geological Society in 1808, published in the Society's *Transactions* and was elected a fellow of the Royal Society in 1813 (Bartrip 2004). His older brother Francis (1778–1817), also educated at Edinburgh University, qualified as a lawyer and, besides being one of the *Edinburgh Review* founders, became a Whig Member of Parliament. In 1809, due to his omnivorous curiosity, he applied for membership, too (Thorne 2004). Ricardo first met him at the Society and his essays in the *Edinburgh Review* were among his first economic readings.

A science in its making

When Ricardo started writing on economic subjects, he had recently become a member of the Geological Society. We may safely assume that he was familiar with the members' ideas on logic, scientific terminology, and causality. Rashid very aptly notes that both political economy and geology

> date their origins to about the same time; economics to Adam Smith's *Wealth of Nations* and geology to James Hutton's paper before the Royal Society in 1785. Economists have generally ignored this period of interaction between economics and geology. It has been easy to move from Newton to Darwin without the earthly interlude.
>
> (Rashid 1981, p. 726)

In Ricardo's case, keeping such interaction in mind can help avoid hasty generalisations that ignore the immediate context. Typical blunders are Ricardo the Benthamite, Newtonian Ricardo, un-philosophical Ricardo and, most recently, Ricardo the 'zealot' without any idea of what science is. One source of such confusion is the prejudice that somebody who was one century's outstanding figure should have had an overwhelming influence on everybody else and that connections with other less famous figures are unimportant. Another is the 'myth of coherence', the idea that what an author says at any point should reveal a system of ideas hidden in his mind.

Ricardo's notorious 'cast of mind' – it will be argued in the following chapters – was a more complicated affair than applying a ready-made 'methodology' to scientific practice. It resulted from influences at several levels and in distinct phases, including shifting connections with three different religious communities, studying chemistry and mineralogy, encounters both at the Geological Society and outside it, with philosophers, that is, writers on human nature, society, government and political economy. Within this context, meta-scientific claims heard at discussions at the Geological Society may have played their role. Those presenting an affinity with considerations expressed in his works and correspondence are: (i) the importance of precise terminology; (ii) a need to correct 'gross indications of the unassisted sense'; (iii) a need to try to approach the same precision as that of algebraic formulas; (iv) a need to distinguish between limited experience and transitory effects on one hand and permanent regularities on the other.

Partial conclusions: the importance of a scientific education

1. Ricardo neither had 'his education to commence' (Mill) nor was he 'an unlettered *pater familias*' (Hutchison) or an 'untutored genius' (Stigler), even less a 'zealot' (Mirowski) without any knowledge of what science is. What happened is that he went through an unusual primary education and found a distinct path to a no less unusual higher education.
2. Ricardo was born into a religious, cultural, and linguistic minority. When he was forced to sever ties with it, instead of integrating into the majority group, he entered into contact with minorities such as Quakers and Unitarians, to no small extent middle-class professionals interested in the new frontiers of science and its application.
3. At the beginning of his activity as a political economist he enjoyed the asset of familiarity with natural science, not the majestic building of Newtonian Physics but rather the humbler, *down to Earth*, and *magmatic* discipline of geology and it was *this* scientific experience that contributed to moulding his 'cast of mind'.
4. There is a connection between the London Geological Society and the Hartley-Priestley philosophy due to Richard Kirwan's close contact with Joseph Priestley; there is a kinship between the meta-scientific claims formulated by Kirwan and his followers in the Huttonian controversy

and the 'logic' of Hartley, Priestley, and Belsham favouring simplicity, reduction of principles and elimination of unnecessary entities.

5. Among the interests of a few members of the Geological Society there were also applications of chemistry to agriculture; it is plausible that the role of the model farm in Ricardo's argument on rent, profit and wages, and on growth and stagnation from which he derives implications for the economy as a whole owes something to Ricardo's early scientific interests.

6. From such an experience he received, instead of a deductive aprioristic attitude or the 'materialist' imprinting required to be Marx's 'forerunner', an awareness of the controversial character of theoretical assumption, the slippery character of scientific entities and the constant interaction between definitions and theory building.

References

Akeyrod, M 2003, 'The Lavoisier-Kirwan Debate and Approaches to the Evaluation of Theories', *Annals of the New York Academy of Sciences*, vol. 988, no. 1, pp. 293–301. DOI: 10.1111/j.1749–6632.2003.tb06110.x.

Annual Biography 1825, 'Wilson Lowry', *Annual Biography for the Year 1825*, vol. 9, pp. 93–107, Longman, London.

Barrotta, P 2000, 'Scientific Dialectics in Action: The Case of Joseph Priestley', in P Machamer et al. (eds), *Scientific Controversies*, Oxford University Press, Oxford, pp. 154–176.

Bartrip, PWJ 2004, 'Horner, Leonard (1785–1864)', in HCG Matthew & B Harrison (eds), *Oxford Dictionary of National Biography*, vol. 28, Oxford University Press, Oxford, pp. 163–165.

Cutler, JC 1976, *The London Institution 1805–1933*, The University of Leicester, Unpublished Ph. D. Dissertation, viewed 30 March 2021, https://figshare.com/articles/thesis/The_London_Institution_1805-1933/10102646

Gentleman's Magazine 1849, 'Lowry Rebeca, 14 December, *The Gentleman's Magazine*, no. 31, February.

Geological Society Library Catalogue, The Geological Society of London, viewed 30 March 2021, http://geolog.cirqahosting.com/HeritageScripts/Hapi.dll/search1?

Goodman, DC 1981, 'Tennant, Smithson (1761–1815)', in Ch. C. Gillispie (ed.), *Dictionary of Scientific Biography*, vol. 13, Smith, London, pp. 280–281.

Greenough, GB 1819, *A Critical Examination of the First Principles of Geology*, Longmans, London.

Guerlac, H 1980, 'Lavoisier, Antoine-Laurent', in Ch. C. Gillispie (ed.), *Dictionary of Scientific Biography*, vol. 8, Scribner's, New York, pp. 66–91.

Guyatt, M 2004, 'Lowry, Wilson (bap. 1760, d. 1824)', in HCG Matthew & B Harrison (eds), *Oxford Dictionary of National Biography*, vol. 34, Oxford University Press, Oxford, pp. 611–612.

Haldimand Marcet, J 1808, *Conversations on Chemistry*, Longman, London.

Heertje, A 2015, 'Life and activities', in H Kurz & N. Salvadori (eds), *The Elgar Companion to David Ricardo*, Edward Elgar, Aldershot, pp. 264–272. DOI: 10.4337/9781784715489.

Henderson, JP 1997, *The Life and Economics of David Ricardo. With Additional Chapters by J.B. Davis*, WJ Samuels & GB Davis (eds), Kluwer, Dordrecht.

Jones, RM 1921, *Later Periods of Quakerism*, Macmillan, London.

King, JE 2013, *David Ricardo*, Palgrave Macmillan, Houndsmill.

Kirwan, R 1787, *An Essay on Phlogiston and the Constitution of Acids*, edn used: Cass, London, 1968.

Kirwan, R 1799, *Geological Essays*, Bremner, London.

Kirwan, R 1807, *Logick; or, an Essay on the Elements, Principles, and Different Modes of Reasoning*, vol. 1, Payne, London.

Kirwan, R 1809, *Metaphysical Essays Containing the Principal and Fundamental Objects of that Science*, Payne, London.

Kirwan, R 1810, *Elements of* Mineralogy, 3d edn., vol. 1, Mackinlay, London.

Knapman, D 2004, 'Sharp, Richard (1759–1835)', in HCG Matthew and B Harrison (eds), *Oxford Dictionary of National Biography*, vol. 50, Oxford University Press, Oxford, pp. 33–35.

Knight, D 2004, 'Davy, Sir Humphry, Baronet (1778–1829)', in HCG Matthew & B Harrison (eds), *Oxford Dictionary of National Biography,* vol. 15, Oxford University Press, Oxford. pp. 506–512.

Knight, DM 1980, 'Davy, Humphry', in C C Gillispie (ed.), *Dictionary of Scientific Biography*, vol. 3, Scribner's, New York, pp. 598–599.

Larsen, K 2017, *The Women Who Popularized Geology in the 19th Century*, Springer, Cham, Switzerland. DOI: 10.1007/978-3-319-64952-8.

Lowry Varley, D 1822, *Conversations in Mineralogy*, Longmans, London.

Lowry Varley, D 1846, *The Engineer's Manual of Mineralogy and Geology*, Weale, London.

Lowry Varley, D 1848, *Rudimentary Mineralogy*, Weale, London.

Malthus, TR 1798, *An Essay on the Principle of Population*, EA Wrigley & D Souden (eds), The Works of Thomas Robert Malthus 1, Pickering, London.

Morgan, MS 2012, *The World in the Model. How Economists Work and Think*, Cambridge University Press, Cambridge. DOI: 10.1017/CBO9781139026185.

Morning Chronicle 1823, 'Mr. Ricardo', *The Morning Chronicle*, Monday September 15, p. 1 (Reprinted in the Appendix of this book).

Partington, JR & McKie, D 1981, *Historical Studies on the Phlogiston Theory*, Arno Press, New York.

Penny Cyclopaedia 1841, 'Ricardo, David', in *The Penny Cyclopaedia of the Society for the Diffusion of Useful Knowledge*, vol. 19, Knight, London, pp. 507–508 (Reprinted in the Appendix of this book).

Phillips, W 1816, *An Elementary Introduction to the Knowledge of Mineralogy*, W. Phillips, London.

Philosophical Magazine 1817, 'Lectures', *The Philosophical Magazine*, vol. 50 (July–December), p. 465.

Rashid, S 1981, 'Political Economy and Geology in the Early Nineteenth Century: Similarity and Contrasts', *History of Political Economy*, vol. 13, no. 4, pp. 726–744. DOI: 10.1215/00182702-13-4-726.

Ricardo, D 1810, 'On Mr Randle Jackson's Speech', in *Works* 3, pp. 145–153.

Ricardo, M 1824, 'A Memoir of David Ricardo', in *Works* 10, pp. 3–15.

Rudwick, MJS 2005, *Bursting the Limits of Time: The Reconstruction of Geohistory in the Age of Revolution*, The University of Chicago Press, Chicago, IL.

Schofield, RE 1975, 'Priestley, Joseph', in CC Gillispie (ed.), *Dictionary of Scientific Biography*, vol. 11, Scribner's, New York, pp. 139–147.

Scott, EL 1973, 'Kirwan Richard', in CC Gillispie (ed.), *Dictionary of Scientific Biography*, vol. 7, Scribner's, New York, pp. 387–390.

Sraffa, P 1955, 'Addenda to the Memoir', in *Works* 10, pp. 16–106.

Thorne, R 2004, 'Horner, Francis (1778–1817)', in HCG Matthew & B Harrison (eds), *Oxford Dictionary of National Biography*, vol. 26, Oxford University Press, Oxford, pp. 159–162.

Thornton, H 1802, *An Enquiry into the Nature and Effects of the Paper Credit of Great Britain*, Hatchard, London.

Torrens, HS 2009, 'Dissenting Science. The Quakers among the Founding Fathers', in CLE Lewis & SJ Knel (eds) *The Making of the Geological Society of London*, The Geological Society of London, London. DOI: 10.1144/SP317.

Usselman, MC 2004, 'Tennant, Smithson (1761–1815)', in HCG Matthew & B Harrison (eds), *Oxford Dictionary of National Biography*, vol. 54, Oxford University Press, Oxford, pp. 124–125.

Usselman, MC 2005, 'Smithson Tennant: The Innovative and Eccentric Eighth Professor of Chemistry', in MD Archer & CD Hale (eds), *The 1702 Chair of Chemistry at Cambridge: Transformation and Change*, Cambridge University Press, Cambridge, pp. 113–137.

Weatherall, D 1976, *David Ricardo. A Biography*, Nijhoff, The Hague.

Weindling, P 1983, 'The British Mineralogical Society', in I Inkster & J Morrell (eds) *Metropolis and Province: Science in British Culture, 1780–1850*, Hutchinson, London, pp. 120–150.

Woodward, HB 1908, *The History of the Geological Society of London*, The Geological Society of London, London.

Wyatt, J 2004, 'Greenough, George Bellas (1778–1855)', in HCG Matthew & B Harrison (eds), *Oxford Dictionary of National Biography*, vol. 23, pp. 608–609, Oxford University Press, Oxford, pp. 608–609.

5   Ricardo's encounter with philosophers and political economists

When he was in his mid-thirties, Ricardo decided that 'the powers of his mind' ought to be 'almost wholly devoted to the elucidation of questions connected with political economy, a study which was at once best suited to the peculiar quality of his mind and most in unison with his daily pursuits in business' (*Penny Cyclopaedia* 1841, p. 507). Previous chapters have reconstructed how Ricardo's family network included more than semi-literate merchants, how a relative encouraged him to pursue a scientific education, and how Quaker relations introduced him to an environment of devotees of the new science. The present chapter reconstructs how, from about 1808, he also established lasting relationships with authors on topics of logic, ethics, government and political economy, or – to use the language of the time – 'philosophers'.

Francis Horner and the Scottish philosophy

Dugald Stewart's common-sense epistemology, ethics and politics

Dugald Stewart (1753–1828), who had succeeded Adam Ferguson in the chair of moral philosophy at Edinburgh University, was the mentor of a whole generation of Scottish intellectuals, including the founders of the *Edinburgh Review*. Stewart worked out a philosophy of mind meant to supply a basis for other disciplines, including ethics, political theory, and political economy. His starting point was Thomas Reid's common-sense realism. His polemical targets included Hume – whose empiricism combined with the association of ideas he believed leads to scepticism – and Hartley and Priestley, whose theory of 'vibrations' he believed trespasses into 'metaphysics' abandoning the safe ground of 'experimental philosophy' (Levi Mortera 2018, pp. 51–64). His criticism did not spare Adam Smith himself, whom he accuses of indulging in scepticism by overlooking in his 'History of Astronomy' the difference between modern natural philosophy that starts with induction from 'individual phenomena' to establish 'general laws' (Stewart 1814, pp. 338) and ancient systems that did not go beyond 'soothing the imagination' by introducing order into the unconnected phenomena that we observe.

DOI: 10.4324/9781003162100-5

Stewart's 'experimental philosophy' programme is a vindication of the 'Newtonian' *regulae philosophandi*, a humble attempt 'to rise slowly from particular facts to general laws' (Stewart 1810, p. xxi). It implies that explanation is not a reduction of phenomena to one principle (Stewart 1814, pp. i–v). Ultimate causes are unknowable, and we should neatly distinguish them from explanatory principles (Stewart 1792, p. 479). Discussion of efficient causes and essences belongs to 'metaphysical speculations' (p. 13) and is out of place in 'experimental philosophy', and thus 'general laws' are not 'operating as efficient causes' (p. 212).

Elements I comments on the status of political philosophy arguing that the art of government is bound to remain forever at a lower level of certainty than the mechanical arts, for the

> difficulties which, in the mechanical arts, limit the application of general principles, remain invariably the same from age to age (...) In the art of government, however, the practical difficulties which occur are of a very different nature. They do not present to the statesman the same steady subject of examination which the effects of friction do to the engineer. They arise chiefly from the passions and opinions of men, which are in a state of perpetual change.
>
> (Stewart 1792, p. 203)

A more extended discussion of the issue is in *Elements II*, of 1814. From 1799 to 1809, Stewart taught a course on political economy closely following *The Wealth of Nations* but adding extensive discussion of Malthus's population theory. Unfortunately, the manuscript revised for publication was destroyed and what we have is a relatively verbose transcript of the lectures (Stewart 1855, 1856). Here he repeats his definition of political economy as an aspect of political philosophy, whose subject matter is not confined to wealth and population but includes virtue and happiness which are the ends pursued by 'good government': a broad definition sharply contrasting with Ricardo's restricted definition of political economy and possibly echoed by Malthus's (Winch 1983; Rashid 1985, 1987; Levi Mortera 2003).

Horner, the Scottish political economist

Francis Horner (1778–1817), the first philosopher with whom Ricardo established a lasting relationship, had studied at the University of Edinburgh and then, after qualifying as a barrister, became an active Whig politician. He was among the *Edinburgh Review* founders and its principal author on economic subjects. After his first election in 1806 followed by re-election in 1807 and 1812, he achieved high authority in Parliament on economic issues and had a softer attitude to the Poor Law and the population principle than the Edinburgh reviewers' approach (Fetter 1965). His reviews were Ricardo's first economic readings after *The Wealth of Nations*.

As mentioned, the London Geological Society provided the occasion for their first meeting. In 1810 Horner was appointed chairman of the Bullion Committee, which had been created to investigate and report on the causes of the 'high price of bullion' (Thorne 2004). The fact that he was the chairman of the Committee may have occasioned his encouragement to Ricardo to publish. The latter had presented in 1809 his views in letters to *The Morning Chronicle*, a newspaper owned by James Perry also a member of the Geological Society (Ricardo, M 1824, p. 7; Henderson 1997, pp. 240–241). Horner persuaded him to write a pamphlet, the usual form of scholarly publication, published with the title 'On the High Price of the Bullion'. Being Ricardo's friend and acquainted with Malthus, Horner may have arranged their first meeting (James 1979, pp. 195–212; Henderson 1997, pp. 296–308) and in the following six years he followed the discussion between them with interest. In a letter to Lord Webb Seymour of 6 July 1807, he mentions Malthus's 'philosophical candour, calm love of truth, and ingenious turn for speculation in his important branch' disclosing his admiration for 'how closely he has taught himself to examine the circumstances of the lower classes of society, and what a scientific turn he gives to the subject' (Horner 1843, p. 404).

In a letter to Mill of 23 October 1816, Ricardo writes:

> I am grieved by a paragraph I see in the newspaper today, that Horner is obliged to spend the winter in Italy for his health. I dined in company with him not long before leaving London, when he coughed in a manner that frightened me. He will be a very great loss – even his absence this winter is grievously to be deplored – when so many foolish, and, I fear, some villainous schemes of finance, will be proposed and listened to.
>
> (*Works* 7, p. 85)

Ricardo may have heard from Horner that the political economist's task is to fight the 'prejudices of the vulgar' (Horner 1803, p. 80) and exert an influence on 'vulgar understandings, in favour of an enlightened policy' (p. 95) by the repetition of concrete examples. He may also have heard about the need to keep 'the labour of accumulating particular facts [...] separated from the more liberal task of generalising these into principles' (Horner 1802, p. 28), in order to avoid 'mixing general principles with particular facts' (p. 30) by introducing principles of a general theory first, then an account of historically given facts, and after that the examination of concrete cases. These were undoubtedly Stewart's concerns but hardly his unique ideas. The analytical-synthetic procedure was an essential item from the Baconian-Newtonian tradition. Though Adam Smith was careful in avoiding philosophical comments in *The Wealth of Nations*, his contemporary Robert Pownall did not doubt that he had constructed his argument along these lines (Pownall 1776, p. 337).

Horner's distaste for James Mill is worth mentioning. The fact that they were both Scottish was not enough to obscure Horner's awareness of Mill's deficiencies; in a letter of 16 July 1810 to Francis Jeffrey, the *Edinburgh Review*'s editor, he complained of Mill's 'deplorable heresies' (*Works* 3, p. 9) and in another of 3 December 1810 implored Jeffrey not to let him 'lay his hands upon us' (p. 10). Horner was Ricardo's first mentor in political economy and encouraged him to publish. Though his mentor's intellectual attitude owed much to Stewart, Ricardo's only mention of Stewart is about a topic treated in his *Philosophical Essays* (Stewart 1810, pp. 53–100), namely an objection to Berkeley's solipsism (to Mill 18 December 1817, in *Works* 7, p. 229) and we lack any evidence of Ricardo's reading of the *Elements*. Ricardo displays no more closeness to Stewart than to Smith, Say and Malthus. In *Reply to Bosanquet*, his attack on 'crude observation and particular facts' draws on widespread commonplaces with hardly anything Stewartian. There is hardly any proof of Ricardo's conforming to 'the method advocated by Stewart' (Depoortère 2008, pp. 103) or of the fact that influence by 'Stewart's pupils' yielded any 'affinity' with Stewart's 'method' (Depoortère 2013, p. 20).

Jeremy Bentham and the philosophic radicals

Jeremy Bentham (1748–1832) is one of those grand figures, more famous today than in their lifetime, who are the typical cause among historians of a widespread ocular disorder – the perception of non-existent influences on everybody living and acting in his century. In our case, the most severe clinical case was Élie Halévy, who forged the myth of Ricardo's Utilitarianism. We will assume that Bentham, unlike lesser-known figures, is known to the reader, so we will deal with him in just a few lines. Bentham conducted a strenuous activity as a writer in ethics, linguistic theory, law and political theory, but he was as bad an organiser of his work as one can be. In 1789 he published *An Introduction to the Principles of Morals and Legislation*, now believed to be his most important work but ignored at the time. Others resulted from the editing of manuscripts by his followers. It was the case, for example, of the *Traités de législation civile et pénale* [Treatises on civil and penal legislation] of 1802 and the *Traité des peines et des récompenses* [A Treatise of penalties and rewards] of 1811 published in French by Étienne Dumont. In 1808 he met James Mill, who had reviewed some of his writings in the *Edinburgh Review*, and hired him as his secretary, a position in which Mill acted as the organiser of a lobby named the Philosophic Radicals.

The novelty of Benthamite ethics was the 'principle of utility' presented in the *Introduction*. The term 'utility' describes 'that property in any object, whereby it tends to produce benefit, advantage, pleasure, good, or happiness [...] to the party whose interest is considered' (Bentham, 1789, p. 12). The principle is no more than an axiom. The fundamental law of psychology says that the motive of action is always to pursue one's pleasure, but this law is the description of a fact, not a prescription. Nevertheless, when we apply the principle to individual cases, we need a specific psychological theory, namely Lockean associationism, on whose basis to perform the 'felicific calculus'. Bentham's legal and political theory stands on the same basis, the principle of utility, psychological hedonism, and self-regarding propensity. In more detail, his theory of government aims at introducing mechanisms apt to make the interests of the many who are ruled check those of the ruling few. In Bentham's lifetime, these theories won international notoriety while his ethics remained virtually ignored. Until 1834, Utilitarianism was the doctrine of a restricted circle including Bentham, James Mill, Francis Place and, with serious reservations, his editors Étienne Dumont and John Bowring. Other fellow travellers came from a broader circle of 'friends of reason' (Campos Boralevi 1990, pp. 109–112; Dinwiddy 1990, pp. 116–118).

Bentham also wrote on political economy but his manuscripts defending a utility-based view of subjective value were left unpublished due to Ricardo's criticism. Though the Marginalist revolution came later as a result of creative use of Benthamite ideas, his other economic writings owe virtually nothing to his utilitarian doctrine (Collison Black 1988; Guidi 1991, pp. 139–141; Bonner 1995, pp. 17–46).

Francis Jeffrey, who reviewed Bentham's *Traités de législation* for the *Edinburgh Review*, argued that his ethics and jurisprudence were less new than they seemed, for there is a broad consensus on utility as the measure of what is morally right. Nevertheless, there is no point in trying 'a bold and rigid investigation into the utility of any course of action that may be made the object of deliberation' (Jeffrey 1804, p. 18). Instead, the moralist and the legislator should rely on 'the old established morality of mankind' (p. 18). Our perception of utility depends on 'sense and feeling' and is no more precise and universal than our shared judgements on right and wrong. Jeffrey's was an isolated criticism since in Britain Bentham's ideas were more ignored than attacked. The reason is that, during the Napoleonic wars, the issue of parliamentary reform was no longer on the agenda and it came back after 1815 in the uneasy company of working-class radicalism during the post-war economic depression. Whig politicians started to fear that radicals might endanger the cause of Reform and were eager to distance themselves from them. This concern inspired a prolix discussion of Bentham's *Plan of Parliamentary Reform* (1817) in the *Edinburgh Review* contending that, even on Benthamite premises, the universal franchise would produce more evils than benefits (Mackintosh 1818).

Bentham's editor John Bowring reports one of his memorable sayings 'I was the spiritual father of Mill, and Mill was the spiritual father of Ricardo: so that Ricardo was my spiritual grandson' (Bowring 1842, p. 498). The same message is in Bentham's letter to Say of 19 October 1823 where he writes: 'Coulson in the Globe-and-Traveller said on morals and politics he had taken his principles from me: which through the medium of Mill was exactly true. Till he knew Mill he was not distinguishable from other Stockjobbers' (Bentham 2000, p. 309).

The facts are that Ricardo and Bentham first met in Spring 1812 (to Malthus 13 August 1811, in *Works* 6, p. 67). When Say visited Ricardo at Gatcomb in 1814, they went together on a visit to Bentham and Mill at Ford

Abbey (to Malthus 18 December 1814, p. 160). An invitation from Ricardo to return the visit is in a letter to Mill of 30 August 1815 (p. 245) and another from Mill of 23 August 1815 mention a meeting at Ricardo's brother's home (p. 235). Despite Bentham's tendency to a secluded life, letters and other evidence offer the picture 'of fairly close personal contact between them over the years, this contact being maintained mainly through Mill' (Sraffa 1952, p. 19). After Ricardo's election to Parliament, the frequency of meetings grew, and the focus of their conversations became Reform. Frequent walks in Hyde Park became the occasion for discussing party politics (to Malthus 25 May 1818, in *Works* 7, p. 263). There are traces of social events involving Ricardo, for example, an invitation to dinner for 13 May 1822 in Bentham's boyish humoristic style (Bentham 2000, pp. 73–74).

Besides reading his economic manuscripts, Ricardo was familiar with Bentham's political works, but no evidence suggests that he ever read his other writings. Three of Dumont's compilations are in Ricardo's library: *Traités de legislation* [Treatises on legislation], *Tactiques des assemblées législatives* [Legislative Assembly Tactics] and *Théorie des peines et des récompenses* (Sraffa 1955, p. 399), and a letter to Trower of 22 March 1818 mentions his reading of the *Plan of a parliamentary Reform* (*Works* 7, pp. 260–261).

The moral is that Mill recruited Ricardo to the Philosophic Radicals, hoping that his economic theory might become a weapon for their arsenal. It resulted in just one more ingredient for their cocktail of ideas, with hardly anything Benthamite in it; Mill felt it was in assonance with their policies since it seemed to play against rent, agricultural protectionism, and the Poor Laws. Mill was an abolitionist while Bentham used to muse about a reformed and, unsurprisingly, authoritarian system of support for the poor (Guidi 1991, pp. 189–195; Sigot 2015, p. 21).

James Mill, between Scottish philosophy and Benthamism

James Mill (1773–1836) entered Edinburgh University when Dugald Stewart held sway over the Scottish Intellect. In 1798 he took Church of Scotland orders but, after losing faith in Christian revelation, he abandoned the ministry and moved to London to earn his living as a journalist. After years of economic hardship, Bentham hired him as a secretary, which allowed him leisure to start working at his *History of British India*. He ended up with a prestigious position at the East India Company, ironically obtained thanks to a book severely critical of the Company. Before he first met Ricardo, he had published a pamphlet on economic subjects, *Commerce Defended*, attacking William Spence's *Britain Independent of Commerce* for denying that foreign trade adds to national wealth and thus trying to 'revive the system of the *Economistes*' (Mill 1808, p. 4). Mill notes that the term *consumption* has a double meaning, the first that of 'absolute destruction of property', the second of 'consumption for the sake of reproduction' (p. 69), or better, *employment*.

He adds that, in the country's interest, 'as much as possible of its annual produce should be *employed*, but as little as possible of it consumed' (p. 70) and the 'production of commodities [...] is the one and universal cause which creates a market for the commodities produced' (p. 81).

Mill enjoyed the enviable asset of education at Edinburgh University and came to London with this viaticum but for several years had no other chance of improving on that dowry, except by the unsystematic omnivorous reading occasioned by his activity as a journalist. Becoming Bentham's lieutenant, he took three items from the Benthamite hoard: the utility principle, the psychological theory and the theory of government, which he grafted – with notable tensions – onto his Scottish dowry. His first publication on philosophical topics is a curious anecdote; it is a review of Belsham's *Elements,* where he attacks everything the author says and neatly sides with Locke and Reid against the Hartley-Priestley philosophy (Bain 1882, p. 41 fn.). While ignoring its necessitarianism and materialism, he concentrates on its philosophy of mind, judging that Locke, Reid, and Stewart had proceeded correctly within the boundaries of the Newtonian 'experimental philosophy' while Hartley, Priestley and Belsham had indulged in aprioristic theorising (Mill 1802, pp. 3–4; cf. Bucchi 2001, pp. 19–20).

The following year, while reviewing Stewart, Mill comes back on his distinction between true and false followers of the experimental philosophy, stigmatising Belsham once more as an author who professes his faith in Newton's *regulae philosophandi* and, immediately after that, fills up his book 'with nothing else than extravagant and unfounded theories' (Mill 1803, p. 569). While reviewing Belsham's book, he also attacks him on adopting the 'self-ish system' (Mill 1802, pp. 10–13), a phrase connoting the theories claiming that enlightened self-love recommends respecting the moral law as a road to happiness. Here Mill attacks Belsham in the name of Stewart's refusal of reduction of moral motives to one inspired by the Scottish aversion from the Cartesian spirit of system, arguing that we act morally at once for several reasons, for example, justice for justice's sake, benevolence or vanity (Mill 1802, pp. 10–11). He quotes Belsham's admission that it 'can never be proved that the interest of the agent himself might not in some instances be promoted by an occasional deviation from the strict rule of truth, justice, and benevolence' (Belsham 1801, pp. 409–410). Such an admission – Mill contends – is enough to destroy Belsham's system of morality since the only remedy left is an appeal to a future life when virtue and happiness will be coincident. However, Belsham himself – he goes on to argue – destroys any evidence of a future life when admitting that such belief is only a matter of revelation. Mill objects that we 'have no conception of moral character in the Divine Being, but from what we experience of moral character in ourselves. We must believe the Divine Being therefore actuated solely by views to his own happiness' and, in this case, we cannot prove that 'the happiness of the Divine Being requires the eternal exercise of beneficence to his creatures' (Mill 1802, p. 12; cf. Bucchi 2001, pp. 20–25). The tone of Mill's objections may be a symptom of his malaise after conversion to unbelief, to which he may have reacted by transferring its source to a scapegoat, in this case, the leader of the most enlightened Christian congregation, a brilliant example of the widely practised tactic of attacking one's closest allies first.

In 1815 there was a U-turn. Until then he had been defending Stewart's philosophy while gradually becoming a Benthamite convert. By 1815, he had consummated his gradual move away from the Scottish philosophy, and the villain had become Stewart himself for failing to follow the rules of experimental philosophy. Mill writes that Stewart's criticism of Utilitarianism is beyond the point. The

> authors who have represented utility as the principle of moral distinctions [...] have proceeded on a plan exactly conformable to that which is pointed out by Sir Isaac Newton, as the only true mode of philosophising. That man pursues happiness, they say, and flies from misery, in other words seeks pleasure, and avoids pain, is a known and acknowledged fact. This fact, they continue, we assert to be completely sufficient to account for all the moral phenomena of human life. We classify these phenomena, and we show that into this fact they all resolve themselves, in the most satisfactory manner [...] Mr. Stewart completely fails in his attempt to show that the fact to which the appeal is made does not account for the phenomena. And [...] he supposes an occult quality [...] a blind, unaccountable propensity to approve or disapprove, which has no dependence either upon reason or experience.
>
> (Mill 1815, p. 195)

Mill turns his previous attack on Belsham upside down in this passage, defending that 'selfish system' whose adoption by Belsham he had stigmatised (Giuntini 1995, pp. 192–205; Bucchi 2001, pp. 89–101). At last, in *An Analysis of the Phenomena of the Human Mind* of 1829, he adopts Hartley's associationism but in a watered-down version, failing to see the point of Hartley's neurophysiological research programme. In conclusion, before and after 1815, Mill adopted a mix of Scottish and Benthamite ingredients in varying doses, with no attempt at a new synthesis for which he lacked time, motivation, and intellectual gifts.

Mill and Ricardo first met sometime before 1810 when Ricardo had not yet published anything, and the former was an established essayist (Weatherall 1976, pp. 72–76; Henderson, 1997, p. 280). The first extant piece of correspondence between them is from 25 December 1810, when Mill sent Dumont's translation of papers by Bentham to Ricardo (*Works* 6, pp. 13–14) and then arranged a meeting to discuss their publication (Henderson 1997, pp. 280–286). The relationship soon evolved into a close friendship. When Ricardo felt lost facing the prospect of writing a book and started complaining about his 'neglected' education (to Trower 29 October 1815; to Mill 24 October 1815, in *Works* 6, pp. 314–316; to Malthus 7 February 1816, in

Works 7, p. 19), Mill almost bullied him into writing the book. He tried to instil in him a sense of guilt for wasting his talents in the country-squire life and promised any help he might need (Mill to Ricardo 23 August 1815; 10 October 1815; 9 November 1815, 1 December 1815, in *Works* 6, pp. 251–252, 309–310, 321–322, 329–333; 14 August 1816; 18 November 1816; 16 December 1816, in *Works* 7, pp. 60, 98–99, 108–109). It is true that 'Mill's letters of the period are full of advice relating to "the art of laying down your thoughts, in the way most easy to apprehension"' (Sraffa 1951, pp. xx) and yet – Sraffa comments – 'Mill's contribution to the making of the *Principles* was less than might have been expected from his promises and encouragement' (pp. xx–xxi).

One of Mill's main accomplishments was Ricardo's political career. As early as 1814, when the latter was planning retirement from business, he started putting pressure on him to enter the House of Commons. Once Ricardo had completed the *Principles*, Mill decided he should teach him the 'science of legislation' as a tool for his political career and, in a letter of 19 October 1817, proposed his *History of India* as 'no bad introduction to the study of civil society in general' (*Works* 6, p. 195). In this work, he intended to apply the Scottish 'philosophical' or 'conjectural' history to the Indian case, with two goals in mind. The first was to explain 'the principles and laws of the social order in almost all its more remarkable states, from the most rude to the most perfect with which we are yet acquainted' (p. 195). The justification for a reconstruction of the history of Indian societies lay 'primarily, not in their particular interest, but in their universal relevance to the history of civil society' (Rendall 1982, p. 59). The kind of competence required – according to him – was philosophical, and he could dispense with such details as knowledge of Indian languages and direct acquaintance with the country. He writes that the 'mental habits' required 'for extracting the precious ore from a great mine of rude historical materials' were 'the powers of combination, discrimination, classification, judgment, comparison, weighing, inferring, inducting, philosophising' (Mill 1817, p. xxiii).

The second goal was to single out the right policies Britain should adopt while shouldering the White Man's Burden, helping a vast mass of barbarians to a higher level of civilisation. Mill writes that to ascertain 'the true state of Hindus in the scale of civilisation, is not only an object of curiosity in the history of human nature' but 'is an object of the highest practical importance' to those charged with 'the government of that great portion of the human species' (p. 17). The main mistake to unmask – he believed – was popular mythology about the Indian civilisation, such as the notions that the Indians invented mathematics or had a philosophy comparable to the Greek philosophy. He deplored the mistake committed 'by the British nation, and the British government', in assuming 'the Hindus to be a people of high civilisation' (p. 225).

Mill tried to accommodate Bentham's claim that legislation, government, and education should be the same for all human societies with the Scottish claim that they vary according to the stage of human history to which a given society corresponds. For stages before commercial society, they should be adapted to the poor conditions of those societies. To formulate his diagnosis, Mill adopts a typically Scottish consideration of the state of laws, religion, and other institutions and practices, which would prove that India is still a country at a barbarian stage, and then – without worrying too much about consistency – he combines it with the Benthamite consideration of the extent to which the principle of utility inspires existing institutions and practices. The beneficent imperialist's task is to teach the Indians the pursuit of utility, which is what entitles us to 'regard a nation as civilised' (p. 224). This passage was the occasion for one of Ricardo's objections as discussed in another chapter.

In 1817 and 1818, after the *Principles* and before the election to Parliament, Ricardo dedicated his time to systematic reading, including history, travel reports, religion and philosophy. Mill contributed a reading list focused on the science of human nature, which in his view should provide the basis for the 'science of legislation' (Mill 1835, p. 145) the knowledge required for Ricardo's political career – albeit not for political economy, a field where he recognised Ricardo as the 'schoolmaster'. Among Mill's suggested readings were Hume's *Essays* and Locke's *Essay on Human Understanding*. Meanwhile, Ricardo read Pierre Bayle without waiting for Mill's suggestion (Mill to Ricardo 19 October 1817, *Works* 7, p. 196). Elsewhere Mill praises Bacon and Dugald Stewart (3 December 1817, *Works* 7, p. 206), and Ricardo alludes to his reading of Thomas Reid and Stewart's *Philosophical Essays* (to Mill 18 December 1817, *Works* 7, p. 229).

After Ricardo's death, John Ramsay McCulloch and Mill went on popularising simplified 'Ricardianism', including claims that Ricardo had never endorsed, or had formally repudiated, such things as a crude version of the principle of population, a 100% labour theory of value and the wage fund doctrine. The reason for such simplifications is Mill's already mentioned dream to appoint Ricardo to supervise the economic branch of Philosophic Radicalism, for he 'was interested in economic theory as a weapon in the service of his political program' (Hollander 1985, p. 28). Simon Patten remarked that 'the creed of James Mill was Calvinism minus God and charity' (Patten 1899, p. 316), and the peculiarities that made him influential

> came from the fact that he was a Calvinist by birth and retained through all his life the characteristics for which men of this type are remarkable. They are noted for the strict way in which they reason, and for the boldness with which they apply their principles into details. Disliking exceptions and compromises, they readily accept disagreeable conclusions if these seem to be deductions from general principles.
>
> (pp. 314–315)

Half a century later, John Stuart Mill wrote that Ricardo's *Principles* 'would have never been published or written' without the 'earnest entreaty and strong encouragement' (Mill 1873, p. 20) from his father. This is fair enough, and Mill's influence on Ricardo's career was significant. Nonetheless, while Malthus was a worthy intellectual partner, Mill, with his 'talent for deduction and logical presentation' (Halévy 1901, p. 186), that is, the talent of an 'an egregious simplifier of complex issues' (Ball 2010, p. 10), was an efficient 'career manager' (Henderson 1997, p. 274) but never the source of original ideas. To conclude, regarding political economy, Mill's 'influence on Ricardo's method rests [...] unsettled in the absence of definite textual evidence' (Depoortère 2013, p. 24).

Thomas Robert Malthus and the Cambridge philosophy

Cantabrigian epistemology and ethics

Malthus is a crucial figure in the history of economic thought and the most influential among Ricardo's intellectual partners. His contributions to population theory and political economy are well known to any reader. Something may yet be said on his ethical and epistemological views.

There was a Cambridge tradition in science and epistemology in the eighteenth century: the 'Newtonian Philosophy', a set of claims marking a third way between radical scepticism and Cartesianism. Colin Maclaurin's *Account of Sir Isaac Newton's Philosophical Discoveries* illustrated one particular version of the Newtonian method that became paradigmatic at the Scottish universities and Cambridge. It downplays Newton's exclusion of hypotheses, arguing that he had ruled out just 'conjectures' or groundless hypotheses (Maclaurin 1748, pp. 29–30) on which the 'old mode of philosophising' was based, consisting of 'imagining systems, instead of learning from observation and experience the true constitution of things' (p. 7). It explains Newton's claim of being able to 'deduce' theories from observation as the assertion that we should '*proceed by the method of analysis, before we presume to deliver any system synthetically*' (pp. 90–91) and defends recourse to analogy when we cannot detect the causes of phenomena (p. 21).

John Keill's *Introduction to Natural Philosophy*, a Cambridge textbook, contrasted 'mechanical' philosophy with Platonism, Aristotelianism, and Baconianism. It claimed that this philosophy avoids idle talk of inexistent substances such as Cartesian ether and abstruse entities such as Aristotelian 'occult qualities' (Keill 1700, p. 4). One more Cambridge textbook was Isaac Watts's *Logick*, adopting the Lockean account of perceptions and ideas and fighting the Aristotelians' practice to use words 'without ideas' (Watts 1725, p. 84).

The average eighteenth-century clergyman had received little training in theology in today's sense of the word. He had studied mathematics, physics, classics and a limited amount of philosophy and, on top of that, Natural Theology, the *philosophical* discussion of God's existence. The existence of natural morality, distinguished from the moral doctrine taught by divine revelation, was a matter of course for Thomism and most Scholasticism but had been rejected by Lutherans and Calvinists. The Cambridge Platonists Benjamin Whichcote, John Smith, Henry More, and Ralph Cudworth, and their fellow traveller Samuel Clarke rescued natural morality by proposing to ground ethics on empirical and rational evidence. Richard Cumberland started a parallel line of inquiry, adopting Grotius's idea of a natural law independent of revelation but combining it with theological voluntarism. Not unlike Nicholas Malebranche and Gottfried Wilhelm Leibniz, he wanted to draw implications from voluntarism opposite to those drawn by the Calvinists, justifying the existence of universal non-arbitrary prescriptions without denying divine omnipotence.

John Gay developed Cumberland's ideas, arguing that the consequentialist criterion is the one adopted by God. At the same time, human beings produce the consequences desired by God following non-consequentialist moral criteria. He claimed that the motive for acting morally is a false question, for the end of action is happiness, and to expect 'a reason, i.e. an end, to be assigned for an ultimate end, is absurd' (Gay 1731, p. 278). John Brown argued along similar lines that human beings tend to seek happiness, and the 'very essence of moral rectitude' is the conformity of actions to this end (Brown 1751, p. 205). William Paley argued that the moral quality of actions depends on the quantity of 'happiness' they bring about (Paley 1785, p. 18). Morality is the tendency of actions to promote happiness, and 'Whatever is expedient is right. It is the utility of any moral rule alone which constitutes the obligation of it' (p. 61). We may discover God's will by enquiring 'into the tendency of the action to promote or diminish the general happiness' (pp. 56–57) for he wants his creatures' happiness and enforces a 'system of moral government' through general laws, the 'laws of nature' (p. 194).

Malthus's ethics and epistemology

Thomas Robert Malthus (1766–1834) graduated from Cambridge, received holy orders and was elected a fellow of Jesus College. There, he received an education that 'was tantamount, in the circumstances of the day, to producing a Newtonian natural and moral philosopher capable of subjecting all theories to the test of observation and experiment' (Winch 1987, p. 18; Cremaschi 2010) and was schooled into the Cambridge theological, ethical and political tradition (Cremaschi 2014, pp. 16–40). This tradition was anti-Calvinist, stressed the essential goodness of human nature, the existence of natural morality and a role for 'utility' as God's key for selecting 'general laws' to enact. In the wake of Cumberland, Gay, Brown and Paley, Malthus declares that motives are always self-interested, the essence of morality is prudence, and God has so organised the world to teach us the right course of action through painful consequences of immoral actions. The moralist's task is 'to distinguish that class of actions, the general tendency of which is to produce misery, but which, in their immediate or individual effects, may produce perhaps exactly the contrary' (Malthus 1803, p. 19). In other words – unlike Bentham – the test of utility is, rather than a criterion for *deciding* what is right and wrong, a criterion for *detecting* whether a maxim is a 'law of nature'.

In 1798 Malthus published the *Essay on the Principle of Population*, a pamphlet against Condorcet's and Godwin's utopian doctrines. The argument was that a 'principle' making the population increase faster than the means of subsistence would make any egalitarian social arrangement founder. In 1803 he published the second *Essay*, a bulky treatise with a rich dowry of empirical data but nonetheless a work in applied ethics using empirical social enquiry as an auxiliary discipline. The work aims to detect moral laws, singling out classes of actions that produce unhappiness, like lack of prudence that prompts early marriages without certainty to be able to provide for the offspring (Cremaschi 2014, pp. 81–84, 119–123).

Malthus follows the Scottish-Cantabrigian epistemology. He contrasts the 'consistent theory of Newton', a result of the new mode of philosophising that requires 'patient investigation, and well authenticated proofs' with the 'old mode of philosophising' that, like the Cartesian theory of vortexes, makes 'facts bend to systems' (Malthus 1798, p. 59). The first *Essay* starts with two 'postulates' (p. 8) concerning the indispensability of food and the stable presence of the sexual drive from which he draws consequences to be confirmed by 'experience' (p. 10). In the second *Essay,* he notes the backwardness of 'the science of moral and political philosophy' but believes that 'the brilliant career of physical discovery' (Malthus 1803, p. 203) provides an example for social science. In the *Principles of Political Economy*, he declares that, though the 'moral and political science' enjoys a privileged status vis-à-vis natural science because its subject matter is more directly accessible, the study of its laws is made more difficult by the impossibility of reducing human 'needs and tastes' to mathematical figures (Malthus 1820, pp. 1–16). Its proofs cannot compete in certainty with 'those which relate to figure and number' since practical results depend upon 'so variable a being as man' and 'so variable a compound as the soil' (p. 1). Consequently, political economy is more similar 'to the science of morals and politics than to that of mathematics' (p. 2). The 'laws which regulate the movements of human society' are different from 'physical laws' because they are continually changing due to 'human interference' (p. 13) and a 'circle of causes and effects' (p. 16). Thus, only general principles partake 'of the certainty *of* the stricter sciences' (p. 8), and others 'require limitations and exceptions' (p. 8). There are three sources of error: 'a precipitate attempt to simplify and generalise' (p. 355), the temptation to mistake 'appearances, which are merely coexistent and incidental' (p. 21) for causes, and the presumption that an 'isolated fact' can refute a 'consistent theory, which would account for the great mass of phenomena observable' (p. 10).

Malthus and Ricardo first met in June 1811 in London when the former was already famous while the latter had just started publishing. In the first two letters, both expressed the wish to settle 'by an amicable discussion in private' (Malthus to Ricardo 18 June 1811, in *Works* 6, p. 21) what appeared to be 'the very few objections' which prevented them 'from being precisely of the same opinion' (to Malthus 18 June 1811, in *Works* 6, pp. 23–24). Malthus then visited Ricardo at Gatcomb Park on three occasions, and Ricardo spent weekends with him at Haileybury. After the Political Economy Club's foundation, they started meeting at its monthly dinners in London (Henderson 1997, pp. 286–336). The correspondence intensified after the publication of Ricardo's *Principles* in 1817. In 1820, Malthus stated his objections in his *Principles* (Malthus to Ricardo 3 December 1817, in *Works* 6, p. 215), and Ricardo responded with his *Notes on Malthus,* which were left unpublished on Mill's suggestion. In the third edition of his *Principles*, Ricardo introduced modifications to his value theory, partly in response to Malthus's objections. The issues discussed were the influence of the currency upon foreign exchanges, the Corn Laws and rent, the possibility of a 'general glut', the inverse proportion between wages and profits, the relationship between exchangeable value and natural value and the possibility of an 'invariable measure' of value. The discussion, not by chance described as aimed at 'settling some important points relating to the metaphysics of Political Economy' (Malthus to Ricardo 9 October 1814, in *Works* 6, p. 139), tackled language and definitions, multi-causality, causes and general laws and the scope of political economy. The controversy was as inconclusive as any other. Complaints of misrepresentation were recurrent, yet it occasioned modifications in their theories (Cremaschi & Dascal 1998, pp. 43–45).

Thomas Belsham and the Hartley-Priestley philosophy

The Hartley-Priestley epistemology

Unlike Belsham and Malthus, few readers would have heard of Thomas Belsham before meeting him in a previous chapter. Besides a Unitarian divine, he is also the last representative of an important eighteenth-century philosophical school.

David Hartley (1705–1757), an Oxford graduate and medical doctor, was the author of the *Observations on Man*, a work ranging from physiology to religion. The work starts with a theory of 'vibrations' as the physical basis of mental life (Hartley 1749a, pp. 5–6). On this basis, it erects a theory of knowledge and language that turns Locke's philosophy upside down. It denies the mind-body dichotomy, reduces mental events to neuro-physiological ones and ideas to a combination of physical vibrations (Allen 1999, pp. 145–153). It claims that neurological processes generate consciousness while making it clear that 'association' is *not* a name for the process by which ideas connect themselves but instead indicates the process through which physical vibrations generate ideas (Giuntini 1995, pp. 71–88; Allen 1999, pp. 93–121, 376–382). In more detail, the 'component particles' of the nervous system and the brain receive impulses from the external world, in turn, governed by attractive and repulsive forces; original vibrations leave weaker vibratiuncles, which leave even weaker ones persisting after the original stimulus has disappeared (Hartley 1749a, pp. 7–13). An implication is that ideas themselves, far from being ultimate data, are *generated* by vibrations. Echoing Spinoza, Hartley answers the objection that his doctrine is materialism claiming that soul and body are the same (Hartley 1749b, pp. 31–32). His theory of language, described in another chapter, reconstructs language in terms of a network of associations between sound or written signs and 'sensible impressions'.

Joseph Priestley (1733–1804), philosopher, chemist and a leading Unitarian divine, sided in philosophy with Hartley against the Scottish common-sense school and the Cantabrigian tradition. He defends a sort of Newtonian Baconianism, the claim that what philosophers should be doing in every field, including 'the study of history, and of human nature', is first 'assuring themselves with respect to *facts*, and then explaining these facts by reducing them to *general principles*' (Priestley 1790, p. 383). He favours mono-causality against unnecessary multiplication of causes, arguing that a 'philosopher supposes no more causes than are necessary to explain effects' (Priestley 1778, p. 31). He endorses 'the universally received rules of philosophising, such as laid down by Sir Isaac Newton'. He mentions the first, that 'we are to admit no more causes of things than are sufficient to explain appearances' and the second 'that to the same effect we must, as far as possible, assign the same causes' (Priestley 1777, p. 221), while omitting the third and the fourth, the one that declares that no hypothesis may be maintained if it contrasts with phenomena. This rule first appears in the third edition of the *Principia*, that is, in 1726. Thus it was still unknown to early popularisers but became the Scottish philosophers' weapon against the Cartesian 'spirit of system'. Priestley also stresses the distinction between 'real appearances' and 'superficial appearances' (p. 221), one example of the latter class being the impenetrability of material bodies. He declares that we may formulate scientific laws even without certainty about the underlying causes; for example, the 'laws of motion are only general rules, to which the facts relating to the approach of bodies to each other, and their receding from each other, are reducible, and are consistent with any *cause* of such approaching or receding' (Priestley 1778, p. 19). He finally proclaims the unknowability of substances, for 'the term *thing*, or *substance*, signifies nothing more than that to which properties are ascribed, and is itself absolutely unknown, and incapable of suggesting any idea whatever' (pp. 23–24); talk of 'properties' of bodies is just a way of expressing 'the unknown cause of the known effects' (p. 31), which is not tantamount to 'real agency' (p. 24).

Thomas Belsham, from 1812 the Essex-Street-Chapel Minister, had been teaching first at the Dissenting College at Daventry and then at the short-lived Unitarian College at Hackney in Eastern London. Manuscript lecture-notes were circulating at the time from a series of courses ranging from Logic to Political Philosophy (Belsham, *Students lecture notes*) and Ethics (Belsham, *Moral Philosophy*). In 1801 he published the *Elements of the Philosophy of the Mind*, a work including an introduction to logic, an exposition of Hartley's philosophy of mind and an ethic close enough to Hartley (Fitzpatrick 1999; Webb 2004).

In his epistemology, the first claim is that 'we know nothing' about 'real essences' or 'that peculiar contexture' of the 'constituent particles' of a thing 'upon which its peculiar properties depend' (Belsham 1801, p. xii). 'Experimental Philosophy', that is, natural science, is based on 'observations of the senses' which do not teach us 'the real essence of substances' (p. xxxii); 'intuition' does play a role in demonstration and is an essential element of science, which is, in a proper sense, knowledge acquired by demonstration (p. xxxiii). He reports Newton's *Regulae philosophandi*, but his list is limited to the three first rules, omitting the fourth (p. 5). Belsham's view of language, described in another chapter, is a kind of nominalism. To sum up, Belsham's epistemology is limited scepticism combined with Hartleyan associationism whence he derives a methodological lesson, namely that, since 'real essences' are unknowable and there are so many causal links in the world, scientific theories are no more than sets of general laws expressing observed regularities.

The Hartley-Priestley ethics

Ethics lies at the centre of Hartley's *Observations*. A centre is a geometrical entity without dimensions, and in this work, not unlike Spinoza's *Ethica*, it is virtually everywhere. Hartley draws a classification of six kinds of pleasures and pains, including sensation, ambition, self-interest, sympathy, theopathy, and the moral sense. The first five can contain positive and negative 'affections' – even theopathy may be either a positive or negative passion since it names the pleasures and pains prompted by elements in the whole collection of things 'religious' – and only the moral sense carries out an always positive function. The virtuous person follows the moral sense, dictated by sympathy and theopathy. Even lower affections may fulfil a useful function in limiting the force of even lower ones. For example, self-interest is a less than virtuous motive and yet a source of reasons for checking the desire for pleasures of 'sensation' and 'ambition', and thus it may be helpful at the beginning of a process of moral education.

The problem Hartley wants to settle is the alternative between theories, the one of Shaftesbury who considers the moral sense an 'instinct' and those that consider it as resulting from 'determinations of the mind, grounded on the eternal reasons and relations of things' (Hartley 1749a, p. 498), declaring that both are partly right and partly wrong. Against the second class, he suggests that the moral sense exists but is a derived rather than primary entity. Against the first, he argues that self-interest, far from primary, is derived from more elementary affections. Thus, self-interest or desire for happiness may be epistemologically primary without enjoying ontological priority. Hartley believes that individual happiness, public happiness, and God's happiness are three sides of a square triangle whose moral sense is the surface (Allen 1999, pp. 44–45). Thus, moral sense should be assumed to arise from association alone and all the pleasures and pains of sensation, imagination, ambition, self-interest, sympathy and theopathy 'beget in us a moral sense' which 'carries its own authority with it, inasmuch as it is the sum total of all the rest' (Hartley 1749a, p. 498).

The decisive point is that moral improvement is self-propelling since it depends on an internal factor, namely the association process that will overcome the effect of the Fall, bringing humankind back to a paradisiacal state. Nevertheless this process, heading to 'perfect self-annihilation, and the pure love of God' (Hartley 1749b, p. 282), albeit understood in religious, indeed mystical terms, involves humankind as a whole. The climax of moral improvement is the restoration of fallen humanity to 'perfect manhood' where all will act 'to increase each other's happiness without limits' (p. 287). The universal character of salvation provides the theological premise of a secularising consequence, namely the admission of the virtuous unbeliever and the independence of morality from religion. Hartley declares that the 'common practice of mankind' suggests the right rule of life, and such a suggestion may be considered even by 'an atheist or sceptic' (p. 196). Virtuous persons who practised benevolence and piety and took the moral sense as the rule of their life, though best exemplified in the Old and the New Testament, were also non-Christians such as Socrates. Hartley concludes that pious and benevolent persons of all kinds own some 'Philosopher's Stone' (p. 344), indicating the path to virtue.

Priestley published an edition of the First Part of Hartley's *Observations* with comments (Hartley 1775). He presented an ethical theory close to Hartley and – despite Bentham's mention of Priestley as one of his sources – far from Utilitarianism. His view of happiness starts with the assumption that the latter is not a measurable magnitude whose parts we can add together. Instead, he writes, echoing Leibniz's 'mirroring' view of happiness, it is an indefinite magnitude multiplied rather than divided when shared among individuals. For 'no man can be happy who lives to himself' (Priestley 1787, p. 143) and 'true happiness' consists 'in having our faculties wholly engrossed by some worthy object, in the pursuit of which the stronger and best of our affections have their full play' (p. 143). The conciliation between self-love, God's love, and love of one's neighbour adopted by Cumberland and his followers is disappointing because it is a solution to a non-existing problem. Hartley's lesson is that there is more identity than opposition between the three kinds of love. Besides, self-love is a hard horse to ride, for it is

> very apt to grow too intense, and is, in fact, the cause of a great deal of the useless anxieties, perplexity, and misery there is in the world, and that, therefore, it ought to be our care, that our minds be engrossed as much as possible by other objects.
>
> (p. 143)

In other words, happiness overlaps with 'the good', which does not mean that 'good' is just another name for 'happiness'. Like Spinoza and Leibniz, true happiness consists of developing all our faculties to their best in activity directed towards some worthwhile goal. We may be happy when acting with the good as a goal. So-called happiness is just the most fully developed form of life, and moral motivation does not depend on *self-love* but coincides with *love*. In fact,

> we are so made, as social beings, that every man provides the most effectually for his own happiness, when he cultivates these sentiments [...] which [...] conduce to the welfare of those with whom he is connected.
> (Priestley 1782, p. 27)

A paradoxical implication is that the best way to promote our happiness is to forget it. Nonetheless, self-love is a self-destructive kind of motivation. It is well-advised not to teach this implication, or at least to recommend forgetting it. Echoing this paradox, Priestley writes that human beings are happy 'but when their faculties are properly exercised in the pursuits of those things which give them pleasure', that is, in 'pursuit rather than enjoyment' (Priestley 1787, p. 129). Active people are 'generally more happy' because they 'have their thoughts constantly employed in the pursuit of some end, which keeps their faculties awake and fully exerted' (p. 131).

Priestley advocates toleration, which is both rational and useful to society (Priestley 1771, p. 133). He claims that society arises out of mutual interest and the government's legitimacy lies in serving individual happiness (p. 13). However, total freedom and equality are impossible, and the acceptable degree of restraint depends on its consequences in terms of the common good. 'Happiness of the whole community' is the sole end of politics (p. 32). 'Virtue and right conduct consist in those affections and action which terminate in the public good' and 'the whole system of right to power, property, and everything else' that may ensure such happiness (p. 12).

Belsham's *Elements* include an ethical theory. Echoing Locke, he argues that 'as moral ideas are equally capable of strict definition with mathematical ideas, demonstration is equally applicable to moral subjects' (Belsham 1801, xlv). He adds that 'the same cause operating in the same circumstances will invariably produce same effects' (pp. lxxxii–iii) and thus also the study of human behaviour may reach the same degree of precision as 'that with which we foretell the effects of physical causes' (p. lxxxiii). Yet in practice 'the evidence of those principles by which human life is chiefly governed, seldom amounts to more than to a high degree of probability' (p. 110) and 'the choice of connections, professions, and situations in life, and even the most important doctrines of natural and revealed religion are more properly the object of rational belief than of certain knowledge' (p. 110).

The starting point of ethical theory is also for Belsham the idea of happiness. His claims are: first, the 'only valuable end of existence is happiness' (p. 369); second, the essence of virtue is the tendency of an action to achieve 'the voluntary production of the greatest sum of happiness, or [...] unlimited benevolence' (p. 379); third, it is only by religion that 'self-love and benevolence can be reconciled' (p. 411) and only belief in God makes virtue and happiness eventually coincide; fourth, this belief may make us confident that 'virtue will ultimately triumph [...] every individual will ultimately attain pure and perfect happiness, and that the world will be restored to a paradisiacal state' (p. 401).

One chapter discusses systems that make virtue coincide with utility, attacking Richard Godwin's proto-Utilitarianism, denouncing the mistake implied by the claim that our interest in the general good provides a motive to virtue.

The mistaken assumption is that the common good is coincident with our own. The criterion of utility might provide a moral standard only from a universalistic point of view, the only one where the agent's happiness and the 'general good' coincide (p. 432). Indeed, 'if the extraordinary case should occur in which I can promote the general good by my death, more than by my life, justice requires that I should be content to die' (p. 440). Nonetheless, no sacrifice of one's good to the general good can be obligatory when there is no prospect of adequate compensation and this

> is possible only upon the hypothesis of a future life, and under the government of a Being of consummate wisdom and benevolence, in which case, to suppose that any being can be ultimately a loser by the greatest sacrifices he can make of self-interest to the good of others would be extravagant and absurd.
>
> (p. 447)

The chapter also attacks Bentham's ethics for failing to justify the greatest-happiness principle; it contends that only if we consider the whole world and assume that there is an afterlife can we justify the principle since only from this point of view is the agent's happiness coincident with the 'general good' (p. 432).

The chapter discusses Paley approving his statement that 'the good of mankind is the *subject*, the will of God is the *rule*, and everlasting happiness the *motive*, of human virtue' (p. 379) or that virtue consists of 'doing good to mankind, in obedience to the will of God, and for the sake of everlasting happiness' (Paley 1785, p. 25). Belsham agrees that the essence of virtue is 'the ultimate happiness of the agent', yet

> the expectation of future reward is so far from being essential to the existence of human virtue, that an explicit regard to it as a motive, is even inconsistent with a state of complete, that is, of absolutely disinterested virtue.
>
> (Belsham 1801, p. 371)

Paley is also unjustified in denying that an atheist may be 'just, temperate, humane, generous, and amiable' (p. 435).

Belsham writes that, while natural philosophy has the task 'to investigate the laws, and to resolve the phenomena, of the material universe', the philosophy of mind 'investigates the laws, and explains the phenomena, of the intellectual world' (p. 1) and the science of politics is one of its parts providing the ruler with 'profound knowledge of human nature' and teaching him how 'to guide the various passions and contending interests of parties, and of individuals, to the general good' (p. 4).

Belsham was also aware of the quick change in the British economy. He mentions 'manufactures' as 'fountains of moral corruption', praises Robert Owen's social experiments (Belsham 1814, p. 12), and gives a non-negative opinion on children's work (Williams 1833, pp. 684–685). In a letter of 19 September 1823, he mentions Ricardo commenting that it is

> really astonishing that a doctrine so absurd and so contradictory to plain and obvious fact as that of Malthus, should have gained a moment's credit with any person of common understanding. And yet it is wonderful to see what numbers are fascinated with it: among others, my late friend, Mr. Ricardo. He made some use of it in his theory of political economy, which I could never well understand.
>
> (p. 749)

Instead – he argues – since the law of supply and demand plays a decisive role in agricultural production no less than in other fields, food production may grow almost indefinitely provided that there is a demand for it. Besides, what lies behind Malthus's principle is 'vested interest'; his principle offers the rich a justification for dissuading the poor from marriage (p. 749).

No correspondence with Ricardo is extant, and no external evidence is available of acquaintance with Belsham's philosophical work. Nonetheless, its absence from the Ricardo Library is no counterevidence. Bentham once said that Ricardo 'would borrow a sixpenny book instead of buying it' (Bowring 1842, p. 498) and, until he moved to Gatcomb, he used to borrow most of the books he read. Thus, even on the wild conjecture that Ricardo's resolve to 'convert' to Unitarianism was the best way to hide his atheism, he may have found Belsham's philosophical ideas justified or unjustified on purely philosophical grounds. Besides, there is internal evidence of his familiarity with ideas close enough to the Hartley-Priestley philosophy on language, causality, scientific laws to discuss in another chapter. The proviso is in order that influences may be overdetermined – for example, Ricardo may have read about explicit definitions and artificial terminology in Richard Kirwan's works and heard about these topics in discussions at the *London Geological Society*. With this proviso in mind, Ricardo may have heard from Belsham that we never attain certainty and the best we may reach is probable knowledge; the knowledge of essences and causes is impossible and we must be content with general laws, and science requires artificial terminology. Besides, he may have heard that the essence of morality is general benevolence. The agent's happiness and public happiness are both obvious goals of action. Virtue is attainable also by unbelievers, and toleration should be unlimited.

Jean–Baptiste Say and the *idéologie*

Jean-Baptiste Say (1767–1832) was a textile entrepreneur, a republican politician and journalist. Thanks to fame won by his economic works, after the fall of Napoleonic regime he became a professor of 'industrial economics' at the *Conservatoire national des arts et métiers* in Paris and, in 1830, was granted the first chair of political economy at the most prestigious French intellectual institution, the *Collège de France*.

His best-known moral and political work is *Olbie, ou Essai sur les moyens de réformer les mœurs d'une nation* [Olbie, or an Essay on the Means of reforming a Nation's Morality] of 1800. Here, the central theme is the conflict, dating back to Nicolas Malebranche, between unruly and enlightened self-love. Within this framework, he addresses the practical question of the eighteenth-century *philosophes*: how to improve a nation's morality and counter self-love's destructive effects (Forget 1999, pp. 35–50; Whatmore 2000, pp. 111–135). He claims that the 'moral man' is the one who follows enlightened self-interest, and the key to moral improvement is not the wise legislator but education, to be more precise, *intellectual* training (Say 1800, pp. 183–193). However, a good education cannot be secured unless we grant the population a reasonable welfare level (p. 197). Lessening the inequality of fortunes is a precondition that such lukewarm remedies as sumptuary laws cannot substitute. A more radical remedy is a reform of 'the whole system of legislation and administration'. Therefore the 'first book of morality is a decent treatise of political economy' (p. 203). The reason for this seeming paradox is that political economy is different from natural science as it belongs to the *sciences morales*, a key-idea for the French *ideologues* (Steiner 1998, pp. 117–125), and it precisely studies self-interest and the ways to govern it in a morally acceptable and beneficial way.

Say became one of the leading figures of the French political economy, a school whose doctrines consisted of the Smithian teachings combined with Turgot's ideas. He gave pride of place to a notion Smith had been careful to avoid: the notion of law. In the Preface to the *Traité*, the reader finds the demanding statement that

> moral and political laws derive from the nature of things with the same degree of certainty as all the physical laws; far from imagining them, we discover them [...] nobody can ever violate them and get away with it.
>
> (Say 1803, p. 17)

Nevertheless, while feeling free to use the term 'law', he proclaims his allegiance to Smith. He believes he has been the first to proceed from 'general facts' to laws, and then to verify 'analytically' that some given fact does have a specific effect as its consequence, adding that, 'before Smith, more than once quite true principles had been advanced, but he has been the first to show why they were the true ones. Besides, he pointed out the true method to detect mistakes' (Say 1803, p. 34). From the second edition onwards, the passage goes on to say that Smith put 'to work in political economy the new scientific method, that is, instead of searching for scientific principles in a void, starting with the most constantly observed facts and reaching those general laws which they imply' (p. 34).

Following a French tradition dating back to Condillac, he gives pride of place to the idea of *utility* and recognises its role as the basis of exchange value, describing it as something more than a subjective appreciation of things since utility is recognised by 'man in society' (p. 79). Once more, while proclaiming allegiance to Smith, he tries to evade the paradox that the latter had recognised, namely that things possessing a high degree of utility such as water have no exchange value, while things of no utility such as diamonds have a high exchange value. The way he takes is to exclude the former kind of things from the subject matter of political economy by a distinction between *natural* and *social* wealth. He argues that there are such things as 'air, water, sunlight' (p. 597) that are devoid of exchange value and may be named natural wealth, and there are 'numberless things that one cannot obtain for free and are the fruit of production, the only ones which may be the subject matter of scientific study' (p. 599). Furthermore, both individuals and families 'cannot avoid drawing a classification of their own needs to satisfy those to which they ascribe greater importance rather than those to which they ascribe a lesser one' (p. 603). The *loi des débouchés*, his most often quoted doctrine, says that a general glut is impossible on principle since 'production of one product instantly creates an outlet for others' (p. 251; cf. Meacci 2015).

The 'Discours préliminaire' to his *Traité* contains an extended methodological discussion. The claims advanced are: some of the facts treated by political economists may be the subject of exact science (Say 1803, pp. 7, 17); a science of 'statistics' may be distinguished from political economy as the former deals with *particular* or *variable* facts while the latter deals with *constant* or *general* facts (p. 11); Smith assembled general and particular facts without drawing a clear distinction between them (pp. 10, 37–41); not unlike other exact sciences, political economy consists of a reduced number of general facts plus a few principles, that is, relationships established through 'analysis' between these facts (pp. 11–12, 34).

Ricardo and Say first met at Gatcomb in December 1814 (to Malthus 18 December 1814, in *Works* 6, pp. 160–161). The meeting gave the start to their correspondence, which was revived from time to time by some publication. They met again when Ricardo visited Paris in 1817 and 1822 (to Malthus 25 July 1817; to Trower 14 December 1822, in *Works* 7, p. 144; *Works* 9, p. 178; Sraffa 1952, pp. 17–18). Their correspondence deals with the theory of value: the distinction between value and riches and the measure of value (Blaug 1958, pp. 64–65, 89–90; Hollander 1979, pp. 500–502). Ricardo read everything Say published in political economy and adopted his *loi des débouchés* (Ricardo 1817, p. 290) but there is no evidence that he ever read his moral and political writings.

Nevertheless, disagreement between them grew steadily concerning mechanisms through which the clearing of markets takes place (Gehrke 2015, pp. 501–503), while Ricardo persuaded himself that Say was stubbornly resisting objections and became more and more disenchanted about his abilities. A source of misunderstanding was a difference in intellectual background. Neither could spell out his own nor fully understand the other's point of view. Thus, apart from shared practical concerns, each was looking in a different direction. Say stressed the preliminary character of economic theory as part of a more comprehensive moral and political science, understanding economic factors as preconditions for a moral reform that could improve both individuals and society with no pre-established boundaries to perfectibility. According to Say, 'mathematical calculation is the most dangerous of all abstractions' (Say 1803, p. 500), and an inductive approach best serves the goals of political economy.

Partial conclusions: a high station among philosophers

1. While describing Ricardo's career in Parliament, Brougham mentioned the universal respect he enjoyed due to 'his high station among philosophers' (Brougham 1839, p. 24). In the following century, Schumpeter nonchalantly remarked that 'his busy and positive mind had no philosophy at all' (Schumpeter 1954, p. 471). A feeling is hardly avoidable that one of these must be wrong. It is as well to note that in language no less than in the universe everything is in flux, and such terms as 'natural philosopher' instead of 'scientist', 'natural philosophy' and 'chemical philosophy' instead of physics and chemistry were still current up to about 1850. So, while 'political economy' had recently become the name of a discipline, its practitioners were still described as scholars who cultivated 'political philosophy' or 'political science', or just 'philosophers'. On the other hand, at the time and place of Schumpeter, to say that Ricardo had 'no philosophy at all' sounded more like praise than reproach.
2. Ricardo's interaction with his partners has been tendentially de-emphasised in the literature for various reasons. One is disciplinary hyper-specialisation, resulting in a lack of interest by philosophers and political theorists for Ricardo and disinterest in Ricardo's context by economists.
3. Another reason is a theory of scientific progress as a one-way route, making historians see a step-by-step process by which the kernel of *science* gets rid of the cork of *philosophy*, and Ricardo as the first 'pure scientist' dropping Adam Smith's meta-scientific ballast.
4. One more reason was a hagiographic view of natural science as 'hard science' and economics as natural science, suggesting that the study of

geology might have been an antidote to early symptoms of Marginalist subjectivism such as could be diagnosed in Say and Malthus.

5. However, thanks to a rich scholarship on the British early nineteenth-century context, we can now see a more nuanced landscape. We may see how the Geological Society was the best place to learn philosophy besides natural science, how Ricardo's 'parson' was the author of a philosophical textbook, and how Say was a complex character with philosophical, political, and ethical views. Sraffa, who rediscovered the existence of Belsham, did not bother to look at his philosophical book because the author was a priest, and the book was philosophical. Ricardo scholars tend to overlook Say's ethical and political contributions for being written in French and being 'extraneous to analysis'. Finally, with the commendable exception of Samuel Hollander, commentators disregard the fact that Ricardo's most important teacher was precisely his opponent Malthus.

References

Unpublished

Belsham, T, *Moral Philosophy*. Manuscript in longhand, Harry Manchester College: MSS. Belsham, Cambridge, 34.

Belsham, T, *Students Lecture Notes Taken at Daventry Academy by Jones Scott of Cradley*. 13 vols. Doctor Williams Library, London, Manuscripts 8.93–105.

Published

Allen, RC 1999, *David Hartley on Human Nature*, SUNY Press, Albany, NY.

Bain, A 1882 *James Mill: A Biography*, The Collected Works of James Mill 7, Routledge/Thoemmes, London & Kinokuniya, Tokyo, 1992.

Ball, T 2010, 'James Mill', in EN Zalta (ed.), *Stanford Encyclopedia of Philosophy* (Winter 2018 Edition), viewed 15 February 20020, https://plato.stanford.edu/archives/win2018/entries/james-mill/.

Belsham, T 1801, *Elements of the Philosophy of the Mind, and of Moral Philosophy. To Which Is Prefixed a Compendium of Logic*, Johnson, London.

Belsham, T 1814, *The Progress of Intellectual, Moral, and Religious Improvement during the Present Reign*, Johnson & Eaton, London.

Bentham, J 1789, *An Introduction to the Principles of Morals and Legislation*, JH Burns, HLA Hart & F Rosen (eds), The Collected Works of Jeremy Bentham 1, Clarendon Press, Oxford, 1996.

Bentham, J 1817, *Plan of Parliamentary Reform*, Hunter, London.

Bentham, J 2000, *Correspondence: January 1822 to June 1824*, C Fuller & F Rosen (eds), The Collected Works of Jeremy Bentham. Correspondence 11, Clarendon Press, Oxford.

Blaug, M 1958, *Ricardian Economics*, Yale University Press, New Haven.

Bonner, J 1995, *Economic Efficiency and Social Justice. The Development of Utilitarian Ideas in Economics from Bentham to Edgeworth*, Elgar, Aldershot.

Bowring, J 1842, *Memoirs of Bentham*, The Works of Jeremy Bentham 10, Tait, Edinburgh.

Brougham, H 1839, 'Lord Brougham's sketch of Ricardo in Parliament', in *Works* vol. 5, pp. 24–25.

Brown, T 1751, 'On the Motives to Virtue', in *Essays on the Characteristics of the Earl of Shaftesbury*, ED Eddy (ed.), Olms, Hildesheim, 1969, pp. 109–239.

Bucchi, S 2001, *James Mill filosofo radicale: analisi della mente e scienza politica nell'Inghilterra del primo Ottocento*, Edizioni di Storia e Letteratura, Roma.

Campos Boralevi, L 1984, *Bentham and the Oppressed*, De Gruyter, Berlin.

Collison Black, RD 1988, 'Bentham and the Political Economy of the Nineteenth Century', *The Bentham Newsletter*, no. 12, pp. 24–36.

Cremaschi, S 2010, 'Malthus's Idea of a Moral and Political Science', *The Journal of Philosophical Economics*, vol. 3, no. 2, pp. 5–57.

Cremaschi, S 2014, *Utilitarianism and Malthus's Virtue Ethics. Respectable, Virtuous, and Happy*. Routledge, London. DOI: 10.4324/9781315819235.

Cremaschi, S & Dascal, M 1998, 'Persuasion and Argument in the Malthus-Ricardo Correspondence', in WJ Samuels & JE Biddle (eds), *Research in the History of Economic Thought and Methodology*, vol. 16, JAI Press, Stamford, Co, pp. 1–63.

Depoortère, C 2008, 'On Ricardo's Method: The Scottish Connection Considered', *History of Political Economy*, vol. 40, no. 1, pp. 73–110. DOI: 10.1215/00182702-2007-047.

Depoortère, C 2013, 'William Nassau Senior and David Ricardo on the Method of Political Economy', *Journal of the History of Economic Thought*, vol. 35, no. 1, pp. 19–42. DOI: 10.1017/S1053837212000612.

Dinwiddy, J 1990, *Bentham*, Oxford University Press, Oxford.

Fetter, FW 1965, 'Introduction: Francis Horner and the Edinburgh Review', in *The Economic Writings of Francis Horner in the Edinburgh Review*, Kelley, New York, pp. 1–22.

Fitzpatrick, M 1999, 'Belsham, Thomas', in JW Yolton, JV Price & J Stephens (eds), *The Dictionary of Eighteenth-Century British Philosophers,* vol. 1, Thoemmes Press, Bristol, pp. 72–73.

Forget, EL 1999, *The Social Economics of Jean-Baptiste Say*, Routledge, London.

Gay, J 1731, 'Concerning the Fundamental Principles of Virtue or Morality', in IA Selby-Bigge (ed.), *The British Moralists*, vol. 2, Dover, New York, 1965, pp. 267–285.

Gehrke, C 2015, 'Say, Jean-Baptiste, and Ricardo', in H Kurz & N Salvadori (eds), *The Elgar Companion to Ricardo*, Edward Elgar, Aldershot, pp. 499–508. DOI: 10.4337/9781784715489.

Giuntini C 1995, *La chimica della mente. Associazione delle idee e scienza della natura umana da Locke a Spencer*, Le Lettere, Firenze.

Guidi, MEL 1991, *Il sovrano e l'imprenditore. Utilitarismo ed economia politica in Jeremy Bentham*, Laterza, Roma.

Halévy, E 1901, *La formation du radicalisme philosophique. 2. L' évolution de la doctrine utilitaire de 1789 à 1815*, Alcan, Paris.

Hartley, D 1749a, *Observations on Man, His Frame, His Duty, and His Expectations*, vol. 1, edn used: Cambridge University Press, Cambridge, 2013. DOI: 10.1017/CBO9781139628617.

Hartley, D 1749b, *Observations on Man, His Frame, His Duty, and His Expectations*, vol. 2, edn used: Cambridge University Press, Cambridge, 2013. DOI: 10.1017/CBO9781139628600.

Hartley, D 1775, *Hartley's Theory of the Human Mind, on the Principle of Association of Ideas with Essays Relating to the Subject of It. By Joseph Priestley*, Johnson, London.

Henderson, JP 1997, *The Life and Economics of David Ricardo. With Additional Chapters by J.B. Davis*, WJ Samuels & GB Davis (eds), Kluwer, Dordrecht.

Hollander, S 1979, *The Economics of David Ricardo*, The University of Toronto Press, Toronto & Buffalo.

Hollander, S 1985, *The Economics of John Stuart Mill*, Blackwell, Oxford.

Horner, F 1802, 'H. Thornton, An Inquiry into the Nature and Effects of the Paper Credit of Great Britain', in FW Fetter (ed.), *Economic Writings of Francis Horner in the Edinburgh Review*, Kelley, New York, 1965, pp. 28–56.

Horner, F 1803, 'Lord King's Thoughts on the Restriction of Payments in Specie at the Banks of England and Ireland', in FW Fetter (ed.), *Economic Writings of Francis Horner in the Edinburgh Review*, Kelley, New York, 1965, pp. 77–95.

Horner, F 1843, *Memoirs and Correspondence of Francis Horner, M.P. Edited by his Brother Leonard Horner Esq. F.R.S.*, vol 2, Murray, London.

James, P 1979, *Population Malthus. His Life and Time*, Routledge, London.

Jeffrey, F 1804, 'Bentham's Traité de Législation civile et pénale', *Edinburgh Review*, vol. 4, no. 7, pp. 1–20.

Keill, J 1700, *An Introduction to Natural Philosophy*, edn used: Thoemmes, Bristol, 2004.

Levi Mortera, E 2003, 'Dalla filosofia della mente alla scienza della società. Dugald Stewart e il metodo dell'economia politica', in L Turco (ed.), *Filosofia, scienza e politica nel Settecento britannico*, Il Poligrafo, Padova, pp. 107–125.

Levi Mortera, E 2018, *Dugald Stewart. Scienza della mente, metodo e senso comune*, Le Lettere, Firenze.

Mackintosh, J 1818, 'Bentham's Plan of a Parliamentary Reform', *The Edinburgh Review*, vol. 31, no. 61, pp. 165–203.

Maclaurin, ECB 1748, *An Account of Sir Isaac Newton's Philosophical Discoveries*, Thoemmes, Bristol, 2004.

Malthus, TR 1798, *An Essay on the Principle of Population*, EA Wrigley & D Souden (eds), The Works of Thomas Robert Malthus 1, Pickering, London 1986.

Malthus, TR 1803, *An Essay on the Principle of Population. The Version Published in 1803, with the Variora of 1806, 1807, 1817 and 1826*, vol. 1, P James (ed.), Cambridge University Press, Cambridge, 1989.

Malthus, TR 1820, *Principles of Political Economy*, vol. 1, J Pullen (ed.), Cambridge University Press, Cambridge, 1989.

Meacci, F 2015, 'Say's Law', in H Kurz & N Salvadori (eds), *The Elgar Companion to David Ricardo*, Edward Elgar, Aldershot, pp. 508–515. DOI: 10.4337/9781 784715489.

Mill, J 1802, 'Thomas Belsham's Elements of the Philosophy of the Mind', *Anti-Jacobin Review and Magazine, or, Monthly Political and Literary Censor*, 1 June, pp. 1–13.

Mill, J 1803, 'Stewart's Account of the Life and Writings of Thomas Reid', *Literary Journal*, vol. 1, no. 18, pp. 567–570.

Mill, J 1808, *Commerce Defended*, The Collected Works of James Mill 1, Routledge/Thoemmes, London & Kinokuniya, Tokyo, 1992.

Mill, J 1815, 'Stewart's Philosophy of the Human Mind', in *'The Political Writings of James Mill: Essays and Reviews on Politics and Society, 1815–1836'*, DM Hart (ed.), The Liberty Fund, viewed 1 March 2020, *http://oll.libertyfund.org/titles/mill-the-political-writings-of-james-mill-1815-1836*

Mill, J 1817, *History of British India*, vol. 1, edn used: Routledge/Thoemmes, London, 1997.

Mill, J 1835, 'A Fragment on MacIntosh', *The Collected Works of James Mill 5*, Routledge/Thoemmes, London & Kinokuniya, Tokyo, 1992.

Mill, JS 1873, *Autobiography*, JM Robson & J Stillinger (eds), The Collected Works of John Stuart Mill 1, University of Toronto Press, Toronto & Routledge/Thoemmes, London, 1981.

Paley, W 1785, *The Principles of Moral and Political Philosophy*, DL LeMahieu (ed.), Liberty Fund, Indianapolis, IN, 2002.

Patten, S 1899, *The Development of English Thought*, Macmillan, New York.

Penny Cyclopaedia 1841, 'Ricardo, David', in *The Penny Cyclopaedia*, vol. 19, pp. 507–508 (Reprinted in the Appendix of this book).

Pownall, R 1776, 'A Letter from Governor Pownall to Adam Smith', in *The Correspondence of Adam Smith*, 2nd edn, EC Mossner & IS Ross (eds), The Glasgow Edition of the Works and Correspondence of Adam Smith 6, Oxford University Press, Oxford, 1997, pp. 337–376.

Priestley, J 1771, 'An Essay on the First Principles of Government', in J Priestley, *The Theological and Miscellaneous Works*, vol. 22, JT Rutt (ed.), Kraus Reprint, New York, 1972, pp. 1-244.

Priestley, J 1777, 'Disquisitions Relating to Matter and Spirit', in J Priestley, *The Theological and Miscellaneous Works*, vol. 3, JT Rutt (ed.), Kraus Reprint, New York, 1972, pp. 197-540.

Priestley, J 1778, 'A Free Discussion of the Doctrine of Materialism and Philosophical Necessity in a Correspondence between Dr. Price and Dr. Priestley', in J Priestley, *The Theological and Miscellaneous Works*, vol. 4, JT Rutt (ed.), Kraus Reprint, New York, 1972, pp. 1-310.

Priestley, J 1782, *Institutes of Natural and Revealed Religion, the Edition of 1782*, in J Priestley, *The Theological and Miscellaneous Works*, vol. 2, JT Rutt (ed.), Kraus Reprint, New York, 1972, pp. xiii-xxxii, 1-383.

Priestley, J 1787, 'The Duty of not Living to Ourselves', in J Priestley, *The Theological and Miscellaneous Works*, vol. 15, JT Rutt (ed.), Kraus Reprint, New York, 1972, pp.121–146.

Priestley, J 1790, 'Preface to 'Experiments and Observations on Different Kinds of Air', in J Priestley, *The Theological and Miscellaneous Works*, vol. 25, JT Rutt (ed.), Kraus Reprint, New York, 1972, pp. 368–384.

Rashid, S 1985, 'Dugald Stewart, 'Baconian' Methodology, and Political Economy', *Journal of the History of Ideas*, vol. 46, no. 2, pp. 245–257. DOI: 10.2307/2709637

Rashid, S 1987, 'Political Economy as Moral Philosophy: Dugald Stewart of Edinburgh', *Australasian Economic Papers*, vol. 26, no. 48, pp. 145–156. DOI: 10.1111/j.1467–8454.1987.tb00453.x.

Rendall, J 1982, 'Scottish Orientalism: From Robertson to James Mill', *The Historical Journal*, vol. 25, no. 1, pp. 43–69. DOI: 10.1017/S0018246X00009857.

Ricardo, D 1817, *The Principles of Political Economy and Taxation*, in *Works* 1.

Ricardo, M 1824, 'A Memoir of David Ricardo', in *Works* 10, pp. 3–15.

Say, J-B 1800, *Olbie, ou Essai sur les moyens de réformer les mœurs d'une nation* [Olbie, or an Essay on the Means of reforming a Nation's Morality], in J-B Say, *Œuvres morales et politiques*, E Blanc & A Tiran (eds), Œuvres complètes/Jean-Baptiste Say 5, Economica, Paris, 2003, pp. 183–265.

Say, J-B 1803, *Traité d'économie politique* [A Treatise on Political Economy], vol.1, C Mouchot (ed.), Œuvres complètes/Jean-Baptiste Say 1.1, Economica, Paris, 2006.

Schumpeter, JA 1954, *History of Economic Analysis*, Oxford University Press, New York.

Sigot, N 2015, 'Bentham, Jeremy, and Ricardo', in H Kurz & N Salvadori (eds), *The Elgar Companion to Ricardo*, Edward Elgar, Aldershot, pp. 17–23. DOI: 10.4337/9781784715489.

Sraffa, P 1951, 'Introduction', in *Works* 1, pp. xiii–lxii.

Sraffa, P 1952, 'Introductory Notes to the Correspondence', in *Works* 6, pp. xiii–xli.

Sraffa, P 1955, 'Appendix (D) Ricardo's Library', in *Works* 10, pp. 389–402.

Steiner, P 1998, *La 'science nouvelle' de l'économie politique*, Presses Universitaires de France, Paris.

Stewart, D 1792, *Elements of the Philosophy of the Human Mind I*, W Hamilton (ed.), The Collected Works of Dugald Stewart 2, Thoemmes Press, Bristol, 1994.

Stewart, D 1810, *Philosophical Essays*, W Hamilton (ed.), The Collected Works of Dugald Stewart 5, Thoemmes Press, Bristol, 1994.

Stewart, D 1814, *Elements of the Philosophy of the Human Mind II*, W Hamilton (ed.), The Collected Works of Dugald Stewart 3, Thoemmes Press, Bristol, 1994.

Stewart, D 1855, *Lectures on Political Economy I*, W Hamilton (ed.), The Collected Works of Dugald Stewart 8, Thoemmes Press, Bristol, 1994.

Stewart, D 1856, *Lectures on Political Economy II*, W Hamilton (ed.), The Collected Works of Dugald Stewart 9, Thoemmes Press, Bristol, 1994.

Thorne, R 2004, 'Horner, Francis (1778–1817)', in HCG Matthew & B Harrison (eds), *Oxford Dictionary of National Biography*, vol. 27, Oxford University Press, Oxford, pp. 159–162.

Watts, I 1725, *Logick: Or, The Right Use of Reason*, edn used: Garland, New York, 1984.

Weatherall, D 1976, *David Ricardo. A Biography*, Nijhoff, The Hague.

Webb, RK 2004, 'Belsham, Thomas (1750–1829)', in HCG Matthew & B Harrison (eds), *Oxford Dictionary of National Biography*, vol. 5, Oxford University Press, Oxford, pp. 42–43.

Whatmore, R 2000, *Republicanism and the French Revolution. An Intellectual History of Say's Political Economy*, Oxford University Press, Oxford. DOI: 10.1016/S0191–6599(01)00037-7.

Williams, J 1833, *Memoirs of the Late Reverend Thomas*, London: Printed for the Author.

Winch, D 1983, 'The System of the North. Dugald Stewart and his disciples', in S Collini, D Winch & J Burrow, *That Noble Science of Politics. A Study in Nineteenth Century Intellectual History*, Cambridge University Press, Cambridge, pp. 23–62.

Winch, D 1987, *Malthus*, Oxford University Press, Oxford.

6 Ricardo on logic and political economy

Ricardian rhetoric

Ricardo 'was not enough master of logic to obtain precision, or even to estimate its importance' (Senior 1836, p. 118), his work is marred by 'inattention to established usage' (p. 62) and 'frequent inaccuracy of language' (p. 118). Such is the court-martial verdict passed by Nassau William Senior, a member of the Oriel School, a group of Oxford academics who wanted to redefine political economy as a deductive science where introspection provides the 'principles' with which to start and deduction does the rest of the work. As happens in court-martials, the one shot at dawn was not the real felon. The fact is that the Oriel School was fighting the Ricardian orthodoxy established by McCulloch and James Mill. Ricardo was a straw man, and understanding his authentic way of proceeding was the last of its worries.

As mentioned, Ricardo was hardly 'unphilosophical'. This chapter will examine his opinions on topics pertaining – in the twenty-first-century lexicon – to logic, epistemology, philosophy of science (known by economists as methodology), cognitive psychology, and research ethics. In the eighteenth and first half of the nineteenth century, Logic was still understood in the broader sense that the Stoics attached to the term: the art of argument at large, including rhetoric. It was hardly astonishing for his readers that Isaac Watts complement his *Logick* with *The Improvement of the Mind*, a handbook on the cultivation of good mental habits (Watts 1724, 1741).

Despite Schumpeter, Ricardo's 'busy mind' made room for considerations on theory and experience, multi-causality, general laws and scientific definitions. One of the reasons for confusion in Ricardian scholarship is that these considerations can neither be found where the reader expects to find them, nor are they a coherent system. In publications between 1809 and 1811, we meet considerations – more rhetorical than logical – centred on 'theory' and 'experience'. In publications from 1815 onwards we hardly meet any meta-scientific considerations, yet the correspondence and unpublished notes from the same period abound in the like. Notably, they drop the language of 'theory and experience', fostering 'pure theory' instead.

DOI: 10.4324/9781003162100-6

In the already mentioned 'On Mr Randle Jackson's Speech', Ricardo writes: 'Merchants may understand the details of business [...] but it does not therefore follow that they are qualified to give sound opinions on points of theory and science' (Ricardo 1810, p. 147). In the *Reply to Bosanquet,* his strategy is to rebuke the 'vulgar charge [...] against theorists' to advance 'speculations before they have been submitted to the test of fact' (Ricardo 1811, p. 160). He conducts an attack on the 'practical men', those who are 'all for fact and nothing for theory', who 'can hardly ever sift their facts' because they 'are credulous, and necessarily so because they have no standard of reference' adding as proof that two sets of 'supposed facts' to which Bosanquet refers 'are absolutely incompatible, and disprove one another' (pp. 181–182).

Yet he does not refrain from attacking the 'practical men' with their own weapons when it proves useful. He asks:

> when the principles of a currency, long established, are well understood; when the laws which regulate the variations of the rate of exchange between countries have been known and observed for centuries, can that system be called wholly theoretical which appeals to those principles, and is willing to submit to the test of those laws?
>
> (p. 160)

He invokes 'opinions grounded on a just theory, sanctioned by practical men, and confirmed by experience' (p. 190) that cannot be 'shaken by one or two solitary facts not perfectly known to us' (p. 165). He takes it for granted that effects observed of the adoption of a forced paper currency 'cannot be accounted for in any other way either by theory or by an appeal to experience' (p. 215). Bosanquet conjectured that banknotes issued in a country with metallic circulation would return immediately to the bank that had issued them because there would be no need for an additional quantity of a circulating medium. This conjecture – Ricardo concludes – is 'contrary to both theory and experience' (p. 218), proving that 'even practical men are sometimes tempted to wander from the sober paths of practice and experience, to indulge in speculations the most wild, and dreams the most chimerical' (p. 239).

We may describe Ricardo's argumentative strategy as a rhetoric of *just theory confirmed by experience* instead of *speculation supported by isolated facts* (Walter 2018, pp. 384–390; cf. 2021, Chapter 2). In those years, mention of *theory and experience* as sources of confirmation for opinions was commonplace, and refusal of *wild speculation* was a legacy of former denunciations of 'enthusiasm', religious at Cromwell's time and 'philosophical' in the years of the French Revolution. What was at stake lies neither in general epistemological principles nor in the right monetary policy. What happened instead was that, under the force of rhetorical description and redescription, a debate over the workings of credit and prices became attached to the debate earlier ignited by Burke, between those who trusted in the 'practice' of a hallowed institution and those who did not because they instead trusted in 'theory'. In this case the Institution was the Bank and the theory was political economy, but the terms of attack were directly borrowed from the earlier debate, where the institutions were Parliament and the Constitution and the theory was the rights of man.

(Walter 2019, pp. 468–469; cf. Walter 2021, Chapter 2)

It may perhaps be true that meta-scientific claims 'supported by Ricardo in his early writings, especially in his *Reply to Bosanquet*, exhibit continuity with the approach advocated by Stewart, Mill, and Horner' (Depoortère 2008, p. 105) except that such claims as those reported above, more than a mark of philosophical affiliation, were received commonplace. Stewart himself was hardly enthusiastic about such jargon. Nothing – he writes –

can be more absurd than to contrast, as is commonly done, experience with theory, as if they stood in opposition to each other. Without theory, (or, in other words, without general principles, inferred from a sagacious comparison of a variety of phenomena), experience is a blind and useless guide; while, on the other hand, *a legitimate theory* [...] *necessarily presupposes a knowledge of connected and well ascertained facts*, more comprehensive, by far, than any mere empiric is likely to possess.

(Stewart 1814, p. 444; emphasis added)

In Malthus's 1798 *Essay* and its enlarged 1803 version we meet evidence of dependence on Stewart, for example, the contrast of the 'consistent theory of Newton' with 'the wild and eccentric hypotheses of Descartes' that represent the 'old mode of philosophizing' based on 'mere conjectures' and make 'facts bend to systems, instead of establishing systems upon facts' (p. 59). Malthus also describes the 'new mode of philosophizing' based on 'patient investigation, and well authenticated proofs' (Malthus 1798, p. 60), or 'experience', the 'true source and foundation of all Knowledge' (p. 10). Yet this evidence is misleading.

Malthus still did not know Stewart's *Elements I* in 1798 and was drawing from earlier shared sources, namely, William Duncan, John Keill, Colin Maclaurin, Isaac Watts, and David Hume (Cremaschi 2010, pp. 6–27). From these shared sources, he inherited different topics from those typical of Ricardo.

There was a change in tone at the time of the *Essay on Profits*. The word 'experience', repeated 12 times in *Reply to Bosanquet*, occurs no more than four times in the *Principles,* where the emphasis shifts to *principles.* Ricardo shifted from a rhetoric of *just theory* and *experience* to a rhetoric of *science,* and his view of the task of the political economist became the discovery of the laws that regulate distribution, thus correcting doctrinal errors by Adam

Smith, as to 'set the science on a firmer basis' (Walter 2018, p. 400). Near the end of his life, in the 'Speech on the Silk Manufacture Bill' of 21 May 1823, Ricardo ferrets out the source of mistaken ideas in dreams that principles may 'change every two or three years' while instead 'the principles or true political economy never changed' (*Works* 5, p. 296).

As Ricardo wrote to Say on 18 August 1815 (*Works* 6, p. 249), the *Principles* should have been no more than an expanded version of the *Essay on Profits*. In the original plan, the work was limited to rent, profits and wages. In the end, it came to include money, prices, and value (to Malthus 7 February 1816, *Works* 6, p. 20). Ricardo's progress was interrupted in the first half of 1816 by Parliamentary commitments, but it was resumed in the summer at Gatcomb, with the help of the English weather, which did its best to keep him at home. He was still obsessed with the 'question of price and value' about which he believed he had been mistaken until then (to Malthus 5 October 1816, *Works* 6, p. 71; to Mill 14 October 1816, *Works* 6, pp. 83–84; Trower to Ricardo 19 November 1816, *Works* 6, p. 95).

Despite the author's reputation as a systematic thinker, the book is far from systematic. The theoretical part consists of the first seven chapters dealing virtually with one topic: value. The remainder is a loose arrangement of chapters covering questions of 'applied' theory. This structure may derive from Ricardo's attitude to his paradigm. He admits that political economy has been 'improved' by Smith, an author whose work 'so justly excites' admiration, with additional contributions by Turgot, Stuart, Say and Sismondi (Ricardo 1817, p. 6). Nevertheless, he feels that they 'afford very little satisfactory information respecting the natural course of rent, profit, and wages', which is 'the principal problem in Political Economy' (p. 5) and believes that Malthus and West's theory of rent supplies the missing piece of the puzzle. Ricardo's task is 'to supply this deficiency' in Smith's work concerning 'the laws of profits and wages' and the 'operation of taxes', thus opening the way to the discovery of 'many important truths' (Ricardo 1817, pp. 5–6; cf. Aspromourgos 2015, pp. 475–477).

Ricardo adopts the typical Kuhnian paradigmatic-scientist strategy. He takes *The Wealth of Nations* as the 'exemplar' or 'paradigm' to which he adds one more item, the theory of rent. This attitude may be one of the reasons why philosophical considerations are missing. Nonetheless, the strategy follows an unspoken rule spelt out in the correspondence: to account for all phenomena in an 'easy and natural manner', that is to reduce Smith's plurality of theoretical accounts of value to a unified theory around which other chapters of political economy may turn.

The main innovations carried out by Ricardo's programme are: (i) the choice of a *labour theory of value*; (ii) the idea of a state of nature as the key theoretical device. Their introduction goes through three steps: the identification of Adam Smith's 'natural price' with 'production costs'; a rough identification of the latter with wages (Sraffa 1951, pp. xxxvi–xxxvii; Aspromourgos 2015, pp. 468–471); a simplified scheme of the evolutionary process going from the state of nature to modern society consisting of only two instead of four stages. The introduction of the first and (partially) the second step happens through definitions. These are typical examples of those 'innovations in language' against which Malthus often reacted. Ricardo innovated in theory, not just language, but Malthus had a distinct idea of the relationship between common and scientific language. In the third step there was an unspoken assumption, probably essential for Ricardo's line of argument, namely that two transitions occurred simultaneously: (i) from a classless to class society; (ii) from an economy where the ratio of *living labour* to *labour embodied* in raw materials is uniform throughout the different lines of production to an economy where this ratio varies from one industry to another. On this assumption, Ricardo attacks Smith for denying the identity of mechanisms regulating prices in the state of nature and modern society. He assumes that capital accumulation and division of labour are of lesser importance and labour costs are still determining relative values. It is well known that – in the third edition – he adds the qualifiers *roughly* and *predominantly* (Henderson 1977, pp. 419–484).

Ricardo's avoidance of meta-scientific considerations in the *Principles* prompted the 'no philosophy at all' verdict by a famous commentator who had not benefited from Sraffa's edition. Ironically, between 1817 and 1820, the correspondence discusses causes and laws, permanent states and intervals, strong cases and realism of hypotheses. The omission of such issues in the *Principles* resulted from deliberate choice dependent on a Kuhnian 'normal science' strategy.

Instead of taking Ricardo's considerations as 'solemn and reliable reflections on the nature of his scientific thought' (Walter 2018, p. 409), we should bear in mind that they were uttered or omitted in context, at a given time, with a distinct audience in mind, which neither detracts from their seriousness nor reduces them to mere 'rhetorical' tricks. Rhetoric is, more than a derogatory term, the name of the theory of plausible argumentation and the shock provoked among economists by *The Rhetoric of Economics* (McCloskey 1985) was an over-reaction. A flaw in McCloskey's claims was a reductive view of rhetoric under-stressing its cognitive dimension, restricting it to style in economic writing (Cremaschi 1996). The idea of a rhetoric of science was hardly a novelty. Ivor Armstrong Richards, Chaïm Perelman and Stephen Toulmin had spread the idea that scientific discourse is more encompassing than the hypothetical-deductive model of explanation and makes room for arguments already studied, since Quintilian's times, by rhetoric, besides what was added by twentieth-century pragmatics (Gross 1990; Dascal & Gross 1999).

Language and definitions

Arbitrary definitions

In the *Principles*, philosophical considerations are absent, but they abound in letters to Malthus. Here we will examine those on language, definitions, and scientific terminology. In the 'Reply to Bosanquet', Ricardo denounces confusion in the use of the word 'excess' referring to paper-money. He assumes that the term was used 'as denoting a quantity greater than the circulation of the country can easily absorb or employ' (Ricardo 1811, p. 228) and contends that in this case disagreement derives more from a misunderstanding on definitions than from different opinions on facts. If we assumed the term excess to have the meaning assumed by Bosanquet, the conclusion would follow that no excess could exist, but the Committee 'must mean the difference in amount of circulation between the sum actually employed, and that sum which would be employed if the pound sterling were to regain its bullion value' (p. 229). Ricardo comments that this distinction is 'of more consequence than at first sight appears' (p. 229).

Malthus's first letter, of 16 June 1811, also refers to the Bullion controversy and precisely discusses definitions. Malthus declares that they are both 'mainly on the same side of the question', that is, against the 'practical men' but objects that Ricardo, yearning to correct the 'absurd notions of the mercantile classes', overlooked 'the real differences between the precious metals and other commodities' (*Works* 6, p. 21). The term 'redundancy' as used by Ricardo (1810–1811, p. 61) conveys 'an incorrect expression of the fact' (*Works* 6, p. 22). Ricardo's answer of 18 June 1811 concedes everything Malthus contends about language, admitting that the word 'redundancy' is not a felicitous choice 'to express the impression' made on his mind 'of the cause of an unfavourable balance of trade' (p. 25).

In their correspondence, the issue of definitions shows up again. In a letter of 13 October 1816 Malthus attacks Ricardo's claim that 'profits depend upon wages' as a 'very vague proposition' or 'a mere truism' (*Works* 7, p. 79) and on 14 October Ricardo attacks Malthus for inappropriate use of language, stating that he calls *nominal* wages what Malthus calls *real* wages (pp. 81–82).

On 26 March 1817, he writes that Malthus may 'object to the correctness' of many of his terms and find them 'fanciful, and not always properly applied' (p. 145) but adds that, apart from different terminology, Malthus may 'agree with much of the matter' (p. 145).

In the *Principles*, a cursory remark reveals a concern about the conditions of meaningfulness for statements. Ricardo writes that, while trying to define the medium in which we estimate a commodity's value, one should avoid that 'no idea can be attached to the proposition' (Ricardo 1817, p. 377). His proposal to split the concept of rent also reveals his awareness of the difference between ordinary and scientific language. He writes that 'in popular language, the term is applied to whatever is annually paid by a farmer to his landlord' (p. 67), but political economists need to distinguish between rent and profit. Elsewhere he declares that if one talks of the high or low value of commodities in different countries without specifying 'some medium in which we are estimating them' (p. 377), the proposition is 'meaningless'. In chapter 32, on rent, he attacks Malthus's improper use of language contending that 'the true and just acceptation' (p. 415 fn.) of the term *real price* is 'cost of production', not 'increase in value relative to all other things' (p. 414; cf. to

Malthus 26 March 1817. *Works* 7, p. 145) and introduces a distinction between *wealth* and *value*.

In a letter to Say of 11 January 1820, he writes that disagreement derives more from misunderstandings on the use of words than different opinions on facts, adding that many of 'the points of difference' between them are 'merely verbal' (*Works* 8, p. 149). In a letter to Malthus of 4 September, he dismisses objections as 'merely verbal' (p. 228). On 25 September Malthus responds denying that their disagreement is 'merely a question of arbitrary definitions' and invoking the test of 'the relative utility of the two definitions' (p. 261). Ricardo's answer of 9 October suggests that their disagreement on the definition of value depends on that on the definition of political economy, defined by Malthus as 'an enquiry into the nature and causes of wealth' and by Ricardo as 'an enquiry into the laws which determine the division of the produce of industry among the classes who concur in its formation' (p. 278).

The publication of Malthus's *Principles* in 1820 marks the beginning of a phase of more explicit dissent. On 4 September, Ricardo comes back to language and meaning dismissing Malthus's objections as 'merely verbal' (p. 228). On 25 September, Malthus responds, denying that his definition of value is 'merely a question of arbitrary definitions' and once more invoking 'the relative *utility*' of definitions (p. 261). On 1 January 1821, Ricardo writes to Mill that Malthus, believing that political economy is not 'a strict science like mathematics', feels free to 'use words in a vague way, sometimes attaching one meaning to them sometimes another' (p. 331).

In the *Notes on Malthus*, he responds to criticism of blurring 'the very important distinction between cost and value'. He objects that 'real value' means what Smith called 'natural price', that is, 'cost of production'; he comments that there is 'nothing arbitrary in this language' and, in a case he is wrong, it depends 'on an error in principle, and not on an error in nomenclature' (Ricardo 1928, p. 35). He insists that Malthus mistakes disputes on words for discussions on facts (p. 225) and insists that the word 'accumulation misleads many persons' including Malthus, who misses the distinction between the economic sense of the term and the vulgar sense of accumulation as 'hoarding' (p. 320 fn.).

In the third edition of the *Principles*, he quotes approvingly Destutt de Tracy's on the measurement of value but adds that he regrets that the latter shared Say's mistaken definitions of 'value', 'wealth', and 'utility' (Ricardo 1817, p. 284).

In the *Notes on Malthus' 'The Measure of Value Stated and Illustrated'*, Ricardo accuses him of falling into a vicious circle by using 'the word value to explain' what he means 'by the word value' (Ricardo 1992, p. 7). He admits that 'all the phenomena of political economy may be explained with any measure however arbitrarily selected' (p. 12) but contends that Malthus's choice of labour as the measure of value 'is an arbitrary selection not founded on any sufficient reason and therefore unsatisfactory as a scientific measure' (p. 14). He repeats these comments in letters to McCulloch of 3 and 11 May 1823 (*Works* 9, pp. 287, 290).

Eighteenth-century theories of language

Malthus and Ricardo addressed questions from a well-known eighteenth-century controversy among British philosophers, with which Malthus was familiar (Cremaschi & Dascal 1998a, pp. 24–26; Cremaschi 2010, pp. 34–45). The starting point was John Locke's linguistic revolution ruling out Aristotelian essences and the Platonic 'mirroring' theory of meaning. He claimed that the immediate 'signification' of a speaker's words consists just in 'his own ideas'. Certain kinds of confusion are inherent in the very nature of language (Locke 1689, pp. 409–420); 'species' do not exist in themselves but are the understanding's 'workmanship' and no generality exists in itself but results from our classifying activity: a choice 'from among the innumerably many similarities' we observe (p. 415).

Besides, as no natural connection exists between words and things, the former are no more than signs of inner affections of the mind. However, these affections are not necessarily the same for all and their connection with specific ideas is established by human beings, through the use of words 'as the Signs of their Ideas' (p. 405). Such imperfection of language still tends to be ignored. People tend to naively ascribe to words not only a reference to their ideas but also a 'secret reference' to things (p. 407), believing that their words are 'marks of the ideas in the Minds also of other Men, with whom they communicate' (p. 406). The concluding recommendation is to find out how other speakers use words and then apply our words 'to such Ideas as common use has annexed them to' (p. 514). Yet this is an insufficient remedy, for common usage depends on beliefs, both past and present. Besides, knowledge advances. Consequently, language needs to be improved, but we can only communicate improvements through the language that already exists. The result is that some amount of uncertainty will survive any language reform.

Locke's view of the mind as a passive receptacle of impressions looked suspicious in terms of religious orthodoxy. In fact William Duncan took care to vulgarise his theory, while avoiding any suggestion that the mind was a passive receptacle. Instead, he argued that we need to communicate the meaning of words that refer to complex ideas and to avoid verbal disputes we should follow the mathematicians' custom of defining the terms they introduce (Duncan 1748, p. 107). Good definitions start with the simple perceptions that lie at the root of simple ideas and reconstruct how we combine them into complex ideas.

Isaac Watts, too, starts with the Lockean account of ideas for reconstructing the nature and function of words (Watts 1724, pp. 45–70). He formulates the following recommendations for their use: first, avoid the Aristotelians' practice of using words 'without ideas' (p. 84); second, avoid the assumption that the 'Essences of things always differ from one another as much as their Names do' (p. 89); third, make definitions explicit to avoid ambiguous or equivocal terms; fourth, 'use every Word as near as possible in the same

Sense in which Mankind commonly uses it; or which Writers that have gone before you have usually affixt to it, upon condition that it is free from Ambiguity' (p. 97).

James Harris, instead of domesticating Locke, reacted to him by rescuing the Platonic theory of meaning. He contends that language results from both nature and convention. His 'Universal Grammar' is the 'analytical' part of the science of language, while Logic and Rhetoric are its 'synthetical' parts. Everybody overlooked the former since in nature causes come first, but effects are more familiar to us. Language consists of sounds with meaning. Animals have a voice with a meaning too and yet, 'whereas the meaning of those animal sounds is derived from Nature, that of the Language is derived [...] from Compact' (Harris 1751, p. 394). Words are not images, and language is not a picture of the universe. It is a medium made of 'symbols', not of 'things without' but of 'something within' (pp. 340–341). Therefore, words cannot be used 'as Mirrors' of the 'real Essences' of things (p. 330) because their adoption results from 'accidents quite arbitrary' (p. 320) and it is as well to stick to the ordinary language since conventional definitions tend to mislead us.

In the opposite mood, David Hartley starts with the claim that the 'arts of logic, and rational grammar, depend entirely on the doctrine of association' (Hartley 1749, p. 270). Language is a network of associations between sounds or written marks by which 'many sensible impressions, and internal feelings, are associated with particular words and phrases, to give these the power of raising the corresponding ideas' (p. 269). Language is not a dictionary to which we associate ideas we already have, for the meaning of sentences is not derivable from that of words, and that of words does not derive from impressions (pp. 278–280). Algebra 'is nothing more than the language which is peculiarly fitted to explain quantities of all kinds' (p. 280) and language itself is 'one species of algebra'.

Belsham, a follower of the Hartley-Priestley philosophy, defines a *nominal* essence, as opposed to the unknowable *real* essence, as 'that collection of properties which constitutes our idea of any substance, and to which the name is constantly applied' (Belsham 1801, p. xii). Abstraction is 'separating from a particular idea those circumstances which render it the representative of a single determinate object, and thereby making it to denote a whole rank or class of things' (p. xiv). It follows that the 'connexion between words and ideas is perfectly arbitrary' (p. xxiii) and meaning consists in the denotation of simple ideas by elementary words, 'beyond which we cannot explain the meaning of terms' (p. xxiv). Scientific language should be artificial, for 'many combinations of ideas occur frequently in the arts and sciences, which do not occur in common life', and this is why terms occur in the sciences that are 'peculiar to themselves' and 'do not occur in common life' (p. xvi).

Dugald Stewart attacks Hartley and Priestley while taking care to keep a distance from Harris's Platonism. He adopts a moderate version of nominalism not far from Smith's theory of language (Stewart 1792, pp. 197, 282–289). He argues that Tooke's discovery of 'the metaphorical origin of by far the greater proportion of words in every cultivated language' (Stewart 1810, p. 227; cf. Tooke 1786–1805) should prompt, instead of an impossible elimination of metaphorical meaning, an admission that words tend to gain meaning only in context. Indeed, many words have no meaning at all out of context, language does not *mirror* thought, and words supply hints to hearers while leaving the mind free to conduct the process of interpretation (Stewart 1814, pp. 5–22). Nonetheless, scientific language consists of general signs used conventionally to formulate theories. The axiomatisation of science is a viable project but one of little use; 'it might be possible, by devising a set of arbitrary definitions, to form a science which, although conversant about moral, political, or physical ideas, should yet be as certain as geometry' (Stewart 1792, p. 203), yet it 'could answer no other purpose than to display the ingenuity of the inventor' (203).

We know that Malthus had Locke and Duncan among his textbooks at Cambridge and Watts in his private library, and it was a matter of course that Haileybury College Library owned such an outstanding work as Stewart's *Elements*. His wish that economic terminology should follow the usage of 'the ordinary and most correct language of society' (Malthus 1820, p. 217) echoes Watts and Harris and is compatible with Stewart's views. Ricardo, instead, defends explicit definitions and artificial terminology with arguments close to Belsham's and echoing Kirwan's and Greenhough's concern with introducing precise terminology into geology.

Laws and causes

A science of laws

In Chapter 2 of the *Principles*, Ricardo mentions the 'laws which regulate the progress of rent' and 'those which regulate the progress of profits' (Ricardo 1817, p. 68. In Chapter 5, he refers to the 'laws by which wages are regulated' (p. 105) and, in Chapter 2 he mentions the 'common principles of supply and demand' (p. 69). The term 'axiom' appears once, referring to the mistaken proposition 'that the price of commodities depends solely on the proportion of supply to demand, or demand to supply' (p. 382). He also uses the term 'tendencies' to describe the 'natural tendency of profits [...] to fall' (p. 120), the tendency of rent to rise at 'every portion of additional capital which it becomes necessary to employ on the land with a less productive return' (p. 78), the tendency of wages to fall in 'the natural advance of society' (p.101) and the concurrent tendency of the price of necessaries to rise (p. 93).

Ricardo had arguably in mind a threefold distinction between primary laws, which he calls 'principles' or 'axiomata', derived laws determining the proportions between rent, profit, and wages, and 'tendencies', that is *contingent predictions* (Cremaschi & Dascal 1996, pp. 459–501).

Primary laws describe necessary and unchangeable relations between causes and effects, such as the law of markets, the law of diminishing returns in agriculture, the principle of population and the 'common principles' of supply and demand (de Marchi 1970, p. 259). These primary laws are unchanging and ubiquitous and thus, as John Davis suggests (Henderson 1997, pp. 591–593), self-effacing. Derived laws establish the *proportions* between rent, profit, and wages at different stages of society's 'natural advance'. They are descriptions of constant regularities, compared in the *Principles* with the law of gravity (Ricardo 1817, pp. 108, 120).

Thus, besides primary and derived laws, there are 'tendencies', 'contingent predictions' deduced from laws (de Marchi 1970, p. 259). Richard Whately noted a few years later an ambiguity in the meaning ascribed to the term, between that of 'a cause which, if *operating unimpeded*, would produce' one particular result and that of 'such a state of things' as may allow the prediction that the same result '*may be expected to take place*' (Whately 1831, pp. 231–232). In other words, he noted that 'tendencies' might be either 'analytical' propositions or historical generalisations (de Marchi 1970, pp. 258–264). Ricardo was aware that the tendencies mentioned are at work in an idealised world. Nonetheless, in a letter to Malthus of 27 March 1815, while arguing the existence of a tendency of the 'corn value' of goods (that is, the value of goods measured by the quantity of corn they can be exchanged with) to fall to that limiting point where there are no more profits, he adds that this principle 'is as certain as the principle of gravitation' (*Works* 6, p. 204). In the speech on the 'Petition of the Merchants of London' of December 1819, Ricardo writes that if 'the profits on capital were higher, and labour more productive in other countries, it could not be doubted that capital would be transferred to those countries: no proposition in Euclid was clearer than this' (*Works* 5, p. 38). In a letter to McCulloch of 18 June 1821, he compares the description of a tendency with 'any proposition in geometry' (*Works* 8, p. 388), but he is just repeating a phrase by McCulloch. We should, however, bear in mind his recurrent admission in the correspondence with Malthus of exceptions and limitations in the real world to any 'principle' (Dascal & Cremaschi 1999, pp. 1156–1161).

In this vein, the scope of political economy is narrower than in Malthus's definition of the discipline. Ricardo limits it to the study of *constant regularities* that we may detect, admitting that no scientific explanation of temporary effects and accidental causes is possible. A letter to Malthus of 9 October 1820 contrasts the latter's definition of political economy as 'an enquiry into the nature and causes of wealth' with Ricardo's as 'an enquiry into the laws which determine the division of the produce of industry among the classes who concur in its formation' (*Works* 8, p. 278). One implication of the second definition may be more limited scope for political economy. Only those *derived laws* that determine the rate of rent, profits, and wages are the proper subject for scientific enquiry. Instead, we should accept more basic principles or axioms as given. Another implication is that *causes* fall outside the scope of enquiry. They undoubtedly lie behind observed phenomena but are so variable and interacting with each other that attempts to establish their precise effects would be delusive.

Multi-causality and the limits to knowledge

In his first letter to Malthus of 18 June 1811, Ricardo mentions causality. The issue discussed – he suggests – far from being a matter of definitions, concerns causes and effects. No 'substantial difference' exists between 'the laws which determine' (*Works* 6, p. 24) the exportation or importation of bullion and those that apply to other commodities. He rejects Malthus's claim that 'redundant currency' is not the 'only cause' of an 'unfavourable balance of trade' (p. 26), contending instead that it is the 'invariable cause' (p. 26) and that money behaves like any other commodity. Since the relative state of the currency regulates commodity demand, changes in the demand for such commodities 'are not causes but effects' (p. 26). In a word, he defends mono-causality against Malthus's preference for multiple causes.

In another letter of 7 October 1815 Ricardo argues that Malthus's preferred asset – multi-causality – is precisely a reason for 'theory' against 'practice'. We may disregard refutations based on 'experience' because on this basis we can disprove any claim whatever, for there are

> so many operating causes in Political Economy, that there is a great danger in appealing to experience in favor of a particular doctrine, unless we are sure that all the causes of variation are seen and their effects duly estimated.
>
> (*Works* 6, p. 295)

A similar appeal to multi-causality is in a letter of 30 August 1814 where he singles out the reason for disagreement with Malthus on the Corn Laws. The 'principal difference' between them – he writes – is about 'the permanence of the effects' (p. 128). High profits do not depend only on the principle of demand and supply, but there are 'many other causes which will occasion profits to be permanently high' (p. 128), for example, they may be higher in a country where there is bad government and consequent insecurity of property. Here appeals to multi-causality are supposed to strengthen the claim that causes are unknowable, and we should be content with general laws.

Between 1815 and 1817, the discussion concentrates on the causes of the growth of wealth. Ricardo comments on 24 January 1817 that 'one great cause' of their disagreement was that Malthus always had 'the immediate and temporary effects of particular changes' in mind while Ricardo used to put these effects aside and fix his attention 'on the permanent state of things which will result from them' (*Works* 7, p. 120). In the *Principles,* he makes a similar point by drawing a neat distinction between 'natural and constant' causes and 'temporary effects' provoked by 'accidental causes' (Ricardo 1817, pp. 91–92, 115 fn.).

Eighteenth-century epistemology

The controversy between Cartesians and Newtonians on the mechanics of the planetary bodies had dictated the agenda for eighteenth-century epistemology. The missing link in Copernican astronomy had been how action at a distance was possible between celestial bodies. The Cartesian theory of vortexes supplied this missing link by introducing a hypothesis that, on the one hand, conformed to the requirements of the new Galilean science but, on the other, paid a heavy price in terms of consistency. The alternative Newtonian theory offered a consistent system that accounted for the movements of celestial bodies at the price of admitting gravitation, a mysterious entity suspected of belonging to the deprecated Aristotelian 'occult qualities' (Hesse 1961, pp. 98–180).

This controversy had a fallout effect on other fields of knowledge. It determined both the emergence of 'philosophy' as a discipline separated from science and the fragmentation of moral and political philosophy into an archipelago of social and human sciences faced by their philosophical counterpart in the moral and political philosophy itself (Louth 2011).

Smith treats the controversy in 'The principles which lead and direct philosophical enquiries' (Smith 1795, pp. 92–100). He argues that Descartes was utterly wrong and Newton made a genial innovation by transferring a simple idea of which we have daily experience, that is, gravity, to the motions of the heavenly bodies (pp. 104–105). Dugald Stewart writes that there is an 'impenetrable veil' hiding the 'hidden machinery' of 'physical causes' (Stewart 1792, p. 309). It is 'proneness to simplification' (p. 180) that prompted Descartes's identification of general laws with efficient causes of phenomena, and his mistaken idea of causality was the primary source of error in Cartesian physics (p. 479). Adam Ferguson writes that any search for causes 'which can be supposed to be occult' (p. 117) is a vain undertaking, something different from the investigation of a 'law of nature, whose very name implies a certain number of facts that are known to exist' (Ferguson 1792, p. 117; cf. Cremaschi 2000, pp. 77–85).

David Hartley and Joseph Priestley also expressed reverence for Newton and accepted the distinction between unknowable essences and laws connecting observed phenomena as a precondition of Galilean-Newtonian science. Thomas Belsham, who was one of their followers, writes that the limits to human knowledge in existence hide 'the unknown cause of known effects which are reducible to certain general laws' (Belsham 1801, p. 320). Distinct implications were drawn from this shared assessment, however. While Priestley derives from the limited character of knowledge a matching of limited scepticism in epistemology with a preference for deductivism as a methodological attitude, Stewart, from the same claim, heads towards moderate epistemological realism and a preference for the hypothetical-deductive procedure, which accords considerable weight to observation and induction.

Among discoverers of strange ideas on Ricardo's 'true method', Halévy still deserves the gold medal for detecting a 'French influence' behind Ricardo's 'systematic and deductive character'. This influence consisted of Physiocracy and Cartesianism, allegedly taught by Stewart, whose lesson Ricardo learnt through Bentham and Mill (Halévy 1901, p. 246). Besides, from the circumstance that the term 'law' is absent from *The Wealth of Nations*, he inferred that Ricardo's definition of political economy is the allegedly French idea of a 'science of laws' (pp. 219–220). However, the famous French historian overlooked the fact that Stewart was Descartes's severe critic (Cremaschi 2000, pp. 83–85).

A more sober view may be that two distinct sets of considerations inspired Ricardo's claims. The first is of a positive nature: he felt he had a promising research programme at hand, that after the discovery of the 'true theory of rent' the way was open simplification and unification of political economy. He could reach such a result by supplementing the theory of rent with his labour value theory, thus amending Smith's mistakes, while the work still waiting to be done was to discover the laws determining the 'natural course of rent, profit, and wages' (Ricardo 1817, p. 5). The second set of considerations had a meta-scientific character: he felt that the positive science of political economy should concentrate on discovering laws, leaving aside the search for causes.

This view echoed ideas from the eighteenth-century epistemological debate. The received view was that Newton's *regulae philosophandi* described the new 'mode of philosophising' opposed to 'old' one, based on execrated conjectures. An implication was that 'causes and essences' should be left to 'the metaphysician' (Stewart 1792, p. 13) and the natural philosopher should instead establish laws corroborated by observation, codifying a division of work between, in Kant's words, 'empirical philosophy' and 'metaphysics'. While the Newtonian *regulae philosophandi* were a shared doctrine, there was yet in British philosophy a division between proponents of epistemological anti-realism like Hume and Smith, Priestley and Belsham and advocates of moderate realism like Thomas Reid and Stewart. Malthus professed epistemological realism at least for social science because he believed that its laws 'relate to objects about which we are daily and hourly conversant' (Malthus 1820, p. 13). His epistemological realism carried a preference for realism of hypotheses and a broader understanding of the subject matter of political economy. Ricardo had heard ideas close to Priestley's at the Geological Society and might have read in Belsham's *Elements* or heard from their author that experimental philosophy rests on observations of the senses that do not reach the real essence of substances. He seems to propend to epistemological anti-realism, a more limited scope for political economy, and a refusal of the realism of hypotheses.

Permanent causes and natural magnitudes

On 24 January 1817, Ricardo notes that Malthus always had in mind 'the immediate and temporary effects of particular changes' while he used to fix his 'whole attention on the permanent state of things which will result' (*Works* 7, p. 120). The choice of the adjectives *permanent* and *temporary* may have been infelicitous as it may have obscured the meaning Ricardo wanted to convey: an asymmetry between two distinct kinds of causes affecting money wages and, therefore, profits. To work out what he had in mind we may think of Priestley's mentioned distinction between 'real appearances' and 'superficial appearances' or Greenhough distinction between 'permanent' and 'transitory' such as the transit of celestial bodies. He meant that in 'no circumstances may imbalances between supply and demand in the labour market offset the effects of changes in the price of wage goods' (Rosselli 1985, p. 242) and, apart from the rise or fall in the demand of labour, 'the money wage rate increases where there is an increase in the price of wage goods' (p. 243). In other words, permanent causes 'are sufficient but not necessary conditions, since the same effects could be brought about by other causes that Ricardo labels as "temporary": neither necessary not sufficient' (Marcuzzo & Rosselli 1994, p. 1258).

Political economy considers only permanent causes. Temporary or accidental ones produce effects that cannot be reduced to lawlike regularities. For Ricardo, unlike Malthus, this is not disregarding the influence of the principle of supply and demand. It is just an awareness of the limits of human knowledge. An implication is that Malthus's dream of a 'moral and political science', whose political economy is a chapter, is nothing but a chimaera. Causes do determine effects, but science does not go beyond lawlike regularities between 'real appearances'.

He writes that, while discussing 'the laws which regulate natural prices, natural wages and natural profits', he disregards *temporary effects* since these laws are 'totally independent of these accidental causes' (Ricardo 1817, p. 92). It is 'absolutely certain' (p. 110) that natural prices, wages, profits, and 'natural value' (Ricardo 1992) are magnitudes resulting '*inevitably and necessarily*' (p. 159) from 'the permanent and systematic forces at work whenever competition operates without restraint' (Signorino 2015, p. 365). The 'natural' price is the purchasing power which a commodity 'would possess, if not disturbed by any temporary or accidental cause' (Ricardo 1817, p. 92) or

> such a price as is necessary to supply constantly a given demand. The natural price of corn is the price at which it can be supplied affording the usual profit. With every demand for an increased quantity the market price of corn will rise above this price and probably is never at the natural price but either above or below it, – the same may be said of the natural price of labour.
>
> (Ricardo 1928, pp. 227–228)

The *natural wage* or *natural price of labour* is, following Smith, the level around which market wages gravitate at a given place and time, in turn, depending on the cost of the 'food and necessaries required by the labourer' (Ricardo

1817, p. 159). It is not 'absolutely fixed and constant' but 'very materially differs in different countries' (p. 96). It depends on the commodities which have become 'essential for habit' to the worker.

A critical point is that the natural wage, for Ricardo no less than for Smith, 'may be established at a level above subsistence' (Stirati 1995, p. 114). Chapter 5 defines the natural wage as the price 'necessary to enable the labourers [...] to subsist and to perpetuate their race, without either increase or diminution' (p. 93). However, he does not always follow this rigid definition consistently for he admits that the natural wage is not identical with the subsistence wage and may vary at different times and places. Permanent causes are *not* the expression of the Physiocrats' natural order doctrine ascribed to the 'classics' by some commentators (Moore 1966, pp. 330–331). Smith's 'natural price' had little to do with natural order since, being Hume's disciple, he was aware that the word 'natural' has different meanings when contrasted with 'artificial' or 'supernatural' or other descriptions and meant just that it is an unintended effect of individual actions in given circumstances. Ricardo, not unlike Trower, inherited the idea from Smith having it clear in mind that the *natural* price is the opposite of the *market* price.

On balance, Ricardo believed that political economy should focus on structural factors in the economy, disregarding the effects of demand and supply. These effects are ubiquitous. We may take them for granted but, when they produce accidental movements in prices, they produce unpredictable effects outside the scope of scientific enquiry. Despite Marx's praise as 'stoical, objective, scientific' (Marx 1967, p. 112) and the Soviet Marxist interpretation of Ricardo as a Spinozist who deduces phenomena for the essence (Ilenkov 1960, p. 165), his search for structural factors is prompted instead by awareness of the limits to human knowledge. The choice of the term *permanent* to indicate the *real* phenomena has led commentators off-track, suggesting a coincidence with the long run. The choice of the term *natural* for economic variables has been less misleading since it had already a technical meaning in Smith. However, it is also to be added that Ricardo's use by no means alludes to the *natural order*, a doctrine professed neither by Smith, nor by Malthus or Ricardo. In the third edition of the *Principles,* there are admissions that the action of economic laws is less rigid than he previously thought (Davis 1989, pp. 473–474). This admission derives from consideration of more causes at work, for example, a rise in consumption standards that may counteract the effects of the 'principle of population' but does not imply that in the first edition economic laws were 'natural laws' in the Physiocratic sense.

Strong cases

Ricardo adopted as a defensive weapon the argument that he was not considering contingent facts but idealised models which, from 1818 onwards he called 'strong cases'. Since transient and accidental phenomena may be overlooked as not amenable to scientific explanation, a consideration of unrealistic cases may be the best way to highlight the action of general laws. As early as 22 October 1811, he had written to Malthus that he contended that the only reason to export bullion in order to pay a nation's debts is its relative redundancy. He adds that the objection that in practice the opposite may happen is no real objection because this 'is *a question of fact not of science*, and might be urged against almost every proposition in Political Economy' (*Works* 6, pp. 63–64; emphasis added).

Ironically, his plea for *science* against *fact* rests precisely on one of Malthus's preferred assets, the already discussed topic of multi-causality, but with opposite implications. On 7 October 1815 he writes to him that, since there are so 'many operating causes in Political Economy', we run a significant risk 'in appealing to experience in favour of a particular doctrine' (*Works* 6, p. 295). On 24 January 1817, he formulates the diagnosis of 'one great cause' of their disagreement. He writes:

> you have always in your mind the *immediate and temporary* effects of particular changes – whereas I put these immediate and temporary effects quite aside, and fix my whole attention on the *permanent state of things* which will result from them.
>
> (*Works* 7, p. 120; emphasis added)

Malthus's response of 26 January 1817 is that referring 'to things as they are' is 'the only way of making one's writings practically useful to society' and avoiding 'falling into the errors of the tailor of Laputa, and by a slight mistake at the outset arrive at conclusions the most distant from the truth' (*Works* 7, pp. 121–122). In *Gulliver's Travels*, Laputa is a flying island whose population is addicted to visionary projects, where Gulliver's host asks a tailor to take measurements for a dress for his guest. The tailor does his job somewhat oddly. Gulliver reports:

> He first took my Altitude by a Quadrant, and then with Rule and Compasses, described the Dimensions and Outlines of my whole Body; all which he entered upon Paper, and in six Days brought my Cloths very ill made, and quite out of Shape, by happening to mistake a Figure in the Calculation.
>
> (Swift 1726, p. 158)

In other words, besides the practical relevance of his theory, Malthus is concerned with the corrective function of realism of hypotheses, assuming that unnoticed mistakes in the initial assumptions may more easily be detected when deductions apply to the real world. In the *Principles,* published three months after Malthus's letter, Ricardo declares:

> I have been desirous only to elucidate the principles, and it is scarcely necessary to observe, that my whole basis is assumed at random, and

merely for the purpose of exemplification. The results though different in degree, would have been the same in principle [...] My object has been to simplify the subject.

(Ricardo 1817, pp. 121–122)

In Ricardo's manuscript *On Torrens*, from 1818, the expression *strong case* appears probably for the first time. Concerning value theory, Ricardo reacts to Torrens's objection, starting with the different durability of different kinds of capital goods, that two commodities 'will be of equal value being the products of equal capitals' (Ricardo 1951b, p. 312). To prove his claim, he considers a 'strong case', an idealised situation with unrealistic assumptions chosen because of its heuristic usefulness. The case considered is that of five men who 'labour to be employed for a year in making iron' (p. 312) compared with 5 men put to 'work in planting a piece of ground, which affords no rent, with acorns' (p. 312). Ricardo argues that the wood produced in 20 years would afford the same profit as the iron produced in one year.

In 1820 Malthus published his *Principles* where he spelt out his divergences with the 'New School'. At this stage, the controversy concentrated again on meta-scientific issues, permanent states and temporary effects (Cremaschi & Dascal 1998a, pp. 21–29) and the 'doctrine of proportions' that had become Malthus's philosopher's stone. He writes that 'all the great results in political economy [...] depend upon *proportions*' (Malthus 1820, p. 430), adding that, since we cannot know where the right proportion lies (pp. 9–10), one of the great sources of error in political economy is the tendency to extremes and every 'rule or proposition' requires 'modifications, limitations and exceptions' (p. 7). Ricardo's objection in a letter of 4 May 1820 is that the opposite recommendation is justified, to enounce scientific laws without admitting any modification, limitation and exceptions, which would mean the end of science. We should be aware instead of the fact that scientific laws imperfectly hold for the real world. He immunises his theory by appealing to its 'unpractical' character, contending that Malthus had assumed that Ricardo's book was 'more practical' than he meant it to be. In contrast, his goal 'was to elucidate principles', and he had 'imagined strong cases' to highlight 'the operation of those principles' (*Works* 8, p. 184).

In a letter to McCulloch of 11 September, he comments on Malthus's inability to understand his distinction between *questions of theory* and *questions of fact*. Malthus's objections on rent – he suggests – are 'a question of fact and degree, not of principle' and he complains that Malthus 'does not answer your principle but wishes to show that you have taken your case so wide, that it could under no circumstances exist' (*Works* 8, pp. 234–235). In a letter to Malthus of 24 November, while commenting on the idea of 'effective demand', he raises the issue of intervals and permanent states, admitting that he can see Malthus's point but objecting that the intervals, on which Malthus 'so exclusively' dwells, do exist 'but still they are only intervals' (*Works* 8, p. 302).

On balance, preference for strong cases depends on a conviction of the limits of science, inspired, in turn, by that kind of limited scepticism with which Ricardo was acquainted through his philosophical frequentations and readings, including his predilected author Pierre Bayle. This preference is certainly *not* a mark of the Cartesian 'method' imagined by Halévy or the Hegelian or Spinozist deductive approach discovered by Marx and Soviet Marxism. It was a sign more of modesty than of arrogance. How it was possible to draw policy recommendations, given the limits of human knowledge, is a different question to discuss in what follows.

The redundancy of utility

In the manuscript Mill sent to Ricardo in 1810, Bentham writes that all

> value is based on utility, on the use we can do of a thing. No use, no value. Thus, since it is always from the point of view of subsistence, defence, or enjoyment that an item of wealth can be of use, it is also from the same point of view that it has any *value*.
>
> (Ricardo 1951a, p. 284)

He argues that paper-money's value, though established by convention, still derives from that of bullion, which instead has intrinsic or use-value. Ricardo's comment is: 'I like the distinction which Adam Smith makes between value in use and value in exchange. According to that opinion, utility is not the measure of value' (p. 284). Bentham did not develop a systematic theory of value, so the father of Utilitarianism never was a 'utilitarian' economist, Here, however, he was pointing in that direction. Ricardo's objection starts with the refusal of any alternative to value as production costs. Stigler (1950, p. 311) wrote that Bentham 'had indeed planted the tree of utility' but, though 'the implications for economic analysis were not obscure', they were overlooked and the 'economists of Bentham's time did not follow the approach he had opened'. Stigler was one more victim of the still surviving assumption that intellectual history cannot avoid teleology, one that justifies such achievements as discovering the marginalist revolution already there in Bentham's manuscripts or general equilibrium foreshadowed in Smith's invisible hand passage.

Ricardo's objection implied that utility is a necessary but ubiquitous condition for value and, as such, cannot account for differences in value between distinct commodities. In the last page of the *Principles*, he declares that one 'set of necessaries and conveniences admits of no comparison with another set; value in use cannot be measured by any known standard; it is differently estimated by different persons' (Ricardo 1817, p. 429). This claim comes back in the correspondence with Say, who gives utility pride of place defining it as 'the quality to be potentially useful' (Say 1803, p. 24 fn.), not an arbitrary quality but a *social* phenomenon, an objective quality recognised by 'man in society' unlike exchange value that is 'arbitrary and ill-determined until it is not recognised' (p. 79). People express their recognition that something embodies utility by proving to be prepared to give something in exchange for it. The

> first basis of the value of a thing is the utility that men see in it. This utility is due to man's physical and moral nature, to the climate in which he lives, to morals, to the laws of the society of which he is a member.
>
> (p. 592)

A rough measure is the price of commodities for, despite variety 'in the tastes and needs of men', there is among them a general assessment of each object's utility, roughly indicated by 'the number of other items they are willing to give in exchange' (p. 25). Besides, material things are never *produced* but just *reproduced* under a different shape. Production is never the production of material things but 'production of utility' (p. 24). In the *Principles*, Ricardo objects that Say has been,

> singularly unfortunate in his definition of riches and value. He considers these two terms to be synonymous, and that a man is rich in proportion as he increases the value of his possessions, and is enabled to command an abundance of commodities.
>
> (Ricardo 1817, p. 280)

He adds that he seems to miss Smith's distinction between value in use and exchange value. Therefore he 'cannot be right in considering value, riches, and utility to be synonymous' (p. 281).

In the third edition, Ricardo adds a reply to Say's additions in the fourth edition of the *Traité* where he had accused Smith of ignoring that, besides the industry of man, natural agents can also concur in producing the value of commodities, 'such as the sun, the air, the pressure of the atmosphere' (p. 285). Ricardo's counterargument is that these agents 'though they add greatly to value in use' of a commodity, 'never add exchangeable value' (p. 285) because, as soon as we succeed in obliging natural agents 'to do the work which before was done by man, the exchange value of such work falls accordingly' (p. 286).

Say wrote to Ricardo on 1 May 1822 that he was distinguishing between 'the quantity of useful things a man can enjoy and that of useful things that we can use to make an acquisition' (*Works* 9, p. 189). He added that political economy studies wealth only to the extent that it is co-extensive with the latter 'because the increase or decrease of this quantity alone is subject to laws which it can assign' (p. 189) and that he believed Ricardo's mistake was failing to draw this distinction. In a letter to Malthus of 16 December 1822, Ricardo comments that Say 'never succeeded in at all understanding what my opinions are' (*Works* 9, p. 249).

In the correspondence with Malthus, disagreement on the same topic emerges with ethical implications. Malthus's strategy for the war on poverty made room for counteracting the effects of the principle of population by raising the living standards of the poor and teaching them a taste for such 'luxury goods' as sugar and tea (Malthus 1820, p. 355). The conviction inspires this proposal that cultural, sociological and moral factors also determine economic and demographic magnitudes, and giving the poor a prospect of being virtuous, respectable, and happy would also motivate them to be provident, delay marriage and set aside savings (Cremaschi 2014, pp. 161–165). Ricardo, who cared no less than Malthus for the plight of the poor, was more sceptical about such prospects for both economic and ethical considerations. Happiness – he objects on 4 September 1817 – is a slippery concept, almost a tautology: 'the object to be desired' (*Works* 7, p. 185). We cannot list its components and should therefore be content with the satisfaction of primary needs, a necessary but insufficient condition for happiness. He concludes that nobody can be sure that, 'provided he is equally well fed, a man may not be happier in the enjoyment of the luxury of idleness than in the enjoyment of the luxuries of a neat cottage, and good clothes' (p. 185). Such considerations are close enough to Smith's remark that happiness

> consists in tranquillity and enjoyment. Without tranquillity there can be no enjoyment; and where there is perfect tranquillity there is scarce anything which is not capable of amusing. But in every permanent situation, where there is no expectation of change, the mind of *every* man, in a longer or shorter time, returns to its natural and usual state of tranquillity.
> (Smith 1759, p. 149)

The weak points Ricardo sees in Malthus's strategy depend on the impossibility of *measuring* happiness. In the *Notes to Malthus*, he writes that the latter is directly correspondent to the abundance of material goods, 'men are happy in proportion as they have an abundance of the commodities they want' (Ricardo 1928, p. 24). The point of such a definition is rebutting Malthus's argument that agricultural labour stands first in a classification of the productivity of distinct kinds of work. Still, an important implication is that happiness is hardly measurable, and we can measure at best its *preconditions* in terms of physical magnitudes, for example, quantities of corn. However, it is not the value of corn but just its physical quantity that affects happiness. The question 'whether it would not also be very desirable to have corn of less value, and in greater abundance' (p. 22) has only one answer which implies, in turn, that value does *not* 'depend' on utility, and greater or lesser value only results from scarcity or the difficulty of production. This answer also has implications regarding Malthus's view of political economy as a part of 'the moral and political science', namely that the point where political economy meets ethics and politics is the extent to which the population has access to essential goods.

On balance, Ricardo's argument against grounding exchange value on utility is twofold. The logical argument is that it is pointless to enquire into casual relationships behind a set of laws plausibly established. This argument is a reformulation of Galilei's refusal to grasp the essence, or Newton's rejection of hypotheses on ultimate causes, or the Razor of Ockham, the rule that we should not multiply entities without necessity. The meta-ethical argument is that happiness is a slippery concept, a view held by mainstream ethics in the seventeenth and eighteenth centuries, against which Bentham was stubbornly rowing.

Rizvi suggests that the reason why Ricardo avoided recourse to the notion of utility is not 'lack of philosophy' (Rizvi 1992, p. 1) but rather a rejection of 'the utilitarian idea that various single objects could all be comparable in terms of utility' because the notion was 'too complicated and multi-faceted to be summed up as a single measure' (p. 1). In more detail, Ricardo had two arguments against utility as a basis for value. The first is the triviality of any account of this kind since exchange value in all cases presupposes utility to the same extent and the only scientific issue left is whether different costs of production may sufficiently account for differences in exchange value or also whether its scarcity should be considered as an additional distinct factor (Rizvi 2015, pp. 135–136). The second argument starts with the impossibility of measuring utility or, in other words, the incommensurability of the utility of one commodity for distinct individuals (pp. 137–139). Both arguments are consistent with Ricardo's recurrent disagreement with Malthus on both the nature of happiness and the scope of political economy, with the rejection of Say's definition of exchange value and the criticism of Mill's 'doctrine of utility'.

Ricardo was hardly 'unphilosophical' and was no disciple of Mill's – either before 1815 when the latter was still a follower of Stewart – or after 1815 when he became adept at Benthamite-Lockean associationism. The Benthamite 'doctrine of utility' is based on Locke's association of ideas. Both the causal account of action and the normative standard or principle of utility rest on this basis. 'Utility' consists of a sum of units of pleasure and pain. Well-being and happiness, the key-ideas of Benthamite ethics, are defined in terms of utility, and the felicific calculus is the procedure through which such magnitudes are determined (Bentham 1789, pp. 38–41). In a letter of 8 August 1823, Mill announced that he was writing 'something considerable towards the exposition of all the phenomena classed under the title of Thought', boasting of having investigated 'all the phenomena called intellectual' (p. 242) and accounted for them 'upon the principles of Hartley' showing that they are 'nothing but sensations, and the ideas, the copies of these sensations, combined in groups by association' (*Works* 9, p. 242). On 30 August 1823 Ricardo replied in his usual polite tone that he would be 'greatly indebted' to him if he would '*make all these matters clear*', for though he had 'occasionally paid a little attention to them' he had '*never been sure that he had accurately understood*' (*Works* 9, p. 374; emphasis added) what the works he had read wanted to say. If we read these words in the light of Ricardo's typical mild irony, the message may be that he fears that any 'science of hu-man nature' is but a delusory enterprise. His sudden death has left us without a record of his reaction to Mill's 'labours' but, keeping his comments to *The History of British India* in mind we might conjecture that his criticism would have been no less sharp.

Ferreting sources is hardly the main task of intellectual history. Nonethe-less, Ricardo's reflections on the nature of happiness, to be discussed in the next chapter, may help to better understand his claim that *objects of utility* are so different that there is no point in *measuring* utility. Any reflective person or any reader of good novels could have concluded that what human beings desire varies from one to another and happiness depends on a hardly pre-dictable combination of elements. However, Ricardo may have also heard an echo of the eighteenth-century discussion on the fragility of happiness (Mauzi 1960, pp. 23–24). David and Priscilla named their first son after the hero of a novel by Voltaire, a writer whose work abounds with illustrations of happiness's delusory character. Ricardo could have heard about similar ideas from Unitarian ministers. The Hartley-Priestley philosophy gave pride of place to Hartley's associationism. As mentioned, this was a doctrine different from that of Locke, Bentham and Mill. It was a physio–neurological account of the origin of ideas laying the basis for an ethical theory incompatible with Bentham's felicific calculus. No evidence suggests that Ricardo ever read an-ything by Hartley and Priestley, but he heard about their ideas from Aspland, Lindsay and Belsham. For example, the last-mentioned declares that happi-ness arises 'from the consciousness of moral worth, from pleasing reflections, and joyful expectations' (Belsham 1801, p. 351), and rational self-interest prompts virtue though not perfect virtue, while self-annihilation 'is essential to perfect virtue, and therefore to perfect happiness' (p. 378 fn.). Lindsay writes that human imagination 'constantly anticipates a happiness, which is for ever eluding his grasp' because the possession of 'present good' is 'precar-ious and transient' (Lindsay 1818, pp. 20–21).

According to Stigler, the cause of Ricardo's failure to adopt 'the concept of utility as a numerical magnitude' is the fact that he 'was not a Benthamite' (Stigler 1950, p. 311). Stigler was right in declaring Ricardo non–Benthamite but was wrong in describing him as 'unphilosophical' (p. 311). On the con-trary, Ricardo's reasons for rejecting utility as both a basis for exchange value and a foundation for ethics were pure philosophical arguments, ones that Malthus believed to be an excessive desire to simplify. By now, we have seen that Ricardo had a more sophisticated intellectual dowry than mere love of simplification. This is not tantamount to saying that Malthus was wrong and Ricardo all the way right. There are points where the preoccupation for con-sistency and intellectual economy blinds him to the point his interlocutors were clumsily making.

The philosophical background of this attack on Malthus and Smith is the impossibility of measuring different sets of necessaries and conveniences against each other because value in use 'is differently estimated by different persons' and 'cannot be measured by any known standard' (Ricardo 1817, p. 429). Nonetheless, Ricardo forgets that Smith estimated the value of the riches produced in terms of value commanded and, despite Ricardo's rejection of value commanded, this was the notion on which Smith's reasoning depends. Ricardo thus fails to see that Smith was 'consistent in maintaining that a *continuous* process of accumulation is the only possible cause of a *permanent* increase in the demand for labour' (Meacci 2014, p. 685) and the ensuing increase in the quantity of goods that a given amount of labour can command (Meacci 2015, pp. 585–586).

Ricardian logic and scientific practice

The vain quest for Ricardo's 'method'

'Method' is a tricky word that may allude to two different things. The first is the gamut of *methods* or *techniques* practised by economists and scientists in general: observation, data collection, measurement and calculus. The second is *methodology*, understood in two ways: the prescriptive Cartesian Method or the critical discussion of scientific practice. The spectre of the *Discours de la méthode* is still hovering over methodological discussion. The Cartesian Method, the roadmap to Truth, is a myth dispelled once and for all by Charles Peirce's critique of foundationalism, but kept circulating for one more century by Logical Empiricist and Popperian crypto-Cartesians.

There are no more roadmaps to the Truth than there are instruction folders for painting the Sistine Chapel or writing the *Divina Commedia*, and science is an as incurably creative affair as any other activity. Methodology is a name still used by economists. Practitioners of other disciplines are aware that there is one called philosophy of science, and some believe that it may be of use to scientists. Economic methodology is acceptable even when taken in the sober sense described by Wade Hands (2001, pp. 7, 396–402), the 'New Economic Methodology' or critical reflection on economists' practice.

So, when it comes to Ricardo, the project of discovering his *method* is a no less vain enterprise than the search for the philosophical school to which he belonged. Instead, pertinent questions are: first, Ricardo's *practices*; second, the contents of his meta-scientific considerations and their relevance for his practices. In his attack on what he named the 'New School', Malthus first criticised the Ricardian Method as a source of confusion between abstractions and the real world (Malthus 1820, pp. 2–7; cf. Cremaschi & Dascal 1998a, pp. 21–24). Senior took Malthus's objections on board, and others continued to elaborate on the *Leitmotiv* of Ricardo's 'otherworldliness'. However, we may take Malthus's attack less seriously than he would have liked. The choice of shifting to questions of method is one rhetorical move among others when somebody lacks objections in matters of positive theory.

Schopenhauer's stratagem no. 19 from his *Eristic Dialectics* or *The Art of Being Right* recommends:

> If the opponent expressly urges us to argue against a particular point of his assertion, but we have nothing suitable, we must put the matter in general terms and then argue against this point. We are to say why a certain physical hypothesis is not to be trusted, so we talk about the deceptive nature of human knowledge and explain it by means of all kinds of examples.
>
> (Schopenhauer 1864, p. 696)

Malthus and Senior were involved in controversies conducted in a dated vocabulary carrying political, social, cultural premises and implications and in the context of the decline of the old élite and the emergence of a new, mainly non-Anglican, urban professional élite. What is worse is that their twentieth-century heirs continued to stock up on their arsenal of anti-Ricardian weapons without much innovation (King 2013, pp. 34–41). Once we take the nineteenth-century context within which such controversies took shape, the effect

> is to undermine accounts of Ricardo's method that treat his statements as amounting to theoretical principles. In the cases studied, such statements have been shown to draw on manipulable, ready-to-hand terms, defined by their uses in intellectual contests and varying depending on Ricardo's contextual needs [...] This should direct attention toward studying the concrete means by which Ricardo produced his arguments in lieu of global characterisations using terms such as 'deductive', 'inductive', 'theoretical' or 'empirical'.
>
> (Walter 2018, p. 29; cf. 2021, Conclusions)

The 'Wealth of Nations' as the paradigm

We have seen how Ricardo first went into political economy with the valuable equipment of experience at the Geological Society, some readings in science and philosophy and experience of the world of finance and how *The Wealth of Nations* and Horner's review essays in the *Edinburgh Review* were his first readings. Later on, after completing the *Principles*, he undertook more systematic philosophical reading. Meta-economic considerations are virtually absent from his main work, but they show up in the correspondence of 1817. Besides, contacts with Horner ended in 1814 and Mill's influence on the book took place after he abjured Stewart's philosophy. These circumstances suggest that Ricardo's 'methodology' took flight – not unlike Minerva's owl – after he had produced his most important contributions.

We may conjecture that he entered a research career the same way Thomas Kuhn illustrates how, after a scientific revolution has taken place and a phase of normal science has begun, scientists proceed by taking one epoch-making work as the exemplar and concentrating on unsolved puzzles. The term 'political economy' was not used as the name of a discipline by Smith, who still understood his work as a contribution to moral philosophy and political theory (Alonzi 2021). Ricardo, Mill and Malthus used it in this sense, a symptom that they believed they were trying to contribute to an established discipline. We may take Ricardo's declaration seriously that he had concentrated on 'those passages in the writings of Adam Smith from which he sees reasons to differ', but this did not detract from his 'admiration which the profound work of the celebrated author so justly excites' (Ricardo 1817, p. 6).

Not surprisingly Ricardo disagreed with Smith on several points, but the tools for manufacturing his arguments were Smithian ones. The *Wealth of Nations* starts with a first step, illustrating a simplified situation such as the economy of the 'age of hunters' or the spinning factory. A second step follows, an illustration of the path the economy would take if it followed its 'natural course'. The third step is the proof that the same principles hold in the eighteenth-century economy. We may describe this procedure in the language of the analytic-synthetic procedure mentioned in Robert Pownall's letter, a process going from a few observed phenomena to hypothetical principles and back from principles to a broader domain of phenomena (Pownall 1776, p. 337).

Thus, Hollander is right when writing that Ricardo believed no less than Smith in the role of theory as an indispensable framework for interpreting historical developments and 'prediction' of the future course of events. He is also right in saying that both proceeded by introducing hypotheses involving limited theoretical commitments through successive steps of idealisation. As a result, the difference between Ricardo and Smith 'on matters of general procedure' is not a tremendous one, 'it was Smith who provided British economics with an archetype of the method of "pure theory" and not by chance Smith was accused too of privileging "system-building" and of reasoning as a "man of system", that is, the characteristics commonly attributed to Ricardo' (Hollander 1979, p. 654).

While defending a different interpretation of the Ricardian economic theory, Kurz makes a similar reconstruction of Ricardo's views on matters of general procedure:

> First, the theory had to be general: it had to deal with the economic system as a whole and with the interdependence between its different parts. Second, it had to come to grips with the modern economy's inherent dynamism, a system that is continually changing from within due to the accumulation of capital, the growth of population, the scarcity of renewable (land) and exhaustible (mines) resources, technical change in all sectors of the economy, a growing social division of labour both domestically and internationally, an expansion of outputs and an increasing heterogeneity and diversity of commodities [...] Third, the analytical method Smith and Ricardo employed in order to investigate the system is known as the long-period method. It focuses attention on situations in

which, in the ideal case of free competition, a uniform rate of profits and uniform rates of wages and of rents for each particular quality of labour or of land obtain.

(Kurz 2015, p. 824)

The relevance of Ricardo's meta-scientific considerations for his practice

As mentioned, Ricardo's considerations on matters of logic came *after* his most important positive contributions. He formulated them to respond to objections in the context of *controversy*. Besides, Malthus introduced considerations of this kind, and Ricardo followed him on this ground because he could not avoid doing so. Nonetheless, when forced to defend his positive doctrines with logical considerations, he was led to an effort of self-clarification with the help of the philosophical notions he had met, first through his cultivation of geology and then by systematic philosophical reading conducted in 1817 and 1818.

Any attempt to establish Ricardo's true philosophical affiliation would be useless. The task was undertaken once and for all by Halévy, with disastrous results. A scientist's career seldom goes under the aegis of one philosophical school – and it is better so – and many of the philosophical ideas taken over by Ricardo were unsurprisingly over-determined. For example, he may have heard about the opposition of 'limited' and 'general' experience from fellow geologists, as well as from Horner and Malthus. The latter was not only his primary opponent but also his most important source. In fact the controversy with Malthus had effects on Ricardo's thought and some modifications introduced in the third edition of the *Principles* are reactions to his objections (Peach 1993, pp. 191–194). It offered Ricardo the occasion to clarify the reasons for his distrust of the realism of hypotheses and his conviction of the impossibility of finding causal links. Thus, Ricardian philosophy was of the magpie kind: a creative attempt to assemble claims on language, causality and scientific laws that he felt would shed light on what he was doing at a positive level. Here again it is possible to single out a common denominator in what he borrowed from various sources, namely first, a tendency to bracket the complexity of phenomena and concentrate on a few supposedly structural determinants of the whole economy; second, a preference for deduction from a limited number of general principles assumed as established; third, a stress on terminological clarity; fourth, the adoption of 'general laws' as opposed to 'causes' in the role of *explanans*; fifth, the option of a more limited scope for science; sixth, a preference for discussing 'strong cases'.

Limited scepticism – or the thesis of the existence of limits to human knowledge – may have been a philosophical doctrine inspiring the above preferences. Besides, the exclusion of an *art* corresponding to the abstract *science* of political economy may also depend on a conviction that scientific knowledge cannot go beyond general principles.

Ricardian style of thought

Henry Brougham wrote that Ricardo's views were 'abundantly theoretical, sometimes too refined for his audience, occasionally extravagant' (Brougham 1839, p. 190), ascribing the origin of these flaws to a

> propensity to follow a right principle into all its consequences, without duly taking into account in practice the condition of things to which he was applying it, as if a mechanician were to construct an engine without taking into consideration the resistance of the air in which it was to work, or the strength and the weight and the friction of the parts of which it was to be made.
>
> (pp. 190–191)

Brougham was Ricardo's contemporary, his vision was conditioned by the restricted angle from which he observed life and, albeit a fellow traveller in matters of civil rights, he was quite distant from Ricardo when it came to class interests. Later commentators were dazzled by this and other judgements by contemporaries, and were thus misdirected into weird discoveries, including Halévy's 'Cartesianism' (Halévy 1901, p. 246), Hutchison's Millian formalist 'methodological revolution' (Hutchison 1978, pp. 26–57, 1995, 50–83) and Foucault's shift of *episteme* with a transition from the pre-scientific to the scientific phase (Foucault 1966, pp. 275–286). First sight judgement is not a vice but a gift, while these and similar blunders resulted from second-sight judgements. Their authors drew ambitious interpretations from insufficient knowledge of primary sources, reliance on already obsolete secondary literature, and unwitting enslavement to prejudice sedimented by past polemical attacks.

What blinded interpreters was Ricardo's style, allegedly the mark of a *truly scientific* mind different from Smith's as yet *pre-scientific* mind. A more sober account is that Ricardo was not really a native speaker of English. He was scared by Horner's invitation to write for the *Edinburgh Review* and terrified at the prospect of writing at all. Mill's 'formal method' was not 'economic methodology' but a style of writing: the art of laying down one's thought by marking in the margin the headings of paragraphs. Besides, Ricardo's publications were 'dominated by immediate practical concerns' and are mainly 'essays taken up with current issues' (Levine 1977, p. 75) and drawn up in a 'clear expository style with a great emphasis given to conclusions and a smaller emphasis given to the logical process by which the conclusions derived' (Gootzeit 1975, p. viii; cf. Dorfman 1989, p. 162; Kerr 2014, p. 540).

Style in writing may, or often may not, correspond to a *Denkstyl*, a system of beliefs shared by a 'thought collective' whose coherence depends on a consistent demarcation line between admissible and inadmissible beliefs (Fleck 1935, pp. 20–52; cf. Cremaschi & Dascal 1998b, pp. 242–246). A group or individual's cultural background is a storehouse from which they may choose 'structures' to organise shapeless phenomena. Ricardo's background included lack of classical education, experience in finance, research in geology, some information on experimental farming. Besides being the exponent of a sub-culture different from that of Malthus, Mill and Bentham, his mind was the result of a unique cultural hybridisation. We may ascribe the distinctive character of his way of producing intellectual artefacts by reassembling pieces from Smith's work to this constellation.

Ricardo adopts straightforward and unilinear representations. The *Essay on Profits* reduces the economy to two substances (corn and manufactured goods), subdividing it into two sectors: rent and profit (Ricardo 1815, pp. 10–22). Such idealisation is not just a simplified description but a rep-resentation of *something else* transferred and mapped on the *set of data* consid-ered. That is, models are metaphors, and what Ricardo does is to *redescribe* values as physical quantities, for example, corn instead of the exchange value of corn. The economy becomes 'a self-regulating and autonomous inner core, within which value magnitudes were isomorphic with physical quantities, controlled not by human volition but by nature itself [...] the forces of and fertility, physical need and human fecundity' (Gudeman 1986, p. 62).

In the *Principles*, the model is different from the *Essay* but no less unidi-rectional. Ricardo writes in Chapter 1 that gold and silver are subject to *fluctuations* (Ricardo 1817, p. 14) and that there was a *fall* in their value, not a *rise* in the value of corn and labour (p. 19). Here, lexicalised expressions em-body frozen metaphors evoking a spatial dimension and substantialisation of labour or value. Following the suggestion by Mirowski (1989, pp. 163–171) that the value-as-substance metaphor is a key to the chapter, the plot would be that value is a *physical magnitude* consisting of labour which remains in-variable through transformation into various commodities (Gudeman 1986, pp. 65–66). Ricardo's model was not a mirroring of the economy of his times; on the contrary, it 're-presented his world as having a specific kind of coherence [...] But this coherence of the model was only a cultural way of formulating experience' (p. 69).

Neither the applauded methodological revolution of Mill nor the dep-recated vice of Ricardo is a historical fact. They are, rather, the fallout of nineteenth-century ideological struggles on to twentieth-century historians. As argued, Ricardo's adoption of 'strong cases' depends on his awareness of multi-causality and option for a restricted number of variables. To gain exact knowledge, we must, in political economy no less than in geology, advance from *art* to *science* but this step is one-way since nobody invented the art of applying science to the real world.

Ricardian logic and policy advice

An appropriate test for the above interpretation is the most shocking of Ricar-do's proposals, namely the redemption of public debt through a tax on capital. His contemporaries had strong reactions to such a 'visionary' proposal, well summarised by Brougham's description as a 'man from another planet' and leaving heavy traces in later criticism (Churchman 2001, pp. 73–74).

Nonetheless, more recent research has modified the picture in important ways. For example, it was discovered that, in a Speech of 24 December 1819, Ricardo proposed a measure to avoid stress on the currency during the time-lapse within which payments would take place, issuing checks 'distinct from the ordinary circulating medium of the country' (*Works* 5, p. 39). It has also been noted that on 11 March 1823 he proposed a schedule for payment of the tax by numerous instalments throughout two, three, six, or twelve months (*Works* 5, p. 271). What is more, a manuscript was discovered elaborating on this scheme for 'saving the use of the circulating medium for this particular purposes' (Asso & Barucci 1988, p. 28).

Apart from all this, Ricardo also had *ethical* issues in mind: fairness in the distribution of fiscal load on the shoulders of different categories of taxpayers and in the calculation of the tax rate on property required to pay off the public debt (p. 28). He had an answer to the objection that his proposal would have been destructive to the existing social order (Churchman 2001, pp. 81–83) and he was aware, as testified by a letter to Sinclair of 11 May 1820, that the real obstacle was the distorted perception of things by social actors – the fact that human beings 'do not like to make an immediate sacrifice for a future good; and they please themselves with imaginary riches, from which they really derive no advantage' since their revenue is something they 'are imme-diately obliged to pay to the tax-gatherer' (*Works* 8, p. 187). On balance, he

> took great care in addressing various detailed aspects of a capital levy, contradicting accusations that he ignored the effect of 'disturbing causes' in applying the conclusions from highly restrictive models directly to the complex real world.
>
> (Churchman 2001, pp. 89–90)

Another example is the Corn Laws controversy. Malthus's overall argument is that considerations of a higher nature than those relating to wealth should also have a say (Cremaschi and Dascal 1998a, pp. 10–13, 45–46). This in-trusion of political or social considerations into economic theory is justified in Malthus's eyes by the conviction that political economy is a part of moral and political science while Ricardo's apparent inability to appreciate such considerations depends on his view of the science as more similar to math-ematics (Cremaschi 2010, pp. 46–48). Looking more closely into Ricardo's argument, it results that he clearly had it in mind that there is a constant in-teraction of multiple causes in determining a state of affairs, and that whether a country will be an importer or exporter of corn depends at different times on population growth, technical development and capital accumulation (Sal-vadori 2020, p. 102). Consequently, in the long run, market mechanisms will take care of international trade and it will be a matter of prudential decisions whether to intervene to remedy inconveniences in the short term (Peach 1993, pp. 99–101; Maneschi 2015, p. 91). Although his contemporaries sitting in Parliament well understood that they were harmful to their interests, the practical conclusions Ricardo drew from the established principles were 'not as ill-founded, as his critics, including Schumpeter, maintained' (Kurz 2017, p. 112).

The adoption of the ideal of the 'abstract science' implies that we cannot *derive* art from science because science only considers permanent states and, when it comes to the real world, there is more to consider. Policymaking implies considerations of expediency, fairness, political feasibility, and thus – not unlike Kant's 'judgment'– policy advice is a game without rules. Nonetheless, 'abstract science' has a function, for 'nothing is as practical as a good theory' (Kurz 1994, p. xx). Its function is ruling out specific policies by proving their impracticability. After that, policymaking is still possible, and justice and humanity have their word to say. What will remain forever unattainable is Bentham's technocratic dream of an 'art' that complements 'science'.

Partial conclusions: a science without an art

1. Ricardo was described by Brougham and other contemporaries as a philosopher. The term, however, had a different denotation from our current usage in that it meant a student of ethics, society, government and political economy. Moreover, as a legacy of the debate on the French Revolution, it still had an ambivalent connotation for pamphleteers as a visionary or 'enthusiast' who indulged in wild speculations.

2. Ricardo came to political economy after an experience in natural science at an extraordinary moment: the scientific revolution in chemistry and the controversy between experimental method and Biblical literalism in geology. This experience left a mark on his cast of mind because geology was still a science in a pre-paradigmatic phase, where discussions were high on the agenda concerning what should count as a fact, how scientific terminology should be fixed, how were causal explanations possible and what was the status of general laws.

3. In his first contributions on monetary policy he did not address philosophical issues because the debate had started within the context of an attack by practical men on wild speculations, the poles of the confrontation being *practice* and *principles* in a framework more ethical and political than epistemological.

4. After the Bullion controversy, he became increasingly aware of the open questions on the scope and status of political economy; he engaged in philosophical considerations resorting to ideas acquired through conversation with fellow members of the Geological Society, some philosophical reading and Malthus's objections, in which he found as much to learn as to criticise.

5. Horner had an important influence on Ricardo's first steps in political economy, offering practical example and discussion of positive issues, yet no evidence suggests that he discussed 'method' with Ricardo.

6. Mill never thought of teaching Ricardo 'method', despite his schoolmaster attitude in writing matters. From their first meeting, he manifested high consideration for Ricardo's superior skills and never dared to think he had anything to teach him in economic subjects.

7. Ricardo looked for suggestions on causality, scientific laws, and scientific terminology where he could find them. In logic no less than ethics and politics, he accepted suggestions to answer specific questions combining them as he felt were compatible with his general intellectual attitude.

8. This attitude may be described as limited scepticism or epistemological anti-realism. Besides echoing Pierre Bayle, it was compatible with Smith's epistemology and Priestley's ideas repeated by Belsham.

9. Ricardo's general way of proceeding in political economy was not far from Smith's and Malthus's; disagreement was in positive doctrine on specific issues.

10. His thought style and his preference for simplified models of the domain of facts examined was, more than the application of a 'method' different from Smith and Malthus, the effect of a distinctive style in scientific representation resulting from a constellation of cultural factors that made him able to *see* the same phenomena *as* something different.

References

Alonzi, L 2021, 'The Term "Political Economy" in Adam Smith', *Intellectual History Review*, vol. 31, no. 2, pp. 321-339. DOI: 10.1080/17496977.2020.1738808.

Aspromourgos, T 2015, 'Ricardo on Adam Smith', in H Kurz & N Salvadori, *The Elgar Companion to David Ricardo*, Edward Elgar, Cheltenham, pp. 466–477. DOI: 10.4337/9781784715489.

Asso, PF & Barucci E, 1988, 'Ricardo on the National Debt and Its Redemption: Some Notes on an Unpublished Ricardian Manuscript', *Economic Notes*, vol. 17, no. 2, pp. 5–37.

Belsham, T 1801, *Elements of the Philosophy of the Mind, and of Moral Philosophy. To Which Is Prefixed a Compendium of Logic*, Johnson, London.

Bentham, J 1789, *An Introduction to the Principles of Morals and Legislation*, JH Burns, HLA Hart & F Rosen (eds), The Collected Works of Jeremy Bentham 1, Clarendon Press, Oxford, 1996.

Brougham, H Lord 1839, *Historical Sketches of Statesmen Who Flourished in the Time of George the Third*, vol. 2, Knight, London.

Churchman, N 2001, *David Ricardo on Public Debt*, Palgrave, Basingstoke, DOI: 10.1057/9780230509016.

Cremaschi, S 1996, 'D McCloskey, Knowledge and Persuasion in Economics', *Pragmatics and Cognition*, vol. 4, no. 2, pp. 425–429. DOI: 10.1075/pc.4.2.15cre.

Cremaschi, S 2000, 'Les Lumières écossaises et le roman philosophique de Descartes' [The Scottish Enlightenment and Descartes's philosophical novel], in Y Senderowicz & Y Wahl (eds), *Descartes: Reception and Disenchantment*, University Publishing Projects, Tel Aviv, 2000, pp. 65–88.

Cremaschi, S 2010, 'Malthus's Idea of a Moral and Political Science', *The Journal of Philosophical Economics*, vol. 3, no. 2, pp. 5–57.

Cremaschi, S 2014, *Utilitarianism and Malthus's Virtue Ethics. Respectable, Virtuous, and Happy*. Routledge, London. DOI: 10.4324/9781315819235.

Cremaschi, S & Dascal, M 1996, 'Malthus and Ricardo on Economic Methodology', *History of Political Economy*, vol. 28, no. 3, pp. 475–511. DOI: 10.1215/00182702-28-3-475.

Cremaschi, S & Dascal, M 1998a, 'Persuasion and Argument in the Malthus-Ricardo Correspondence', in WJ Samuels & JE Biddle (eds), *Research in the History of Economic Thought and Methodology*, vol. 16, JAI Press, Stamford, CO, pp. 1–63.

Cremaschi, S & Dascal, M 1998b, 'Malthus and Ricardo: Two Styles for Economic Theory'. *Science in Context*, vol. 11, no. 2, pp. 229–254. DOI: 10.1017/S0269889700003008.

Dascal, M & Cremaschi, S 1999, 'The Malthus-Ricardo Correspondence: Sequential Structure, Argumentative Patterns, and Rationality', *Journal of Pragmatics*, vol. 31, no. 9, pp. 1129–1172. DOI: 10.1016/S0378–2166(99)00026-0.

Dascal, M & Gross, A 1999, 'The Marriage of Pragmatics and Rhetoric', *Philosophy & Rhetoric*, vol. 32, no. 2, pp. 107–130. DOI: 10.1353/par.1999.0001.

Davis, JB 1989, 'Distribution in Ricardo's Machinery Chapter', *History of Political Economy*, vol. 21, no. 3, pp. 457–480. DOI: 10.1215/00182702-21-3-457.

de Marchi, NB 1970, 'The Empirical Content and Longevity of Ricardian Economics', *Economica*, vol. 37, no. 147, pp. 257–276.

Depoortère, C 2008, 'On Ricardo's Method: The Scottish Connection Considered', *History of Political Economy*, vol. 40, no. 1, pp. 73–110. DOI: 10.1215/00182702-2007-047.

Dorfman, R 1989, 'Thomas Robert Malthus and David Ricardo', *Journal of Economic Perspectives*, vol. 3, no. 3, pp. 153–164. DOI: 10.1257/jep.3.3.153.

Duncan, W 1748, *An Introduction to the Elements of Logick*, edn used: The Scholar Press, Menston, 1970.

Ferguson, A 1792, *Principles of Moral and Political Science*, vol. 1, edn used: Garland, New York, 1978.

Fleck, L 1935, *Genesis and Development of a Scientific Fact*, transl. F Bradley & TJ Trenn, RK Merton & TJ Trenn (eds), Foreword by T Kuhn, University of Chicago Press, Chicago, IL, 1979.

Foucault, M 1966, *The Order of Things: An Archaeology of the Human Sciences*, no translator, 2nd edn, Routledge, London, 2002.

Gootzeit, M 1975, *David Ricardo*, Columbia University Press, New York.

Gross, A 1990, *The Rhetoric of Science*, Harvard University Press, Cambridge, MA.

Gudeman, S 1986, *Economics as Culture – Models and Metaphors of Livelihood*, Routledge, London.

Halévy, E 1901, *La Formation du radicalisme Philosophique 2: L'évolution de la doctrine utilitaire: de 1789 à 1815*, Alcan, Paris.

Hands, DW 2001, *Reflections without Rules. Economic Methodology and Contemporary Science Theory*, Cambridge University Press, Cambridge. DOI: 10.1017/CBO9780511612602.

Harris, J 1751, *Hermes or a Philosophical Inquiry Concerning Universal Grammar*, Nourse & Vaillant, London.

Hartley, D 1749, *Observations on Man, His Frame, His Duty, and His Expectations*, vol. 1, edn used: Cambridge University Press, Cambridge, 2013. DOI: 10.1017/CBO9781139628617.

Henderson JP 1997, *The Life and Economics of David Ricardo. With Additional Chapters by J.B. Davis*, WJ Samuels & GB Davis (eds), Kluwer, Dordrecht.

Hesse, MB 1961, *Forces and Fields: The Concept of Action at a Distance in the History of Physics*, Nelson, London.

Hollander, S 1979, *The Economics of David Ricardo*, The University of Toronto Press, Toronto.

Hutchison, TW 1978, *On Revolutions and Progress in Economic Knowledge*, Cambridge University Press, New York. DOI: 10.1017/S0022050700105042.

Hutchison, TW 1995, *The Uses and Abuses of Economics*, Routledge, London. DOI: 10.4324/9780203050521.

Ilenkov, E 1960, *Dialektika abstraktnovo i konkretnovo v Kapitale Marksa* [The Dialectics of Abstractness and Concreteness in Marx's Capital], Izdatel'stovo Akademii Nauk SSSR, Moskvà.

Kerr, MPM 2014 'Good Terms: The Style of Ricardian Political Economy', *The Review of English Studies*, New Series, vol. 66, no. 275, pp. 540–563. DOI: 10.1093/res/hgu097.

King, JE 2013, *David Ricardo*, Palgrave Macmillan, Houndsmills, Basingstoke. DOI: 10.1057/9781137315953.

Kurz, H 1994, 'David Ricardo', in D Ricardo, *Über die Grundsätze der Politischen Ökonomie und der Besteuerung*, H Kurz & C Gehrke (eds), Metropolis Verlag, Marburg, pp. xi–lxx.

Kurz, H 2015, 'David Ricardo: On the Art of "Elucidating Economic Principles" in the Face of a "Labyrinth of Difficulties"', *European Journal of the History of Economic Thought*, vol. 22, no. 5, pp. 1–34. DOI: 10.1080/09672567.2015.1074713.

Kurz, H 2017, 'Is There a "Ricardian Vice"? And What Is Its Relationship with Economic Policy Ad"vice"?', *Journal of Evolutionary Economics*, vol. 27, no. 1, pp. 91–114. DOI: 10.1007/s00191-016-0468-2.

Levine, D 1977, *Economic Studies. Contributions to the Critique of Economic Theory*, vol.1, 2nd edn, Routledge, London, 2011.

Lindsay, J 1818, 'Of the Spirit of Man Compared with the Spirit of Beasts', in J Lindsay, *Sermons on Various Subjects*, Hunter, London, pp. 1–28.

Locke, J 1689, *An Essay Concerning Human Understanding*, edn used: H Nidditch (ed.), Clarendon, Oxford, 1975.

Louth, J 2011, 'From Newton to Newtonianism: Reductionism and the Development of the Social Sciences', *Emergence: Complexity and Organization*, vol. 13, no. 4, pp. 63–83.

Malthus, TR 1798, *An Essay on the Principle of Population*, EA Wrigley & D Souden (eds), The Works of Thomas Robert Malthus 1, Pickering, London 1986.

Malthus, TR 1820, *Principles of Political Economy*, edn used: J Pullen (ed.), Cambridge University Press, Cambridge, 1989.

Maneschi, A 2015, 'Corn Laws', in H Kurz & N Salvadori, *The Elgar Companion to David Ricardo*, Edward Elgar, Cheltenham, pp. 85–92. DOI: 10.4337/9781784715489.

Marcuzzo MC & Rosselli, A 1994, 'Ricardo's Theory of Money Matters', *Revue économique*, vol. 45, no. 5, pp. 1251–1268.

Marx, K 1967, *Theorien über den Mehrwert*, vol. 2, Marx Engels Werke 26.2, Dietz, Berlin.

Mauzi, R 1960, *L'idée du bonheur dans la littérature et la pensée françaises au 18. Siècle* [The Idea of Happiness in Eighteenth-Century French Literature and Philosophy], Colin, Paris.

McCloskey, DN 1985, *The Rhetoric of Economics*, Harvester, Brighton.

Meacci, F 2014, 'On Adam Smith's Ambiguities on Value and Wealth', *History of Political Economy*, vol. 44, no. 4, pp. 663–689. DOI: 10.1215/00182702–1811379.

Meacci, F 2015, 'Wealth', in H Kurz & N Salvadori (eds), *The Elgar Companion to David Ricardo*, Edward Elgar, Cheltenham, pp. 581–586. DOI: 10.4337/9781784715489.

Mirowski, P 1989, *More Heat than Light: Economics as Social Physics, Physics as Nature's Economics*, Cambridge University Press, Cambridge. DOI: 10.1017/CBO97805 11559990.

Moore, S 1966, 'Ricardo and the State of Nature', *Scottish Journal of Political Economy*, vol. 13, no. 3, pp. 317–331. DOI: 10.1111/j.1467–9485.1966.tb00399.x.

Peach, T 1993, *Interpreting Ricardo*, Cambridge University Press, Cambridge, 1993. DOI: 10.1017/CBO9780511559525.

Pownall, R 1776, 'A Letter from Governor Pownall', in *The Correspondence of Adam Smith*, EC Mossner & IS Ross (eds), The Glasgow edition of the works and correspondence of Adam Smith 6, Clarendon Press, Oxford, 1997, pp. 337–376.

Ricardo, D 1810, 'On Mr Randle Jackson's Speech', in *Works* 3, pp. 145–153.

Ricardo, D 1810–1811, The High price of Bullion, in *Works* 3, pp. 47–127.

Ricardo, D 1811, *Reply to Mr. Bosanquet's 'Practical Observations on the Report of the Bullion Committee'*, in *Works* 3, pp. 155–256.

Ricardo, D 1815, *An Essay on the Influence of a Low Price of Corn on the Profits of Stock*, in *Works* 4, pp. 9–41.

Ricardo, D 1817, *The Principles of Political Economy and Taxation*, in *Works* 1.

Ricardo, D 1928, *Notes on Mr. Malthus's Work 'Principles of Political Economy Considered with a View to their Practical Application*, in *Works* 2.

Ricardo, D 1951a, 'Notes on Bentham's "Sur les Prix"' 1810–1811', in *Works* 3, pp. 267–341.

Ricardo, D 1951b, 'Fragments on Torrens Concerning Value 1818', in *Works* 3, pp. 303–318.

Ricardo, D 1992, *Notes on Malthus' 'Measure of Value'*, PL Porta (ed.), Cambridge University Press, Cambridge.

Rizvi, SAT 1992, *Ricardo's Resistance to Utility and the Association of Ideas Debate*, Mimeo, University of Vermont, Burlington, VT.

Rizvi, SAT 2015, 'Exchange Value and Utility', in H Kurz & N Salvadori (eds), *The Elgar Companion to David Ricardo*, Edward Elgar, Cheltenham, pp. 135–140. DOI: 10.4337/9781784715489.

Rosselli, A 1985, 'The Theory of Natural Wage', in G Caravale (ed.), *The Legacy of Ricardo*, Blackwell, Oxford, pp. 239–254.

Salvadori, N 2020, *Ricardo's Theory of Growth and Accumulation. A Modern View*, Routledge, London. DOI: 10.4324/9781003009511.

Say, JB 1803, *Traité d'économie politique*, vol. 1, edn used: E Blanc et al. (eds), Economica, Paris, 2003.

Schopenhauer, A 1864, *Eristische Dialektik*, in A Schopenhauer, *er Handschriftliche Nachlass*, vol. 3, A Hübscher (ed.), Deutscher Taschenbuch Verlag, München, 1985, pp. 669–695.

Senior, NW 1836, *An Outline of the Science of Political Economy*, Farrar & Rinehart, New York, 1939.

Signorino, R 2015, 'Natural and Market Prices', in H Kurz & N Salvadori (eds), *The Elgar Companion to David Ricardo*, Edward Elgar, Cheltenham, pp. 364–370. DOI: 10.4337/9781784715489.

Smith, A 1759, *The Theory of Moral Sentiments*, DD Raphael & AL Macfie (eds), The Glasgow Edition of the Works and Correspondence of Adam Smith 1, Oxford University Press, Oxford, 1976.

Smith, A 1795, 'The Principles Which Lead and Direct Philosophical Enquires', in A Smith, *Essays on Philosophical Subjects*, WPD Wightman, JC Bryce & IS Ross (eds), The Glasgow Edition of the Works and Correspondence of Adam Smith 3, Clarendon Press, Oxford, pp. 31–129.

Sraffa, P 1951, 'Introduction', in *Works* 1, pp. xiii–lxii.

Stewart, D 1792, *Elements of the Philosophy of the Human Mind. I*, The Collected Works of Dugald Stewart 2, Thoemmes Press, Bristol, 1994.

Stewart, D 1810, *The Essays on Philosophical Subjects*, The Collected Works of Dugald Stewart 5, Thoemmes Press, Bristol, 1994.

Stewart, D 1814, *Elements of the Philosophy of the Human Mind. II*, The Collected Works of Dugald Stewart 3, Thoemmes Press, Bristol, 1994.

Stigler, GJ 1950, 'The Development of Utility Theory I', *Journal of Political Economy*, vol. 58, no. 4, pp. 307–327. DOI: 10.1086/256962.

Stirati, A 1995, 'Smith's Legacy and the Definitions of the Natural Wage in Ricardo', *Journal of the History of Economic Thought*, vol. 17, no. 1, pp. 106–132. DOI: 10.1017/S1053837200002327.

Swift, J 1726, *Gulliver's Travels*, edn used: P Turner (ed.), Oxford University Press, Oxford, 1971.

Walter, R 2018, 'The Enthusiasm of David Ricardo', *Modern Intellectual History*, vol. 15, no. 2, pp. 381–409. DOI: 10.1017/S1479244316000044.

Walter, R 2019, 'The Bullion Controversy and the History of Political Thought: Experience, Innovation and Theory', *Intellectual History Review*, vol. 29, no. 3, pp. 1–22. DOI: 10.1080/17496977.2018.1526452.

Walter, R 2021, *Before Method and Models: The Political Economy of Malthus and Ricardo*, Oxford University Press, New York.

Watts, I 1724, *Logick: Or, The Right Use of Reason*, edn used: Garland, New York, 1984.

Watts, I 1741, *The Improvement of the Mind*, Selected Works of Isaac Watts 7–8, Thoemmes, Bristol, 1999.

Whately, R 1831, *Introductory Lectures on Political Economy*, Kelley, New York, 1966.

7 Ricardo on ethics and political economy

Moral impressions and the rational pursuit of happiness

Moral impressions

'Moral impressions' are the first source of moral obligation that reason confirms and to which religion adds further support. It would be a 'libel upon human nature to say otherwise' (*Works* 5, p. 327). Ricardo uttered these words in Parliament in 1823. It is a statement incompatible with both the Calvinist view of human nature as utterly depraved and the Benthamite view of moral judgement in terms of pleasure and pain.

There are traces left of Ricardo's discussion of ethical topics, besides the correspondence and speeches, in the *Commonplace Books*. The latter are two notebooks of reading notes (Ricardo Papers) tendentially slighted by commentators. Weatherall (1976) and Henderson (1997) ignore them completely, Milgate and Stimson (1991, p. 23) and King (2013, p. 33) dismiss them in half a page. Sraffa, as careful as ever, lists their contents accurately (*Works* 10, pp. 393–398). What emerges from the list is that 40% of Ricardo's reading consists of modern history and travel journals and 60% of logic, religion, ethics and theodicy.

Natural morality

In recent literature, the reader may meet strong assertions about Ricardo's 'unreligious mind' (Hartwell 1971, p. 36), his profession of 'atheism' (Depoortère 2002, p. 501) and his 'agnostic' tendency (Henderson 1997, p. 163). There are obvious objections to these: first, Ricardo never disclosed his atheistic or agnostic opinions; second, when discussing theological issues, far from hinting at privately held Atheism, his arguments are consistent with his public image of 'rational believer', and third, the thesis he repeatedly asserts – namely that *natural morality* is independent of *religious morality* – is the Unitarian divines' favourite claim.

In correspondence with Hutches Trower, Ricardo comments on a pamphlet – a reprint of letters to the *Times* from 'Laicus' and 'an East India Proprietor' – the

DOI: 10.4324/9781003162100-7

pen names of the Evangelical lawyer John Poynder and Trower himself. Poynder insists that India needs Christianity and that the Gospel should replace the absurd, cruel and immoral Hindu superstitions that allow infanticide, the burning of widows and human sacrifices (Trower 1813, pp. 3–4). He adds that the East India Company should establish an Episcopal Government in India and grant additional facilities to Missionaries so they can reach that country (pp. 5–10). Trower illustrates the dangers of such steps, arguing that 'any attempt to convert the Hindoos to Christianity' (p. 48) would be both impossible and counterproductive. He denies that the Hindus are 'in the most dreadful state of moral depravity', addicted to 'every vice which can degrade our nature' (p. 38), concluding that 'their vices are not attributable to their religion' (pp. 14, 39), their moral character 'is not deserving of the severity with which it is censured' and it 'may be improved without their conversion' (pp. 86–87).

After manifesting 'very great interest', Ricardo declares: 'My opinion coincided with yours before I read your letters and it is now very much strengthened by the facts and reasoning which you have brought forward' (to Trower 8 November 1813, *Works* 6, p. 96). From this admission, we may infer adhesion to the following opinions: we cannot force people to believe something; morality can be improved independently of adhesion to any given set of religious beliefs; the moral character of non-Christian nations is not necessarily corrupt; the moral character of Christian nations is not by definition at the same height as the Gospel.

In the *Commonplace Book* for 1817, Ricardo wrote down a select list of chapters from two works by Pierre Bayle with excerpts copied in full (Ricardo Papers; Sraffa 1955c, p. 393). The first is *Pensées diverses sur la Comète* [Various Thoughts on the Comet]. The topics Ricardo thought worth examining are– in chapters XLVI, LXXXIV, XCIX, C, and CVIII – that despite having already been refuted by experience, opinions continue to be shared simply because of their antiquity, and that even visions firmly believed by several witnesses turn out to be patently false (Bayle 1682a, pp. 130–133, 219–221, 266–273, 292–293). In chapter LXIX we read that right reason teaches us to honour God not by ceremonies but by the practice of virtue (pp. 179–182); in chapters LXXXI and XCI, that religion is continuously used by rulers either to defend themselves or to manipulate their subjects (pp. 205–209, 242–244); in chapter LXXXVIII, that conversions obtained by force or bought with money are counterproductive (pp. 228–235); in chapters CXX, CXXIII and CXLVI, that idolatry is more obnoxious than irreligion and that Atheism does not necessarily lead to corruption of morals (pp. 315–318, 1862b, pp. 5–8, 37–39). In chapters CXXXIV–CXXXVIII, we read that experience shows that religion fails to correct vicious inclinations because, more than on principles they profess, men tend to act on particular judgements dictated by the passion prevailing at the moment (Bayle 1682b, pp. 8–18).

The second work is the *Dictionnaire historique et critique* [Historical and Critical Dictionary]. From this book, only two passages are reported. The first, from note B to the entry *'Anabaptistes'*, says that excesses by this sect offered the Roman party an occasion to defame Reformation and, to face competition from Catholics, the reformers 'shouted with all their strength' against the Anabaptists (Bayle 1697a, p. 200). The other passage reports note 1 to the entry *'Gregoire* I' which tells the anecdote of a monk who described Giangaleazzo Visconti's grave at the Pavia Chartreuse as that of a 'great saint'. The monk justified his description by referring to the maxim followed in his country to 'call saints all those who do us good'. Bayle comments that this maxim, far from being typically Italian, 'is followed at every time and in every country' (Bayle 1697b, p. 598).

The *Commonplace Book* for 1818 includes an excerpt from chapter 14 of Locke's *Reasonableness of Christianity*. It declares that, although among the ancient Heathens some philosophers cultivated the knowledge of one God, few went to their schools to learn 'their duties' and most were content with sacrifices celebrated by priests who 'made it not their business to teach them virtue' (Locke 1695, p. 147).

Besides, there are two excerpts from Hume's *Natural History of Religion*. The first declares that religious conviction has in all ages been 'more affected than real', commenting that 'the assent in these matters is some unaccountable operation of the mind between disbelief and conviction, but approaching much nearer the former than the latter' (Hume 1757, p. 72). The other declares that the virtuous man 'is drawn to his duty without any effort or endeavour' by the force of the natural ties he has with his family and community and a 'sentiment of order and moral beauty' without any 'pretence to religious merit', adding that virtuous conduct is 'no more than what we owe to society and to ourselves' (p. 82).

Reading notes follow from two works by Richard Watson, the Bishop of Llandaff, *An Apology for Christianity*, a rejoinder to Edward Gibbon, and *An Apology for the Bible*, a rejoinder to Thomas Paine. An excerpt from the first says that it is 'just as illiberal in Divines, to attribute the scepticism of every Deist to wilful infidelity; as it is in the Deists, to refer the faith of every Divine to professional bias' (Watson 1776, pp. 86–87).

Another excerpt is from *An Examination of the Bishop of London's Discourse concerning Prophecy* by Conyers Middleton, a Cambridge fellow with a taste for theological controversy. It argues that 'the foundation of all religion' lies in 'those practical, social and real duties, which our reason and senses prescribe in common to all' (Middleton 1750, pp. 196–197), and religious writers should avoid 'questions, wholly speculative, fruitless and inexplicable' (p. 197).

Self-deception

One ubiquitous trait of human nature – Ricardo believes – is improvidence, a flaw provoked by limited ability to foresee events and a constant tendency to self-deception. In a letter to Trower of 27 January 1817, he notes that 'poor and rich all have confidence in their good fortune and whilst their affairs are prosperous never dream of a reverse' (*Works* 7, p. 126). On 24 February, Ricardo adds that 'the chances of a reverse of fortune are always considerably undervalued by all of us' and 'the fear of falling into poverty can have very little influence on the mind of any man whose wages are such as to enable him to save a part of his earnings' (*Works* 7, p. 134). In a letter to Mill of 6 January 1818, he mentions 'the astonishing self delusion which prevents men from seeing in their own acts those very qualities which they are so loud in condemning in the acts of others' (*Works* 7, p. 197). On 30 January, he writes to Malthus that he knows 'the strong disposition of every man to deceive himself in his eagerness to prove a favourite theory' (*Works* 7, p. 251). On 11 February 1823, he declares to Maria Edgeworth that, among the 'moral evils of society', there is none which he is 'more anxious to see removed than the improvidence of the lower classes' (*Works* 9, p. 299).

Paradoxes of morality

In a letter of 10 November 1821, Maria Edgeworth reports a conversation between Ricardo and Thomas Smith 'about cases of conscience', particularly concerning truthfulness. She adds that William Paley, the Anglican authority of the time, was 'of course quoted' (Edgeworth 1971, p. 261). Paley's starting point in his discussion of truthfulness is that a lie is the breach of a promise since the very fact of engaging in communication is an implicit promise of truthfulness. Conforming to his consequentialist approach (Cremaschi 2014, pp. 16–40), Paley argues that the evil of lying is the damage it carries – whether the specific damage to somebody or 'the destruction of that confidence which is essential to the intercourse of human life' (Paley 1785, p. 107).

However, he concedes that there are falsities that are not lies, namely those not implying deception and whose addressee has no right to know the truth. On the other hand, there may be lies that do not need falsity to be such, for it 'is the wilful deceit that makes the lie' (p. 110). Edgeworth does not report what was argued by Ricardo, but at least the fact that he discussed a classical issue from casuistry is proof of acquaintance with the philosophical literature of his time.

In another letter of 14 November, she mentions a conversation on the effects on happiness of rank and wealth. She reports that Ricardo said that, in case

> anybody offered him for himself or any of his children such an increase of fortune as should take them out of their rank of life he would not accept it. There would be a necessity for living according to new habits and spending according to the expectations of others instead of according to his own taste &c. At the same time he allowed that if he had been born Lord Lansdowne or any nobleman of great possessions he might have been as happy as he is now.
>
> (Edgeworth, 1971, p. 264)

In another of 22 November, she describes a 'delightful conversation' between Ricardo and Thomas Smith, 'mixed with placid deep philosophy now and then from Ricardo' referring to Adam Smith's theory about the

> inclination which people feel to sympathise with persons in high rank − rich and prosperous − why and how is this compatible with *envy* of riches − of the envy felt for those who rise to a rank or fortune to which they were not born.
>
> (p. 271)

She adds that Ricardo commented 'beautifully and *nobly* on this subject − on the fault and unhappiness of each party − and he has avoided all these faults. No one envies − all admire him' (p. 271). This report informs us that Ricardo was familiar with Paley's *Principles of Moral and Political Philosophy*, a work he also cites in speeches and Smith's *Theory of Moral Sentiments*, of which he owned an exemplar (Sraffa 1955d, p. 399).

Ricardo's argument may have been as follows. A paradox of morality is our inability to reach perfect impartiality; there are laws of human nature steering our ability to share small and great pains and joys; we are more ready to sympathise with little joys and great pains than with great joys and small pains (Smith 1759, pp. 15–16); with joy, we sympathise up to that point at which it starts provoking envy, and we have even greater sympathy with great pains while we hardly feel any sympathy with small ones (p. 45).

We might better understand this argument in light of Smith's theory of sympathy. He assumes that our ability to formulate moral judgements depends on 'sympathy' or 'the exchange of situations'. Such origins fatally undermine the possibility of absolute impartiality because the degree of impartiality we can reach depends on the afore-mentioned greater or lesser ability to sympathise with pleasures and pains. Imperfect impartiality yet is a reason for the fragility of happiness. As the 'chief part of human happiness' comes from the consciousness of being loved, it is improbable that a sudden change of fortune would make us happier because, in such circumstances, real-world spectators would hardly feel any sympathy.

In a letter to a 'young lady' of 20 April 1822, Ricardo drops a casual remark on the good life. He wishes her as much wealth, 'and no more, as will make [her] happy and contented' (*Works* 10, p. 165). He recommends books, for they 'teach us how to think justly, and to think justly is one of the best sources of happiness' (p. 165) and concludes by mentioning other 'concomitants' of happiness, that we may easily guess to be the joys of virtuous love and family life.

Another grain of moral theory is in a letter of March 1815 to Abraham Delvalle, a wine-merchant and probably a relative with whom his wife had had an unpleasant argument. Ricardo remarks that a

> man of integrity should be quickly alive to any attack upon his honesty, but the consciousness of the purity of his views should secure him against

that extreme touchiness which on the slightest grounds makes him suspect that thoughts are harboured to his disadvantage. Such extreme instability is a torment to the possessor of it and a mortal foe to peace and harmony. It is ever prone to strike the first blow on a vague supposition that hostility is intended and must be promptly guarded against.

(*Works* 10, p. 142)

Behind this casual remark, the idea that 'the chief part of human happiness' depends on how we mirror ourselves in our fellows seems to lurk once more.

Two objections to Utilitarianism

In the correspondence, Ricardo formulates objections to Utilitarianism. While discussing Mill's *History of British India*, he mentions critically 'the doctrine of utility or expediency'. On 19 October 1817, Mill had written that he believed his *History* might be 'no bad introduction to the study of civil society in general' (*Works* 6, p. 195). As mentioned, Mill's diagnosis of Indian society considers the extent to which its institutions conform to the principle of utility as a criterion of civilisation. On this criterion, he believes that he can prove that India is a barbarous country whose ingenuity is 'wasted on contemptible or mischievous objects' (Mill 1817, p. 224). In his usual deferent mood, Ricardo first compliments Mill on his performance but, after reading a few chapters, starts raising sharp objections. On 6 January 1818, he writes that India's British domination went through two steps, first, 'to get our troops into the dominions of our allies for a stipulated monthly payment', second, to seize 'all the powers of Government'. He agrees that the first step was the most injurious to the Indian people since, by consolidating the power of tyrannical rulers, it 'opened the door to all manner of misrule and oppression'; the second step instead had the desirable consequence of establishing more efficient and just administration. Yet – he objects – the dilemma is that,

in the first step, stipulating that your ally shall have the service of your troops in consideration of his paying for it, there may be a want of policy and wisdom, but there appears to be no injustice, – but in the second step there is the greatest injustice although it is demonstrable that it may greatly promote the happiness of the people.

That which is free from the taint of injustice is the cause of misery to the people, – that which is manifestly unjust is the cause of their happiness. Are we to fix our eyes steadily on the end, the happiness of the governed, and pursue it at the expence of those principles which all men are agreed in calling virtuous?

(*Works*, vol. 7, p. 241)

In a word, Ricardo contends that the principle of utility ends up with destructive moral nihilism as it implies that the production of happiness is the sole criterion of moral judgement disregarding those most obvious rules about which there is universal agreement. Thus, he seems to be defending traditional morality against Bentham's 'new morality'. Indeed, he was formulating what became a classical critique, independently formulated by the English philosopher William Whewell (1852, pp. 210–215) and the Italian writer Alessandro Manzoni (1855, vol. 3, pp. 337–339, 400).

In the same letter, Ricardo formulates one more objection. He writes that

> the difficulty of the doctrine of expediency or utility is how to balance one object of utility against another – there being no standard in nature, it must vary with the tastes, the passions and the habits of mankind.
>
> (*Works* 7, p. 242)

Utility is, for Bentham, a capacity of things, actions and institutions to 'produce benefit, advantage, pleasure, good, or happiness or [...] to prevent the happening of mischief, pain, evil, or unhappiness' (Bentham 1789, p. 12). Ricardo objects that, since 'utility' is a property far from universal and invariable, the felicific calculus is impossible because we cannot reduce various kinds of utility to one standard. He adds: 'This is one of the subjects on which I require to be enlightened' (*Works* 7, p. 242). Note the kind of speech act performed: he is shifting the burden of proof on Mill while hiding mild irony under a coat of apparent deference.

Let us examine extant counterevidence. The first alleged proof of Ricardo's adhesion to utilitarian ethics is in a letter of 9 September 1821 to Francis Place, the radical activist who had become Bentham's follower, where he defends Malthus trying to show that his use of the words 'right' and 'law of nature' could be read as roughly equivalent to 'utility' or 'the good of the whole'. To stress his closeness to Place, he adds that he is, no less than him, 'a disciple of the Bentham and Mill school' (*Works* 9, p. 52). The statement, when read literally, sounds like information about Ricardo's philosophical beliefs. If we read it as a concession made to a partner in a discussion, it sounds like a less cogent utterance, a part of an argumentative move aimed at stressing convergence points while trying to gain the partner's assent on what is really at stake. Here, he concedes that, strictly, the *law of nature* and *innate rights* are meaningless phrases while 'the good of the whole' is instead a meaningful one. The latter phrase, however, does not belong to Benthamite jargon. Besides, he contends that, all in all, Malthus and Place might have reached the same conclusion expressed in different words. A distinction often advanced in his correspondence with Malthus, the one between questions of language and questions of fact, may have been something he had in mind also here. His admission may have been more a remark on terminology than a profession of adhesion to Utilitarianism.

The second apparent proof is in a letter to Edgeworth of 13 December 1822. After discussing remedies to famines, among them the cultivation of potatoes as a means of securing more food, Ricardo expresses what sounds like adhesion to the principle of utility. After declaring that he is not sure that potatoes afford safer and more abundant provision of food without the risk of frequent famines, he adds that the

> argument, that the failure of the potatoe crop is only occasional, and that at all other times there will be in the world a much greater number of happy and contented beings, appears to me defective. Judging by my own feelings, if for five, six, or seven years of easy competency, with respect to food, I had to endure one year of famine, and to witness the sufferings of my family and friends for that one dreadful year, I would rather that I had never been born.
>
> (*Works* 9, p. 238)

He concludes: 'Give me these securities and I will fight with you till death in favor of the potatoe, for my motto, after Mr. Bentham, is "the greatest happiness to the greatest number"' (pp. 238–239). Two remarks are in order. The quote refers just to the phrase, not to the doctrine. Besides, the utterance's addressee is *not* a Benthamite, and the dramatic promise to fight 'till death' makes the following sentence sound as ironical as the former. Behind the veil of irony, the serious theoretical issue Ricardo has in mind is the comparatively heavier weight to ascribe to risks of unhappiness *vis-à-vis* prospects of happiness, that is, one of the difficulties in which he believes Bentham's felicific calculus incurs because of its lack of qualifications in the definition of pleasure and pain. Ricardo seems to advance two criteria for practical judgement: first, the *certainty* of happiness, a feature which we may safely include in Bentham's requirements for the felicific calculus; second, a comparatively *higher weight* to be assigned to unhappiness *vis-à-vis* happiness, which could hardly fit in Bentham's requirements. The difficulty he feels here concerns the possibility of measuring happiness, the same kind of objection he had made to Mill. In other words, the quoted passage formulates, instead of a profession of Benthamism, an objection to Bentham.

On balance, we should not take occasional Benthamite phrases at face value. They are moves in a conversation with a specific partner. In such cases, the meaning of a speech act may be reconstructed only from the context. The utterance may have several Gricean *implicatures*, that is, things that are said tacitly not by logical implication but relying on either the partner's background knowledge or what the partners had already said during the conversation, or the partner's ability to understand the kind of speech act performed. In the correspondence with Place, Ricardo was interested in establishing contact points at the price of leaving aside matters of language and definitions. Though an Anglo-Irish aristocrat who tended to turn up her nose at London middle-class scribblers, Edgeworth was a humane spirit and a keen observer of human characters. Only with her does Ricardo adopt an ironic tone with regard to Bentham and Mill. In correspondence with Bentham, he had always been respectful, with Mill he was always friendly, though occasionally ironical, for example, in the choice to systematically substitute the phrase 'You are wrong' with 'I want to be enlightened'. With Edgeworth, the game carried a double asymmetry. She was an aristocrat confronting a delightfully exotic sample of humanity named Ricardo while chatting about a half-mad London lawyer and a semi-barbaric Scottish literate. Her mild jokes may have induced Ricardo to engage in the art of poking fun at his fellow travellers. Another chapter noted Ricardo's irony in his semi-serious mention, in this very letter, of Mill's 'formal method'. His mention of 'the greatest happiness to the greater number' here was more than 'a gesture to what he found uncontroversial and vaguely comprehensive' (Bonner 1995, p. 2). It was another name for the widely shared ideal of 'public happiness', a phrase adopted by a cohort of eighteenth-century writers uncontaminated by as yet non-existent Utilitarianism, from Ludovico Antonio Muratori, a Catholic priest, to such no less devout Christians as Antonio Genovesi and Joseph Priestley (Cremaschi 2020).

The fragility of happiness

Ricardo's view of happiness has little to share with Bentham's definition in terms of a positive balance of pleasures and pains over a lifetime. In a letter to Trower of 25 December 1815, he argues that his addressee 'must necessarily be a happy man' enjoying 'exercise both of the body and of the mind', 'living in a healthful country', being ignorant of boredom and 'surrounded by a charming family' (p. 344). However, he adds, 'love of distinction is so natural to man' that 'emulation and ambition' (*Works* 6, p. 344) will encourage Trower to take the responsibilities expected from a gentleman.

Besides limits to knowledge and foresight, Ricardo assumes indolence to be a fundamental trait of human nature. In a letter to Malthus of 4 September 1817, he questions his proposal of encouraging luxury consumption among the working classes, so that the poor would tend to delay marriage until they have saved enough to secure a comparatively high standard of living for their families. The argument is that it is true that happiness 'is the object to be desired', but each of us has his view of what happiness is and

> we cannot be quite sure that provided he is equally well fed, a man may not be happier in the enjoyment of the luxury of idleness than in the enjoyment of the luxuries of a neat cottage, and good clothes.
>
> (*Works* 7, p. 185)

On 7 August 1817, congratulating Mill on his literary accomplishments, he adds a semi-serious consideration on happiness. He writes:

> I hope then that your purse may at least be as well lined as mine is, provided it does not inflect upon you the cares and anxious responsibility of

wealth. If it would have that effect then I wish your wealth to be limited
to that point at which it will be most productive of happiness.

(Works 7, p. 170)

In the same letter, he drops a remark on another ingredient, once more
the joys of family life. He describes his satisfaction on his return to Gatcomb after 'extended travels', adding that 'happiness is made up of an infinite number of particulars', which, in turn, might be found nowhere 'in
such great abundance as at home. Novelty has its charms, but an isolated
being in a foreign country will very soon exhaust its pleasures, and will
naturally turn his eyes towards the scene of all his agreeable associations'
(p. 170).

The rational pursuit of happiness

In Ricardo's correspondence and speeches, we also find normative claims. In
a bitter letter of 12 September 1803 to Edward Wilkinson, his father-in-law,
he reproaches him for being seen by his children as a tyrant, 'instead of the
guardian, and anxious promoter of their happiness' (*Works* 10, p. 121). On a
couple of occasions, he declares that the right conduct of life consists of the
rational pursuit of happiness. He writes to Mill on 9 November 1817 that his
interest in the study of the progress of human society, about which he expects
to learn from the latter's *History of British India*, is prompted by the desire to
understand the 'causes which are constantly obstructing man in the rational
pursuit of his own happiness' (*Works* 7, p. 204). In another of 1 January 1821,
while commenting on the birth of grandchildren, he expresses a wish that
'succeeding generations may be more wise than the present, and may be
better able to avail themselves of the means of happiness which this world
affords' (*Works* 8, pp. 329–330). On 17 September 1822, he writes that his
son Ralph 'is a good fellow and is wise in knowing how to choose a judicious
path to happiness' (*Works* 9, p. 163). The idea that the rational pursuit of happiness includes doing the good in our power to do is expressed in another of
14 October 1820, where he justifies his refusal of nomination to the East India Company's governing body. He writes that he would 'act very unwisely'
if he deviated from 'the quiet sober path' in which he was then moving and
concludes: 'it is not one in which I can do *much* good, but still it affords me
opportunities of doing *all* the good which I am capable of performing' (*Works*
8, p. 282).

Available evidence suggests that Ricardo had to his credit some good reading in ethics and some clear ideas in his mind: that the just rule of life is
the rational pursuit of happiness, that happiness is a complicated and fragile
gift, that its reduction to a measurable magnitude is a vain enterprise, that
wealth may contribute to happiness up to a certain point, that happiness
includes promoting the happiness of others and – reversing Paley's dictum –
that whatever is expedient is *not* always right.

Just war

Ricardo's opinions on a classical issue of casuistry, just war, may be found in a handwritten marginal note to *The Sinfulness of War* by Unitarian Minister Benjamin Travers, one of the 'oddments' in his library (Sraffa 1955d, p. 402). The moral justification of war had become a hot topic since wars with France had begun. A pacifist alignment which had coalesced in the 1770s, at the time of the American War, made of Unitarians, Baptists, Congregationalists and Quakers acted in the 1790s as a pressure group on the most liberal Whigs in Parliament under the name of 'The Friends of Peace' (Cookson 1982, p. 2). Unitarians, being a part of this body, in some cases suffered from rising anti-Jacobin hysteria. For example, Joseph Priestly found himself forced to leave his hometown and then emigrate to America.

In this broad alignment, the Quakers represented a more radical pacifist trend co-existing with a more moderate one inspired by traditional just-war doctrine. This doctrine, dating back to Cicero, was stated by Augustine in an overly permissive version, redesigned by Aquinas with more demanding conditions, then by Francisco de Vitoria with extremely demanding conditions for *jus ad bellum*, the conditions under which recourse to war is admissible, and *jus in bello*, the admissible practices in the conduct of war (Johnson 1981, pp. 121–189).

Travers's pamphlet criticises a sermon by John Jortin, a Church of England prelate author of a defence of the Christian faith, a history of the Church and a biography of Erasmus of Rotterdam (Young 2004). In this sermon, Jortin defended traditional just war doctrine, contending that war is always admissible once certain traditional conditions are respected. He suggests that we should not interpret many of Jesus's precepts 'literally and with extreme rigour', for example, 'If a man smite thee on the one cheek, turn to him the other'. The Gospel 'contains many precepts and counsels, commands and prohibitions, expressed in general unrestrained terms, which must admit various exceptions and limitations' (Jortin 1771, p. 46). He concludes that what is required is that we 'love our enemies; that is, we must have a favourable disposition of mind towards them, which will always incline us to be just and charitable in our dealings with them', which, in terms of practical consequences implies that our 'anger must be short in its continuance, and harmless in its effects' (p. 49). However, it neither follows that 'Christian nations may not wage war with their enemies' (p. 44) nor 'that men may not in the defence of their own lives take away the lives of those who unjustly assault them' (p. 45).

Travers intends to condemn the 'sinful practice of war' as such. However, he introduces the exception of self-defence by the argument that 'resistance, in case of invasion, is not, strictly speaking, to be denominated war – it is self-defence – it is self-preservation, and which is justly styled the first law of nature, and therefore not only lawful, but justifiable' (Travers 1814, p. 11).

The Monthly Repository, the Unitarian publication whose editor was the already-mentioned Robert Aspland, treated the pamphlet nicely, writing it intended to convince Christians that they

> ought on no account whatever [...] to hire themselves, or suffer their children to hire themselves, if in any way they can prevent it, for the express purpose of carrying on offensive war. Alas! How little chance is there of the still small voice of reason and humanity being heard amidst the universal and perpetual dim and clang of arms!
>
> (*Monthly Repository* 1815)

Ricardo, not too impressed by the reviewer's authority, expressed a different appraisal in the mentioned handwritten note to a page where Travers writes that Jortin 'very ambiguously' declares that

> we must forgive our enemies and pray for them, that they may repent and return to a better mind; but it does not follow from hence that we may not fight against them [...] From hence, it appears, that the good Doctor thought we were *warranted* to *destroy* them, but not to do them *any harm*! Alas! Such is the infirmity of our nature, and the difficulty of serving two masters.
>
> (Travers 1814, p. 9 fn.)

Ricardo's note is:

> This remark is as appliable to B.T. as to the good Doctor.

His point seems to be that it is challenging to defend pacifism without condemning self-defence as well. To define self-defence as something different from war is – foreshadowing what will become one of his favourite phrases – *a matter of words, not of theory*. This note also reveals a style that will be apparent in his later correspondence with Malthus. It resorts to a '*tu quoque*' argument, one of those for which Ricardo will manifest a preference (Cremaschi & Dascal 1998, pp. 249–250).

In the same years, Belsham wrote that 'the horrors of war will eventually be the means of putting an end to that destructive calamity'. Human beings 'will see that wars of aggression [...] are not only cruel and unjust, but even unwise' and, though defensive wars 'must indeed always be lawful, and are often unavoidable', at last, 'human beings will see that it is in their interest not to have recourse even to the most just and necessary defensive wars' (Belsham 1814, p. 13).

A casual remark in a letter to Trower of 4 July 1821 also reveals Ricardo's concern with peace expressing the opinion that, together with free trade and 'liberal' policies, it would mark the road to European countries' prosperity. He writes:

> I cannot but flatter myself with the hopes of a continuance of peace in Europe [...] I hope nations are becoming wiser, and are every day more

convinced that the prosperity of one country is not promoted by the distress of another – that restrictions on commerce are not favorable to wealth, and that the particular welfare of each country, as well as the general welfare of all, is best encouraged by unbounded freedom of trade, and the establishment of the most liberal policy.

(*Works* 8, p. 4)

We may also note that Ricardo's life choices had been consistent with his marginal note's spirit. From 1798 to 1801, we know that he volunteered to join the Loyal Lambeth Infantry Association, a territorial defence corps (Sraffa 1955a, pp. 46–47; Weatherall 1976, pp. 35–38).

Penal law and private morality

Ricardo's comments on the Queen's affair also deserve notice. Caroline of Brunswick, the Duke of Brunswick's daughter, was married in 1795 to George III's eldest son without ever seeing him before engagement. Nine months later, she had a child, Princess Charlotte. In 1806, rumours that Caroline had a lover led to an investigation with a verdict denying any foundation to such rumours. In 1814 Caroline moved to Italy, where she took as a servant a man called Bartolomeo Bergami, who was soon suspected of being her lover. Her husband set up a second investigation on her alleged adultery, which got buried under a heap of '*non mi ricordo*' [I don't remember] uttered by Italian witnesses. The Prince tried to divorce her by having the Tory government submit an ad hoc bill to Parliament. In 1820, he became King, and Caroline returned to Britain intending to assert her right to be crowned together with him, but he had her barred from entering Westminster Abbey. The same day she fell ill, dying shortly after. Her will declared her desire to be buried in Brunswick but the decision to preclude the funeral procession from crossing central London caused a riot.

Ricardo manifested his opinion that 'this unfortunate business' should not have become 'an affair of state' (to Trower 21 July 1820 *Works* 8, p. 206). On 15 September, he writes to Trower that, in the light of 'the cruel usage she has received', the Government could not pretend that, whatever 'her conduct may have been', 'the country's real interests required a bill of pains and penalties' (p. 273). To McCulloch, Ricardo writes that the question 'of her innocence or guilt' was not so relevant since she had been 'abominably treated' and 'this disgusting enquiry' was neither 'just, or necessary for the public good' (p. 240). He expresses the wish 'that the Queen may be able to prove her innocence' (to Mill 18 September, p. 184) and, shortly after, rejoices at the prospect that, since her defence appeared to be going well, the Lords could not pass the bill, and the Commons would be relieved from the nightmare of discussing the case (to Malthus 9 October, p. 276). Ricardo writes that the Queen's defence was 'still much more satisfactory' than one would have expected, and the fact was surprising that 'the Queen preaches pure radicalism' (to Mill 14 October, p. 284). Then he comments favourably the Government's decision to withdraw the bill (to Mill 16 November, pp. 295–296). On 26 November, Ricardo expresses disagreement with Trower's suggestion that Parliament pronounced at least a censure because 'never had a woman so many reasons of justification to urge in extenuation of her fault' (p. 303). After the riot occasioned by the funeral, he deplores the Government's insane obstinacy in trying to hamper the people's wish 'respecting the course of the procession' (to Trower 22 August 1821, *Works* 9, p. 39).

In a word, Ricardo had it clear in mind that the existence of a crime must be *proved* before punishment, *moral persuasion* does not justify censure, not to mention legal sanction, even in case of guilt there may be extenuating circumstances and, above all, we should distinguish a breach of private morality from a crime. This is the lesson of Pietro Verri and Cesare Beccaria that he seems to have understood better than others.

Slavery

Another sensitive issue on which Ricardo pronounced himself is slavery. After the Wilberforce campaign, the Slave Trade Act of 1897 declared the trade illegal in all British dominions. However, slavery was still a legal institution in the dominions and remained so until 1834 when, after a campaign headed by Quaker Joseph Sturge – the great uncle of philosopher George Edward Moore – it was abolished. In a speech of March 1823 at the East India Company General Court, Ricardo declares that

> he really was inclined to blush with shame, to hide his face, when West-India slavery was mentioned. […] It was a stain on the otherwise pure character of the country, which he ardently desired to see wiped away. […] The question of slavery was one of infinite importance […] On this day, he believed, a petition would be presented to Parliament by a most benevolent individual (Mr. Wilberforce) in favour of that unfortunate race of men, who were subjected to the horrors of slavery. He hoped the application would produce its just effect, and that this grievous stain would be removed from the national character.
>
> (*Works* 5, p. 483)

From this report we learn that, though Marx believed Ricardo was the working class's enemy (Marx 1897, p. 507), he was the West Indian slaves' friend. Besides, he thought it proper to address the issue as ethical rather than economic; it was not Adam Smith's argument against the rentability of slave plantations to which he had recourse but the equality of human beings.

Unlimited toleration

Brougham wrote that Ricardo's most striking opinions were, more than his defence of free trade, 'his extreme opinions upon questions connected with the reform of the constitution in Church and State' (Brougham 1839, p. xxxiv). Commitment to unlimited freedom of opinion was for Ricardo a matter of course, first as a Jew by birth, second as a Quaker's husband and third as a Unitarian by choice. Unitarians campaigned for unlimited toleration for obvious reasons: the 1689 Toleration Act did not cover anti-Trinitarianism, which until 1813 still fell under the penal law, and it was not until 1829 that the Corporate and Test Act depriving Dissenters of full rights was abolished.

Ricardo made a remarkable comment in a letter to Mill of 9 September 1821 after a visit to Gatcomb by Sydney Smith, an *Edinburgh Review* editor, mentioning James Lindsay's principle, that is, 'unbounded freedom of opinion'. His guest – he writes –

> is always on the liberal side, but has a strong propensity to halt halfway – he is for tolerating all religions, but is inclined to be intolerant to those whom he supposes to have no religion. I contended for Dr. Lindsay's principle, that even the Atheist should be heard.
>
> (*Works* 9, p. 60)

On 26 March 1823, in support of a petition for the release of Mary Ann Carlile, who was imprisoned on a formal accusation of having sold atheist literature, Ricardo declares in Parliament that 'a fair and free discussion ought to be allowed on all religious topics' (*Works* 5, p. 288). On 4 April 1823, in a letter to Isaac Lyon Goldsmit, a leading campaigner for Jewish emancipation, he comments:

> I carry my principles of toleration very far; – I do not know how, or why any line should be drawn, and am prepared to maintain that we have no more justifiable ground for shutting the mouth of the Atheist than that of any other man.
>
> (*Works* 9 278)

In 1823 Ricardo delivered a Speech in support of the 'Christians' Petition against the Prosecution of Unbelievers' whose 'prime mover' was Robert Aspland. Starting with the argument that 'belief does not in all cases depend upon the will', the petitioners asked the Honourable House to act 'to abolish prosecution of unbelievers' (*Christian Reformer* 1823a, 224). MP Joseph Hume introduced the petition (*Christian Reformer* 1823b; *Monthly Repository* 1823a; Sraffa 1955a, p. 41). The discussion revolved around Ricardo's Speech reported in *Hansard*, the periodical dedicated to parliamentary debates, and then summarised in the Unitarian *Monthly Repository* (1823b) and reprinted in Sraffa's edition. Ricardo vindicated 'a more large and liberal spirit of toleration' (*Works* 5, p. 324) while quoting Paley and other Anglican authorities to the effect that the law should not establish *any* limit to discussion on religious doctrines. He added that the public authority has no competence to judge whether such discussion is conducted with respect or instead 'levity and ribaldry', and the law should admit 'unfettered liberty of discussion' (p. 331). His first argument is that imposing belief in a future state as a precondition for legal admissibility of testimony is self-defeating. In case a witness was asked:

> 'Do you believe in a future state?' If he were a conscientious man, enter-taining seriously such an opinion, his answer must be in the negative, and the law said he should not be heard; but if he were an immoral man, and disregarded truth, and said, 'I do believe in a future state,' although in his conscience he disbelieved in it, then his evidence was admissible, and his hypocrisy and falsehood secured him credibility.
>
> (p. 327)

The second is that, on such

> abstract religious subjects, upon which it was quite impossible to obtain universal assent, no man had a right to say to another, 'My opinion upon religion is right, and yours is not only wrong when you differ from me, but I am entitled to punish you for that difference'.
>
> (pp. 324–325)

The third is that moral obligation does not arise necessarily from religion. Ricardo declared that he believed in the possibility that somebody could respect all essential obligations to the community and still not assent to belief in a future state. He admitted that 'religion was a powerful obligation, but he denied it to be the only obligation – it was, in fact, one which was superad-ded to the general force of moral impressions' (p. 327). The argument insists on the distinction between opinions on purely theoretical questions and the capacity to perceive the moral quality of actions, for 'a man might be very sceptical upon doctrinal points, and yet very positive in the control of moral impressions distinct from religious faith' (p. 328).

Finally, he introduced a distinction between positive sciences like astron-omy, in which criteria for ending controversies exist, and religious subjects bound to remain forever the battlefield of unending struggles. In these fields, we lack 'one unerring criterion to which the common credence of mankind bowed', for religion is, unlike 'the rising sun, or any of the other phenomena of nature, which were bound by indissoluble and indispensable laws', 'a sub-ject open to conflicting opinions' (p. 329).

Ricardo's arguments are precisely those endorsed by 'rational believ-ers'. The essence of religion is morality, not speculative truth; acceptance of theoretical claims is a matter of rational persuasion, not of will; the non-believer may act on strong moral motivation deriving from 'moral impressions' independent of religious belief; human nature is sufficiently uncorrupted to allow the unbeliever to perceive moral impressions; no closure is possible of religious controversies by appeal to some infallible criterion; nobody has the authority to silence his opponent in religious matters and any attempt to force the profession of religious belief would be self-defeating and demoralising.

Good government

The extension of the suffrage

Ricardo and Trower often discussed politics with recurrent professions of Whiggism by Trower and corresponding refutations by Ricardo. One point of disagreement was human nature. In a letter of 15 July 1816, Ricardo manifests his disagreement with Trower's opinion 'that the war has had much effect in degrading the morals of the people'. He argues that the people 'are less outrageous [...] then they formerly used to be', adding that 'as they increase in knowledge they will more clearly perceive that the destruction of property aggravates and never relieves their difficulties' (*Works* 7, p. 49). On 22 March 1818, he argues that there is no class 'whose interests are so clearly on the side of good government as the people' and, therefore, the

> suffrage must be extensive to secure the voters against corrupt influence and the voting must be by ballot for the same reason. There must be an intimate union between representatives and their constituents in order to destroy the dependence of the former on the executive government.
>
> (*Works* 7, p. 261)

On 27 June 1818, he reassures Trower that he does 'not go so far as Mr. Bentham'. Then, paraphrasing Edmund Burke (1770, p. 255) adds that 'the people may err but it can never be from design' (p. 261). After writing that 'Parliament should really represent the good sense of the nation', he declares, with an appeal to another Whig authority, that his programme 'is contained' in Sir Samuel's Romilly's 'system of Reform': 'to extend the suffrage to all householders, to limit the duration of parliament to three years, and to vote by ballot' (*Works* 7, p. 273).

In a letter of 2 November 1818, he remarks that 'the only legitimate end of all government' is 'to promote the happiness, and prosperity, of the people' (p. 319). On 20 December, he insists that, since the end is 'the happiness of the people', Reform should aim to put the Government under the influence of 'all wisdom and virtue of the country' (*Works* 7, p. 366). These goals were those indicated by Paley, who had written that 'the final view of all rational politics is to produce the greatest quantity of happiness in a given tract of the country' (Paley 1785, p. 587), a claim repeated by Malthus (1798, p. 36) when referring to the 'the aggregate mass of happiness' that the legislation is likely to produce. These letters show that Ricardo was familiar with Paley and Burke and rejected the Whig myth of the British mixed constitution.

The science of legislation

In a letter of 23 August 1815, Mill had written that Ricardo's mission after retirement should become to serve the cause of 'good government, that is human happiness'. He suggests that Ricardo's political education will not be a demanding task, for there is 'not much difficulty in finding out the principles on which alone good government must of necessity depend' (*Works* 6, p. 263). Ricardo objects that Mill is 'unjustly severe' for 'there are many venal men in Parliament who get there with no other view but to forward their own personal ends' yet, 'as a body they have more virtue than you are willing to give them credit for' (to Mill 30 August 1815, p. 263). He argues that the influence of public opinion may act as a constant motive for virtuous conduct, the remedy to existing evils should be 'so to constitute Parliament that no particular interest should be predominant' and that nobody could 'better promote his own happiness than by serving the public' (p. 264). The most important asset would be 'general information': everybody should understand what makes for real 'happiness and welfare' and people should accept 'a judicious compromise by which each in giving up a little will best secure to himself the greatest attainable sum of good' (p. 264).

On 10 October, Mill reaffirms his dim view of human nature. It is common prejudice – he says – 'that virtue is attached to high station, and vice to low', going on to assert that 'the steady operation of the laws of human nature' acts so that anybody 'with the same bad education', 'the same powers', 'the same motives' would behave as badly. He then concludes that, since 'the performance of the duties' can only depend on their coincidence with interest, we should trust not so much in enlightenment as in a Parliament constitution that would make 'interests' and 'duties' converge (p. 307). On 24 October, Ricardo objects that the principle is correct but that Mill 'applies it too rigidly' for the 'effect of public opinion, and the consciousness of deserving approbation' have at least as much weight as the 'stimulus of money' or the desire of 'praise of Princes' (p. 311). He admits that some held 'these latter rewards' to be so valuable that 'there are no difficulties which they will not incur to obtain them'. In nations that enjoy 'a free government' there is 'a natural corrective which will considerably ameliorate the evil of its institutions' and, 'in some measure' education teaches us 'to raise our thoughts above the mere covetousness of money' (p. 311).

As mentioned, Mill recommended his *History of British India* as introductory reading for Ricardo's political education, and the book provided the occasion for Ricardo's afore-mentioned objections to Utilitarianism. It was also the occasion for discussing the elusive character of the 'science of legislation'. In a letter of 9 November, after the customary compliments, Ricardo strikes his blow writing that legislation 'would be comparatively an easy science if it were not so much influenced by the characters and dispositions of the people for whom it is to be undertaken'. If we want to influence people's behaviour, however carefully 'we may have examined the end to which all our laws should tend', we need 'thorough knowledge of the peculiar habits, prejudices and objects of desire of such people, which is itself almost an unattainable knowledge' (p. 204). We are so influenced by our 'peculiar habits and prejudices' that we 'frequently see these things through a false medium' and, as a result, legislation becomes

> a most difficult science, for first you have to study the objects which ought to be attained to promote the general happiness, and then the nature of the materials on which you have to act for the attainment of that end.
>
> (p. 204)

Mill's remarkable claim of 3 December is that 'legislation is essentially a science the effects of which may be computed with an *extraordinary degree of certainty*' (p. 211). Ricardo responds on 18 December that though legislation 'may not be so difficult' as he imagines, he feels one of 'the great difficulties of the science' to be that 'the Government and laws of one state of society' are 'often very ill adapted for another state' (p. 229). On 27 December, Mill tries to limit the implications of this objection, arguing that, once we have a standard of excellence, it will not be too difficult to determine what is to be done in all cases since, once we have established the aims, what is left is just 'the choice of the means' (p. 235). Ricardo counterattacks, contending that Mill's book lends 'too much weight' to 'self-interest' or 'self-preferment' and is 'too severe' in claiming that we can seldom meet with 'knowledge and talent' in places such as Parliament, 'where much either of money or power is to be enjoyed'. He adds that it would be true if money and power were the only things desirable to man, but the 'sanction of public opinion' has more weight than money and power for those who appreciate 'public sympathy'. Moreover, since this sanction is 'much valued by all ranks of men', they have sufficient motives for 'the acquirement of knowledge and talent independent of the power and money' (to Mill 30 December, p. 239).

The mechanics of good government

The 'Reform' invoked by both progressive Whigs and Radicals implied a new electoral system, extended franchise, newly defined constituencies, a revision of the relationship between Church and State and a solution to the Irish and Catholic questions. Bentham's idea was to introduce institutional arrangements that would keep the interest of 'the few' under control by the interest of 'the many'. The desired effects were economy, transparency, accountability and the maximisation of the diligence, morality and intellectual qualities of public officials (Bentham 1822, p. 272). The 'securities against misrule' to secure such effects were extended suffrage, frequent elections, the secret vote and unlimited freedom of speech (Bentham 1817, pp. 80–101,

171–182). Such a framework would bring about an artificial convergence of interests, so that the people's representatives would promote their interests by promoting those of the people (Bentham 1776, p. 485). Permanent checks on the mechanism through the sanction of the 'Public Opinion Tribunal' would be secured by freedom of the press (Crimmins 1994, pp. 262–263). As mentioned, Ricardo owned a copy of the Dumont edition of Bentham's political writings and read his *Plan of Parliamentary Reform* (Bentham to Ricardo 28 October 1819, *Works* 8, p. 116).

In 1820 Mill published his essay on *Government*. He was writing under commission for the Supplement to the *Encyclopaedia Britannica* whose editor was MacVey Napier, a Whig who had no intention of leaving Mill free to write whatsoever he felt proper. The result is that the essay's critical part sounds Benthamite and its positive part Whiggish (Fenn 1992, p. 147). The essay starts with these axioms: the end of government is the greatest happiness of the many; the science of human nature teaches us what happiness is; Government is necessary, but securities against abuse are required because an 'inherent principle of human nature' is to make those in power 'infallibly have the strongest motives to make a bad use' of it (Mill 1820, p. 16). A representative body is an appropriate check to those in power yet there is a danger that its members will also 'ill use their powers not for the advantage of the community, but for their own advantage' (p. 18). Mill suggests two remedies. The first is to shorten the duration of elected offices (p. 18). The second is to assign the task of electing the representatives to 'the most wise and the most virtuous part of the community, the middle rank' (pp. 31–32) assuming that, because of the coincidence of their interests, they will *virtually represent* the lower ranks.

On 27 July, Ricardo, after praising the essay as 'excellent, and well calculated to serve the good cause' (*Works* 8, p. 211), objects that Mill should have also discussed the influence of public opinion, 'one of the checks, and a most powerful one in such a government as ours', stressing the importance, even in case 'the right of suffrage is given to the people generally', of 'the securities for a good election' (*Works* 8, p. 211). Besides, commenting on 14 October 1821on Mill's *Liberty of the Press* (Mill 1821a), Ricardo manifests surprise at his defence of 'the liberty to be allowed of exhorting the people by means of the Press to resist their Governors, and to overthrow the Government' (*Works* 9, p. 102) – an old item from Whiggish rhetorical weaponry that Ricardo feels incompatible with an argument for a representative Parliament. In a letter to Mill of 10 August 1819, Ricardo had written that 'Reform is the most efficacious preventative of Revolution' (*Works* 8, p. 49). On 28 August 1821, he reiterates the same idea: the 'only prospect we have of putting aside the struggle which they say has commenced between the rich and the other classes, is for the rich to yield what is justly due to the other classes' (*Works* 9, p. 45), so that justice will prevail without violence because 'the expediency of the rich, will make it necessary even in their view' (p. 45).

Parliamentary reform and the secret vote

On 23 September 1818, Mill suggested that Ricardo, as an exercise for his future parliamentary activity, should draft essays on political issues (*Works* 7, pp. 301–302). In 1824, after Ricardo's death two political essays were published on Mill's initiative (Henderson 1997, pp. 562–568).

The 'Observations on parliamentary reform' argue three points. The first is that virtue and interest may coincide if we eliminate temptations not to be virtuous. Following a Benthamite idea, the sanctions of religion, public opinion, and the law could have this effect; the perfect state is the one 'in which all these sanctions concur to make the interest of all men to be virtuous' or 'to use their best endeavour to promote the general happiness' (Ricardo 1824a, p. 500). The second point is that the way these checks work is either unreliable or 'irregular' since they are subject to the effects of corruption. For example, it is easy for the Government to have a majority in the House of Commons 'by giving a portion of these lucrative places to those who have the choice of the majority of the house of Commons' (p. 496). The third is that, of all classes, 'the people only are interested in being well-governed' and only their happiness tends to coincide with 'general happiness' (p. 499).

Consequently, the right to vote should cover everyone who does not have 'interests contrary to the general interest' (p. 498). This right should be denied only to those who have too small an income since they may believe that removing the safety of property would be a solution to their problems (p. 501). Since 'good government' is the end and the extension of suffrage is the means, 'an extension of the suffrage, far short of making it universal, will substantially secure to the people the good government they wish for' (p. 502). Universal suffrage yet is a viable strategic goal since the effects of the above measures

> would have so beneficial an effect on the public mind, would be the means of so rapidly increasing the knowledge and intelligence of the public, that, in a limited space of time after this first measure of reform were granted, we might, with the utmost safety, extend the right of voting for members of Parliament to every class of the people.
>
> (p. 503)

Ricardo here goes one step beyond what he admitted in the letter to Trower of 22 March 1818. He clarifies that the extension of franchise is necessary as a part of a learning process in which the people will realise that good government is a consequence of extended suffrage, and most potential voters will become aware that good government, not anarchy, promotes their interests.

'Defence of a plan of voting by ballot' illustrates the evils provoked by the existing electoral system. One is the fact that a 'rude and brutal populace [...] surround the hustings, and heap every sort of insult and indignity on the candidate who happens not to enjoy their favour'. Another arises 'from the influence exercised over the voters at elections' (Ricardo 1824b, p. 505) so that the elector cannot vote as he thinks appropriate and it is 'not he who has the vote, really and substantially, but his landlord' (p. 506). To make sure that the representatives support the electors 'and their interests, and not those whose interests may, on many occasions, be in direct opposition to theirs' (p. 512), he proposes that 'the secret mode of election, be substituted for the open mode' (p. 508).

Though the essays deserve consideration as authentic expressions of Ricardo's thought, they are less dependable than published material, since the author never saw them through publication. Reports of speeches in Parliament or at public meetings are, on the one hand, more dependable as expressions of Ricardo's real opinions but, on the other, are reported by a third party. The most extended was on 24 April 1823 about Lord John Russell's motion for a Parliament reform (*Works* 5, pp. 283–289). It argues two points: first, that the antiquity of institutions is not a merit, and it would be unreasonable that 'the present generation ought to be bound down by all that had been done by their ancestors' (p. 283); second, that the government of Britain was a 'compromise between the aristocracy and the Crown' (p. 287), and that even the House of Commons was 'the representative of the aristocracy of the country' (p. 286). The remedy is frequent elections by secret vote and the extension of suffrage. The former is indispensable to put the 'inferior class of tradesmen' in a position to 'withstand the threats and terrors which might be put into execution, to prevent them from voting according to their conscience' (p. 285). The latter carries no danger since the 'people at large now possessed so much more information than they ever before possessed, that they were entitled to be better represented in parliament than they had ever before been' (p. 287). Ricardo adds that 'all men, in all situations, acted under the influence of motives' (p. 288) and thus, the members of Parliament and the ministers themselves would act in the interest of the people if 'they could not do otherwise' (p. 288). The conclusions quote Montesquieu's description of the Athenians and the Romans as proof that the people, 'if left to the unrestricted exercise of their choice' (p. 289), instead of electing demagogues 'would act wisely and prudently' (p. 289).

A Speech of 6 December 1819, on the 'Seditious Meetings Prevention Bill', argues for the citizens' right to participate in public meetings. The right to petition is a right to meet 'in such numbers, and showing such a front to ministers as would afford a hope that bad measures would be abandoned, and that public opinion would be respected' (*Works* 5, p. 28). A more effective check to disturbances could be exercised 'only by a reform of parliament' that made the House of Commons 'the best check which any government could have' (p. 29). In a speech of 18 April 1821, Ricardo defends 'voting by ballot, which [...] would be greater security for the full and fair representation of the people than any extension of the elective franchise' (*Works* 5, pp. 112).

Milgate and Stimson (1991, p. 61) advanced three plausible claims about Ricardo, followed by a questionable one. The former are that he never was a utilitarian, he formulated his political theory *before* Mill's *Essay on Government* and he had a more markedly pro-poor attitude (p. 119). The latter claim is that he was the author of a 'modern' market theory of democracy. While agreeing that Ricardo was not a Benthamite, others commented that he was more radical and pro-poor than Bentham or Mill, was aware of society's conflictual character and the need for politics to represent conflicting interests. They noted that there were other sources besides Whiggism and Benthamism, including the Scottish tradition of civic humanism, the legacy of Jacobinism and the new social radicalism heralded by Robert Owen (Winch 1983; Fenn 1987, p. 106; Tribe 1992, p. 722; Peach 1993, p. 1339).

We may add that Ricardo appreciated Bentham's projects to make the interests of 'the many' check those of 'the few', which did not imply accepting Bentham's philosophy as a whole. Unlike Peach (1997, pp. 226–230), we might feel that he was more radical than Bentham or Mill on both toleration and social justice. He certainly objected to Mill's philosophical assumptions: the limited character of human knowledge implies that legislation cannot be an axiomatic science; human nature is not as depraved as Mill believed; psychological egoism is a false thesis; people are more rational than Mill assumed and education may improve them; indirect representation is nonsense, and the virtues of the middle rank are less exemplary than Mill believed; finally, the right of resistance is nonsense too, and incompatible with a representative system.

Ethics and the uses of political economy

Ethics in business

Besides other things, Ricardo's merits lay 'in his acquiring a splendid fortune by the application of his own talents, by his coming through the dangerous ground of the money-changers without a stain, or a whisper of accusation', so that 'no man could attach to his principles, or his conduct, a single stigma' (*Sunday Times* 1823). By 'his talents', he had acquired a 'princely fortune, which was gained honourably' (*Monthly Repository* 1823c). Nobody 'who knew him ever talked of his possessions without, at the same time, acknowledging that he had earned them fairly' (Ricardo, M 1824, p. 11). His integrity was such that, when a

> Bank proprietor, he argued strenuously and warmly against the inordinate gains of that body; he defended the cause of the fund-holders when he had ceased to be one; he was accused of an attempt to ruin the landed interest after he became a large landed proprietor

(p. 13)

These are judgements from early sources. A legend circulated yet about one million pounds acquired in one day by an unknown 'mister R.' by speculating on public debt after the battle of Waterloo. The legend grew with a snow-ball effect in the popular press in two parallel versions, with a speculator named either Rothschild or Ricardo (Parys 2020, pp. 36–40). Even Whittle Harvey seems to lend credence to the legend dropping the remark that, upon 'a single occasion' – the Waterloo battle – 'he is said to have netted upwards of a million sterling' (*Sunday Times* 1823). The snowball got bigger, including manipulation of the market by spreading news of a defeat the day before the official messenger reporting victory reached London, became an avalanche under the pen of anti-Semitic scribblers and even crept into twentieth-century academic literature (Parys 2020, pp. 35–38). There is not yet a shred of evidence in its favour. Even fluctuations before and after Waterloo in the public-debt market were incompatible with such great-scale speculations (pp. 53–57). Besides, Ricardo's extremely prudent conduct allowed him no more than limited gains (Sraffa 1955b, pp. 70–74, 80–84; Parys 2020, pp. 46–57), and he had already acquired his considerable landed property before 1815. On top of all this, there is evidence that he acted to raise the Stock Exchange ethical standards when he was one of its most influential members (Sraffa 1955b, p. 69; Parys 2020, pp. 41–45; Parys 2021).

Philanthropy

Early sources also mention 'his exemplary benevolence to the poor' (*Gentlemen's Magazine* 1823), the fact that his princely fortune 'was used generously' (*Monthly Repository* 1823c), contributing 'to almost every charitable institution in the metropolis', and supporting 'at his own expense, an alms-house for the poor, and two schools for the instruction of the young in the vicinity of his seat in the country' (McCulloch 1846, p. xxxi).

Ricardo's humanitarian ventures included educational institutions. He contributed money and organisational work to implement the project of a day-school intended to apply the Lancaster system 'to the higher branches of learning, for the use of the middling and higher ranks in life' (Bentham 1817, p. 1; Ricardo to Bentham and Mill 15 July 1814, *Works* 6, p. 125), a project finally abandoned because of the inability to find a plot of land on which to build the school (Sraffa 1952, p. xxix; Weatherall 1976, pp. 107–113). As soon as he moved to Gatcomb, he founded a school for girls and one for boys supervised by his wife. There are bills for construction work, stationery, the teacher's salary and 'hair-cutting for the boys' (Ricardo Papers). While describing her visit to the schools, Edgeworth (1971, p. 260) reports that 'the chief thing that struck' her 'was that the school rooms were comfortably warmed' and 'no flogging' was allowed.

Besides education, savings banks were one of the nineteenth-century social reformer's front lines. Ricardo writes that they are 'excellent institutions and calculated to improve the condition and morals of the poor' (to Trower 4 February 1816, *Works* 7, p. 16). In other letters, he describes a project of a saving bank in Gloucestershire and reports its successful start (to Trower 10

December 1817, p. 221), expressing his hope that these institutions may 'convert the thoughtless spendthrift into the cautious and prudent economist' (to Trower 9 February 1817, pp. 129–130).

A more traditional initiative was the establishment of two alms-houses for the old and disabled. There is a list of payments relating to their building, a £200 receipt for construction work and an estimate for building a cistern and a shed (Ricardo Papers). Ricardo's comment on private beneficence also deserves reporting. On 9 November 1921, he writes to Richard Place that he disagrees with him on the opinion 'that private benevolence would degrade the poor man more than the aid he receives, from the poor rates' quoting Malthus's admission that it can be a useful measure of relief (*Works* 9, p. 52).

On balance, Ricardo had inherited from the religious traditions that contributed to shaping his vision of life a keen sense of property as stewardship and 'giving' as an essential duty. Yet there was a degree of tension in his choices: on the one hand, he did something as traditional as contributing to charities and alms-houses while, on the other, he engaged in such front-line initiatives as schools and saving banks. We may feel that, not unlike Malthus, he wavered between two diverging strategies: a disciplining strategy to instil a sense of respectability and an empowering strategy to promote self-reliance.

The Poor Laws

When Malthus and Ricardo discussed the Poor Laws, they were facing an issue with immediate policy implications. Poor relief had been a duty for both the aristocratic ethos and Christian preaching, yet in the eighteenth century the prevailing attitude to poverty changed from compassion to reproof. Malthus's *Essay* of 1798 was both an expression and a source of such change. It illustrated the Poor Laws' perverse effects of encouraging population growth among the most unfortunate part of society, pushing wages down while hindering labour-force mobility. In a sense, it implied an attack from the left on existing institutions and their paternalism while attacking enemies on the left, like Godwin and Condorcet. Malthus's concern was to defend traditional liberties from a 'disgusting tyranny' and 'tyrannical laws' enacted by monarchical absolutism and republican despotism (Malthus 1798, p. 36).

After 1798, through the combined effect of the principle of population and rent theory, the prevailing vision turned increasingly bleak (Winch 1996, pp. 10–16). Malthus's approach yet became softer, with the increasing weight for the 'moral restraint' as a check to population and the admission of cultural factors as determinants of consumption patterns. In the 1817 edition of the *Essay,* he writes that the '*gradual* abolition' of the Poor Laws should have been consistent 'with humanity' (Malthus 1803a, p. 138), a mark of his shift from the punishment of the poor to the investment in the poor as human resources (Jensen 1999, p. 450; Cremaschi 2014, pp. 157–165). Nonetheless, despite prevailing pessimism, the real world had been evolving in a direction opposite to overpopulation, widespread poverty and the stationary state and, by the 1830s, 'the recognition that subsistence had increased faster than population was to discredit much of the Malthusian analysis' (Poynter 1969, p. 242). Middle-class reformers who had become self-appointed advocates of the population principle did not take the trouble to read Malthus's reformulations and stuck to abolitionism. The result was that the New Poor Laws came too late and were a downward compromise between abolitionism and reform, and the resulting enforcement of the reformed laws turned out even worse than unqualified abolition would have been (Lees 1998, pp. 115–152).

Ricardo remained faithful to a 'pure' version of the principle of population until the third edition of his *Principles*, at a time Malthus had already modified it adopting the view that the effects of the principle of population are not as immediate and inexorable as he had supposed in 1798 (Opocher 2015). In 1816, at a time of acute distress caused by a bad harvest, Ricardo was still a hard-liner. On 17 November, he writes to Mill that he is 'sorry to see a disposition to inflame the minds of the lower orders by persuading them that legislation can afford them any relief' (*Works* 7, p. 90). On 24 February 1817, he writes to Trower that the 'only good that the most sanguine can expect' from 'Provident Institutions' such as the savings banks is the spread of more 'independent feelings' among the poor, but a necessary condition for a significant effect would be to raise 'the general rate of wages' (p. 134). He insists that a result 'gratifying to every friend of the poor' would be a situation where a man's wages were sufficient not only to maintain himself and family but also to enable him to lay up a provision for such 'extraordinary cases' as illness or invalidity (pp. 134–135).

On 26 January 1818, he shows first signs of softening, writing that he would accept 'such a change in the Poor Laws as should restore them to what appears to have been the original intention in framing them; namely, the relieving only the aged and infirm and under some circumstances, children' (p. 248). He adds that a system based on voluntary contributions would be no alternative, to 'relieve the poor by an extended exercise of private charity would hardly be less objectionable than the evil of which we now complain' since 'the selfish would pay nothing, and the whole burden would fall on the generous and humane' (p. 248). The same year he is still giving signs of rigour, writing about Brougham's mentioned plan for infant schools in London. He would have 'most serious objections' if it was intended 'to feed as well as to take care of and educate the children' (to Mill 12 December 1818, p. 359), though Mill's letter of 18 December 1818 (p. 363) informing that there was no provision for free meals persuaded him that he might give a £50 contribution without detriment to his abolitionist conscience.

In the *Principles*, Ricardo makes an admission mirroring his discussion with Malthus, that the 'natural price' of labour 'essentially depends on the habits and customs of the people' (Ricardo 1817, pp. 96–97) and the 'friends of humanity cannot but wish that in all countries the labouring classes should have a taste for comforts and enjoyments' because there is no 'better security against a superabundant population' (p. 242).

On 21 October 1817, Ricardo writes to Malthus that he had read the *Essay* carefully for the second time (*Works* 7, p. 201), which means that he had read the new edition, where Malthus considerably softens his position. After that, Ricardo seems to have adopted the softer version of the population principle. He starts criticising oversimplified cause–effect relationships and makes room for cultural and social conditioning to the action of the principle of population. A symptom of this softer attitude is in a letter to James Brown of 13 October 1819. He writes that he is worried about 'the present distressed situation of the labouring classes in this country'. He adds that 'the remedy is not very apparent' to him (*Works* 8, p. 103) because immediate enforcement of measures conforming to the correct principles of political economy, for example, the end of agricultural protectionism, would produce at least more damage than benefit to the working classes.

On 26 June 1819, a meeting was held at Freemasons Hall to discuss a plan for the 'employment and improvement of the poor' proposed by Robert Owen, the promoter of a utopian experiment in New Lanark, an industrial settlement with a cotton mill and a village for the workers with better than average working conditions and an avant-garde welfare system (Siméon 2017, pp. 45–86). The plan recommended establishing something like *kibbutzim*, agricultural villages of the same size as New Lanark's industrial village to resettle the unemployed with enough land to cultivate under collective responsibility, a shared kitchen and messrooms, and a children's house. Ricardo reluctantly agreed to be a member of the committee in charge of examining the plan (*Works* 5, p. 467). He declared that Owen's 'zeal for the public good' was 'worthy of the highest praise' and his plan was likely to be successful to a 'limited degree' in producing 'considerable happiness, comfort, and morality by giving employment and instruction to the lower classes' (pp. 467–468). However, he concluded that he did not believe that it would ameliorate 'the condition of the lower classes to such a degree' (p. 468) as its author envisaged.

On 16 December 1819, Ricardo spoke in the House of Commons on a motion to appoint a select committee to examine 'Mr. Owen's plan for ameliorating the condition of the lower classes'. On this occasion, while omitting recognition of Owen's good intentions, he went straight to points of disagreement: 'a theory inconsistent with the principles of political economy' inspired the plan that would 'produce infinite mischief to the community' (*Works* 5, p. 30); promoting 'spade husbandry' to increase the demand for labour was a mistaken idea; 'machinery did not lessen the demand for labour' (p. 30) while, both in agriculture and industry, the crucial precondition to increase it was an increase of the capital available (p. 32). In a word, he paid attention to Owen's practical experiment, admired his commitment to humanitarian purposes, and yet mistrusted his plans, believing that they ignored basic principles of political economy.

In his correspondence with Mill, objections to the latter's tendency to simplification became increasingly explicit. Mill had remained faithful to the original version of the population principle, besides the love of simplification, for political reasons since it looked like a weapon for middle-class radicals against both the establishment and working-class radicalism. In the machinery chapter – which did not fail to arouse reaction in both Mill and McCulloch – Ricardo makes a crucial concession, revising what he had been contending for, namely that it is true that machinery may lower demand for work and the working classes have good reasons to complain (Ricardo 1817, p. 388). On 29 March 1820, Ricardo reminds Mill that the 'distress of the poor' is not 'synonymous with diminished resources' for there may be situations when the 'annual revenue, and with it the means of expenditure and enjoyment of the higher classes of society would increase but would be accompanied with a diminution of happiness, if not positive misery to the great mass of the people' (*Works* 8, p. 171).

On 28 August 1821, while denouncing the Whigs' inconsistency, he writes to Mill that the only prospect 'of putting aside the struggle which they say has commenced between the rich and the other classes, is for the rich to yield what is justly due to the other classes' (*Works* 9, p. 39). His 'Notes on Mill's Elements of Political Economy' point out that the 'power of employing labour depends on the increase of a particular part of capital, not on the increase of the whole capital' (Ricardo 1821, p. 127). This specification implies that what he had always been saying was inaccurate and that unemployment and poverty are less necessary evils than he had admitted before. He also objects to a rigid application of the population principle admitting that social and cultural factors may stem the population growth. For example, in a prosperous country, 'the demand for nurses, and female servants of all descriptions, lessen the number of childbearing women', so that 'there are not a sufficient number left to augment the population in the same proportion' (p. 126).

In a letter to Francis Place of 9 September 1821, he denies one of the original premises of Malthus's population theory, namely that 'under a system of equality population would press with more force against the means of subsistence than it now does' (*Works* 9, pp. 49–50). Instead, 'mankind would increase much faster than it now does, but so would food'. What will happen is that a 'larger proportion of the whole capital of the country would be employed in the production of food-necessaries, and a less proportion in the production of luxuries' (p. 50).

Ricardo's new vision kept elements of his former vision: the need to teach foresight and self-reliance, the 'true' theory of population albeit in a softer version, and the need to abolish the Poor Laws albeit with increasing prudence. Besides these constants, there are variables. The first is an increasingly hesitant attitude (Poynter 1969, pp. 343–345). As soon as 1817, while supporting the abolition of the Poor Laws, he adds that 'he is the best friend of the poor, and to the cause of humanity, who can point out how this end can be attained with the most security, and at the same time with the least violence' (p. 107). However, as he admits in the letter to James Brown, the remedy to the present distress is far from obvious, and amending 'errors in legislation' would afford no immediate relief to the working classes and carry 'additional difficulties' (*Works* 8, p. 103). The second variable is an increasingly severe judgement on the wealthy classes' expectations, not only those who live on rent but also those who earn profits. In the already quoted letter to Place, he writes that the workers 'are often cruelly calumniated' (*Works* 9, p. 54). On 9 July 1821, he writes to Mill that 'the labouring class, in Agriculture, and Manufactures, are doing well, we must console ourselves for the misfortunes of landlords and tenants – they form but a small proportion of the whole population' (*Works* 9, p. 13). To Trower, he writes on 22 August 1821 that 'masters say they do not get their usual profits – by usual I suppose they mean unusual and exorbitant profits' (*Works* 9, p. 40).

In Ricardo's strategy against poverty, the key idea is that by removing factors that distort market mechanisms, the market itself will offer workers the opportunity to earn enough. This strategy – whether realistic or unrealistic – was justified by a moral criterion. An example is a letter to MP Wilmot Horton of 19 January 1823 commenting on a plan to support paupers' emigration to Canada. He writes that 'the most important consideration' is that, by diminishing the burden of the poor supported by Parishes, the plan would raise the workers' bargaining power and

> could not fail to make the wages of labour more adequate to the support of the labourer and his family, besides *giving him that as wages which is now given to him as charity.*
>
> (*Works* 11, p. xvi, emphasis added)

The miscarriage of all social theodicies

On Bayle's refutation of theodicy

Theodicy is the attempt to explain why a benevolent, almighty, and all-knowing God permits evil. The name was coined by Leibniz but the topic was already present in Augustine. Primarily metaphysical in nature, the topic is also relevant to ethics. Towards the end of the eighteenth century, most philosophers, echoing Kant's argument on the miscarriage of all trials in philosophical theodicy, started to admit that the question on evil has no answer, and the theodicies of Paley, Malthus, and John Sumner were expressions of a rear-guard battle (Cremaschi 2014, pp. 77–99, 135–145). As mentioned, Ricardo may have heard from Unitarian divines that theodicy is a difficult question to answer.

Besides those reported in the *Commonplace Books*, Ricardo read other entries from Bayle's *Dictionnaire*. In letters to Mill of 12 September and 9 November 1817 (*Works* 7, pp. 190, 206), he mentions those on '*Manichéens*' (Bayle 1697c, pp. 302–307), '*Pauliciens*' (pp. 624–636) and '*Marcionites*' (pp. 314–319), which discuss doctrines that set the New Testament merciful God against the Old Testament merciless God. Bayle argues that it is hard to account for evil without allowing for two original co-existing principles, and besides, to refute such admission is more difficult for a Christian than for a polytheist. The reason is that a Christian is bound either to deny God's omnipotence or to make him the author of evil.

Another reading recorded in the *Commonplace Books* touches on theodicy. It is *Apology for the Bible* by Richard Watson (1796, pp. 367–369) where he argues that Deism runs into the same difficulties as revealed religion: 'the existence of evil, moral and natural, in the work of an infinite being, powerful, wise, and good' (p. 369), and besides, 'the gift of freedom of will, when the abuse of freedom becomes the cause of general misery' (p. 369).

On theodicy and Atheism

In letters to Mill, Ricardo diagnoses, in Kant's words, the 'miscarriage of all philosophical trials in theodicy' while rejecting Mill's implication that this miscarriage leaves Atheism as the only option. On 9 November 1817, he writes:

> On these difficult points I keep my mind in a state of doubt from which *in this world* I never can be relieved. To account for evil in a world governed by a Being of unbounded benevolence and power is or appears to be impossible. It is as puzzling a question now as in the early times of which Bayle writes. Is it much different from the Manichean heresy to say that the Creator's benevolence is unbounded, but that his power is limited – and thus to account for evil?
>
> (*Works* 7, p. 206, emphasis added)

King (2013, p. 32) comments that, though we cannot assess Ricardo's views on religion, this letter proves that he was 'agnostic on the problem of evil'. The comment is misleading since *Agnosticism* claims that we cannot answer the question of God's existence or non-existence, not the question of evil, and besides, Theism without theodicy is a significant current of thought to which both Bayle and Kant belong. Mill's answer of 3 December is that he entirely agrees with Ricardo's remark, that supposing that God's power is limited implies 'that there is some power in the universe, which the Deity cannot controul, and which has a tendency to produce evil' (*Works* 7, p. 212). However, while Ricardo had implied that theodicy is a question with no answer but that we can, at most, hope for an answer *in a world to come*, Mill typically ignores what Ricardo had said and repeats that this impossibility is a water-proof reason for Atheism, moreover, making it the occasion for attacking Malthus's alleged hypocrisy by adding:

> Poor Mr. Malthus – If I am not mistaken, it is he who solves the difficulty about the existence of evil in this manner. What a misfortune – what a cruel misfortune, it is, for a man to be obliged to believe a certain set of opinions, whether they be fit, or not, to be believed!
>
> (*Works* 7, pp. 212–213)

That is, Mill *presumes* that Malthus, albeit aware of the irresistibility of the argument for Atheism based on the existence of evil in the world, goes on teaching what he cannot believe just to keep his 'prebends' – a line of action in stark contrast with Mill's own characteristically virtuous choice of abandoning the Ministry. Besides the usual arrogance, the comment is ill-informed in assuming that in 1817 Malthus's theodicy was still the one of the 1798 *Essay*, ignoring changes in the second *Essay* of 1803 and further changes in its 1817 edition (Cremaschi 2014, pp. 79–81, 94–99, 145–151).

Ricardo tactfully avoids discussing Mill's presumptions. He shifts instead to the *History of British India*, of which he had read the first two books.

In one chapter, Mill reconstructs the origins and evolution of Hinduism (Mill 1817, pp. 282–375). As mentioned, he starts with a pre-comprehension of Indian civilisation as 'barbarism', the second stage in the history of civilisation. In coherence with this view, he interprets Hinduism as an inconsistent mixture of barbarism with relics from the primitive stage. Following Hume and Adam Smith, he writes that the primitives believe they have found a cause for a natural event when they ascribe it to the action of 'designing and invisible beings who preside over the powers of nature' (p. 321). After the primitive explanation of extraordinary natural events, the second step is considering 'all the objects of nature' as a whole and asking 'whence did the whole proceed' (p. 283). The ancient Indians did so when they first started elaborating their cosmologies. However, 'in answering the question respecting the origin of the universe, it is impossible that men should not be guided by their previous ideas' (p. 284). Such a ballast of primitive ideas in a somewhat more advanced worldview is why it is impossible to extract any 'coherent system of beliefs' (p. 283) from Brahman cosmology, a 'chain of unmeaning panegyric', the 'religion of ignorant men' (p. 318), a 'gross and disgusting picture of the universe' (p. 329). As an alternative to this gross picture, Mill sets the rational response to the question of 'the origin of the universe' (p. 284) containing 'high and refined notions of an All-perfect being' (p. 341) offered by Monotheism, that is, the Biblical description of the world's creation, the Greek, Roman and European philosophy, and even the 'more rational and simple doctrines of Mahomet' (p. 326).

The most charitable reaction Mill's performance suggests is that the four-stages theory had become in his hands a toolbox, or better a grinder, out of which the texts he had read in English translation emerged in pieces. In the midst of a historical reconstruction, Mill drops a demanding philosophical claim, that 'just and rational views of God can be obtained from two sources alone: from revelation; or, where that is wanting, from sound reflection upon the frame and government of the universe' (p. 329). However, only correct science and philosophy can yield a refined idea of the Divinity, while populations that entertain 'absurd, mean, and degrading' ideas about God's works cannot devise 'elevated ideas of the author of those works' (p. 329). Was he serious while making the above assertions? Since he had long rejected both the Christian faith and natural theology, he was just paying lip-service to his readership's beliefs, but what he cared for was that Greek-Christian Theism was *civilized* religion while Indian polytheism was *barbarous* religion. To put it in a paradox, he was a Calvinist Atheist persuaded that he had even more reason not to believe in *false* religions since he did not believe in the *true* religion.

In his letter of 18 December, Ricardo comments that Mill's comparison of Hinduism with what the religion of an enlightened and civilised people should be is 'curious, and instructive, and is in an uncommon degree clear, and perspicuous' and he is 'temperate' but 'powerful in argument' when attacking 'the received opinions too, on which the multitude are so exceedingly susceptible' (*Works* 7, p. 228). He notes that Mill's account of the process through which humankind became 'acquainted with the idea of a Supreme Being is much the same as that of Hume' and agrees that 'the language in which they speak of him, and the adulatory expressions in which they address him afford no proof whatever of any just or sublime conception of him' (p. 229). An obvious comment is that Ricardo, polite as usual, was saying that Mill was wrong. Mill's repeated use of such expressions as 'sublime hypothesis', 'just and rational views', 'exalted notions' to denote what the Hindus lack was his typical way of characterising more advanced civilisation. *Just, rational, sublime* ideas are the Greek, Roman and European philosophical monotheism. Even Islam is on a higher level than Hinduism. Whether being *rational, exalted* and *sublime* also implies that a doctrine is *true* is a different issue that he avoids challenging. Ricardo is careful to avoid asking unpleasant questions, but he had clearly in mind what Mill's and Malthus's beliefs were and wanted to be respectful of both. Thus, his mention of the 'just or sublime conception' of God may conceal a subtle irony that Mill was unable to grasp.

On Sumner's moral theodicy

In a letter to Trower of 26 January 1818, Ricardo mentions John Bird Sumner as 'a clergyman, the author of a clever book on the Records of Creations, in which Malthus's system is defended not only for its truth but also for its affording proofs of the benevolence and goodness of the Creator' (*Works* 7, p. 247). The 'clever book' was a treatise of theodicy, the *Treatise on the Records of Creation*. Paley's theodicy argued that the total sum of goods in the world outweighs that of evils, defined respectively as pleasure and pain, including pleasure and pain felt by other sentient beings besides human beings (Paley 1802, p. 491). Sumner restyles Paley's argument adding Malthus's principle of population, and contends that we may reach the same conclusions as Paley less extravagantly if we define evil and good in terms, respectively, of pain and moral improvement. Evil, to some extent, arises 'from the law of nature', and suffering is necessary 'to make men look beyond the present day' (Sumner 1816, p. 258). The main 'cause of the greatest evil of the poor is ignorance' (p. 292), and evil is also the result of inappropriate institutions that discourage the learning of 'prudence' (p. 301). Significant improvement in the human mind is, however, possible through education, and thus the correct way to assist the poor is 'to make them agents in bettering their condition' (pp. 338–339, cf. Cremaschi 2014, pp. 135–139).

In his usual tone, Ricardo qualifies the book as 'clever', though – being persuaded of the impossibility of any theodicy – he is convinced that its argument is fallacious. The following is his charitable comment:

> I am sorry to hear that Mr Sumner does not intend writing any more on Political Economy – his whole attention in future is to be devoted to the study of Theology. Whether in this future pursuit he will have an equal chance of benefiting mankind, as in the former, I have great doubts, or rather have no doubt at all.
>
> (*Works* 7, pp. 247–248)

What Ricardo is implying here is that *theology* (not *faith*) is a vain pursuit. The clarification may be useful that what was meant by 'theology' at the time was either *natural theology* (the philosophical discussion of the existence and attributes of the Deity) or *revealed theology* (the discussion of the above topics in the light of assertions taken from the Bible). Thus understood, theology had been the *bête noire* of eighteenth-century *Aufklärer* as an impure mixture of unwarranted metaphysical claims and assertions about God allegedly found in the Bible. Belsham, much in the same spirit, used to teach that faith is a *practical*, not a theoretical attitude. Since human knowledge is limited, it is useless to inquire into subjects 'without the grasp of the human mind', for example, 'the mode of the divine existence' (Belsham 1827, p. 55), and we should not require 'rational knowledge' but rest content with 'rational belief' on 'the most important doctrines of natural and revealed religion' (Belsham 1801, p. 110).

On Malthus's theological Optimism

In the *Essay on Profits*, Ricardo mentions Providence while drawing opposite implications from a claim by Malthus. He notes that

> it has been remarked, in reference to a single country, that if the crops are bad in one district, they are generally productive in another [...] and, by this compensating power, Providence has bountifully secured us from the frequent recurrence of dearths. If this remark be just, as applied to one country, how much more strongly may it be applied to all the countries together which compose our world?
>
> (Ricardo 1815, p. 31)

To be fair, mention of God is made here in the context of a *tu quoque* argument and thus cannot be assumed to imply an unconditional acceptance of his existence. However, a more explicit admission is in the *Notes on Malthus*. Ricardo's objection concerns the qualification of rent as a 'bountiful gift of

Providence', and the argument is that rent comes from limited resources, not from unlimited ones, and it is scarcity instead of usefulness to give a price to scarce resources. Thus, the problem for a political economist is not

> whether the Creator did not consult our real happiness by limiting the productive powers of the land, but whether the fact be not, that he has so limited it, – while He has given us an unbounded supply of water, of air, and has set no limits to the use we may make of the pressure of the atmosphere, the elasticity of steam and many other services rendered to us by nature.
>
> (Ricardo 1928, p. 210; cf. pp. 337–338)

The direction of the argument is in favour of a more value-free approach as contrasted with Malthus's moralising. Nonetheless, Ricardo does mention the Creator here as he had not hesitated in mentioning Providence in the earlier quote. He makes both comments for the sake of argument since he is drawing implications from Malthus's assertions heading to a *reductio ad absurdum*. His main concern seems to be to rule out not so much religion as 'metaphysics', that is, the alleged discovery of a teleological order in the world. In more detail, he wants to confine human knowledge to the formulation of general laws. Thus – in Malthus's words turned upside down – he claims that political economy has *less* 'resemblance to the sciences of morals and politics' than to 'the science of mathematics' (Malthus 1820, p. 518).

On Owen's Deistic Optimism

Robert Owen was no stranger to these problems, either. A table-talk remark by Ricardo on Owen's views reported by John Lewis Mallet in his diary (14 January 1820) is as follows:

> Ricardo knows Owen intimately. He says that he is a thorough necessitarian; but being at the same time a Deist, he believes that all works for the best. It were to be wished, upon this principle, that he would be less pertinacious in his efforts to alter the state of society.
>
> (*Works* 8, p. 153)

Ricardo may have been implying: first, Optimism – in eighteenth-century jargon, the belief in the existence of an answer to the question of evil – carries a paradox, the same Adam Smith had detected in Stoicism, for it makes moral judgement redundant since Providence draws good results even from evil deeds; second, Optimism derives from a combination of necessitarianism and Deism; third, on these assumptions, any effort to do the good we can do is pointless. No less than those in the correspondence and the *Commonplace Books*, this comment highlights theodicy's relevance to the social question.

Public happiness without social theodicy

Ricardo's views on the possibility of faith and the impossibility of theology, the independence of morality from religion and unlimited toleration are part of the background of his contribution to political economy, and the crucial topic for historians of economic thought is the most abstruse theological theme: theodicy.

As mentioned, young Malthus had introduced a new kind of theodicy to respond to the new evil he had discovered, the asymmetry between the growth of resources and population. He had been attacked on every side and had conducted an egregious retreat in several steps, claiming he had always been right. The fifth edition of Malthus's *Essay* of 1817 was in the Ricardo Library (Sraffa 1955d, p. 399). We may assume that he read the work in this edition, where he met Malthus's theodicy in its third version (Cremaschi 2014, pp. 153–155). Besides, Ricardo started reading Bayle's work in 1817, and the discussion of theodicy with Mill also dates from that year. This coincidence suggests that Ricardo's interest did not arise out of conversion from economic to religious interests but was an attempt to untie a tangle, the bond between riches and poverty or the question on the causes of social evil and the possibility of discovering its function or *social theodicy*. Eighteenth-century population theories were of a theological kind, exploring the role of divine providence behind the growth and decrease of population, shifting from the discussion of the causes of human finitude, suffering, and wickedness to that of the causes of misery and vice unavoidably going with misery (La Vergata 1990, pp. 20–40).

Malthus's discovery of the population principle had occurred in the context of a refutation of a new kind of theodicy, the atheistic *anthropodicy* of human perfectibility proposed by William Godwin and Nicolas de Condorcet (Cremaschi 2014, pp. 79–84). Malthus's discovery was one step in an on-going process transforming theodicy from a highly abstract discussion into 'applied theology'. His 1798 theodicy tried to prove that evils deriving from the population principle were *partial* evils that prompted exertion and transformation of matter into mind (Malthus 1798, pp. 97–101; Cremaschi 2014, pp. 64–67).

His 1803 theodicy proves that there is a moral order in the world suggesting a way out of the evils carried by the population principle through prudence and chastity: a world where passions were under control. That would be a comparatively happy place, and its Creator would prove to be omniscient, benevolent and omnipotent (Malthus 1803b, pp. 88–95; Cremaschi 2014, pp. 94–99).

The third version of Malthus's theodicy, of 1817, is a response to criticism from Evangelical authors John Sumner and Thomas Chalmers. It assumes that in the divine design, moral improvement is the variable to maximise, and the principle of population's constant threat is there to compel 'moral constraint', that is, delayed marriage without 'irregular gratification', made possible by education, self-respect and self-reliance (Malthus 1803a, p. 19, 1803b, pp. 214–215, 251; cf. Cremaschi 2014, pp. 145–155).

James Mill was not immune to such concerns. According to his son's account, his unbelief was provoked by a 'state of perplexity' facing a 'world so full of evil' that made it impossible to believe that it 'was the work of an Author combining infinite power with perfect goodness and righteousness' (Mill 1873, p. 43). Oddly enough, in his *Elements of Political Economy*, he smuggles in a social theodicy. In a factual tone, he argues that the condition of the 'great body of the people' can be made more comfortable either by quickening the rate at which capital increases or by slowing down the rate of population growth (Mill 1821b, p. 44). In case we cannot secure 'human happiness' by making capital increase as fast as the population, the practical problem is to find a way to limit births (p. 65). He goes on to argue that besides economic factors a sociological one should also be considered. The possibility that humankind may advance in knowledge and discover ways to secure the means of happiness depends upon the existence of a class of people who can cultivate and enlarge knowledge. He then shifts abruptly from cause-effect relationships to value judgements, adding that it is the

> men of middle fortune who, having their time at their own disposal, freed from the necessity of manual labour, subject to no man's authority, obtain, as a class, the greatest sum of human enjoyment. For *the happiness, therefore, as well as the ornament of our nature*, it is peculiarly desirable that a class of this description should form as large a proportion of each community as possible.
>
> (p. 64, emphasis added)

Here, after the Malthusian principle in its original version − already abandoned by its author − he also applies the Benthamite principle of utility in its crudest form, with the *total amount* of happiness as a moral criterion. The twofold effect is, first, to transform a discussion of economic laws into a normative theory of justice and, second, to smuggle in a Calvinist-Atheist doctrine of predestination according to which salvation is only for a few and everyone else should rejoice in their good luck.

Note that Ricardo's rejection of theodicy would have implied a rejection of Malthus's 1817 theodicy, which justifies evil as a spring of moral improvement. Ricardo's mature view was that we *ought* to reduce social evils, even though no consideration makes them tolerable and that the war on poverty is a moral imperative despite awareness of the tragic nature of the human condition. The claims he seems to reject are:

(i) all works for the best (in Voltaire's phrase, *tout est bien*);
(ii) evil is out there as a means to our moral improvement;

while the claims he seems to endorse are:

(iii) evil is a hard fact for which no account is available;
(iv) nevertheless, it is a duty to promote our neighbour's happiness.

For several reasons, Ricardo disagrees with Mill, Owen, and Malthus. In his sociology of religion, Max Weber points at one primary function of religions, answering the question of evil. The '*Zwischenbetrachtungen*' argue that the tension becomes obvious between a rationalised economy and a rationalised religion. Thus,

> the religions of salvation have had a tendency to depersonalize and objectify love in the unique sense of acosmism. Yet have watched with profound suspicion the deployment of economic forces which [...] have likewise become impersonal.
>
> (Weber 1915, p. 331)

In such religions, love becomes universal and every human being becomes a brother or sister. Such universalism is bound to clash with market logic, where every human being tends to become one more element 'in a quantified economy in a no less universal way'. Money is

> the most abstract and 'impersonal' element that ever existed. The more the world of the modern capitalist economy follows its own immanent laws, the less accessible it is to any imaginable relationship with a religious ethics of brotherliness.
>
> (p. 331)

Ricardo somehow sensed Weber's tension and felt the need for a solution. However, he felt that logical fallacies vitiated all social theo- or anthropodicies. His mature views in social policies were fairly close to Malthus, but there was still theological disagreement. Even a *moral* theodicy that turns social evil into the source of moral progress is logically unwarranted and morally repugnant. We may conjecture that his only acceptable answer to the questions of why there are diseases, destitution and high rates of mortality was: we do not know. While some commentators, like Senior and Bagehot, deprecated his mistaking idealised assumptions for the real world, and others admired him as 'stoic, objective, scientific' (Marx 1910, p. 112) or execrated his lack of 'human feeling' (Stephen 1900, p. 222), Ricardo's research programme stands out as an awareness of the *limits* of knowledge and concern for its *usefulness*.

Partial conclusions: neither a utilitarian nor theological optimist

1. Ricardo believed that, besides pain and pleasure, human nature is governed by imagination and sympathy. He also believed that happiness is more elusive and frail than Bentham's measurable magnitude, since it is a complex and unstable condition where the mirroring relationship between individuals plays a crucial role.

2. He advocated a *natural morality* independent of religion. Albeit aware that religion teaches morality, he claimed – not unlike Voltaire, Pietro Verri, Adam Smith and Kant – that the latter is *autonomous*.
3. He was sure that 'moral impressions dictate moral principles' which reason confirms and religious teaching reiterates. He rejected the doctrine that happiness is a reward for virtue but believed that the rational search for happiness and doing as much good as we can for others is the correct way to live.
4. Far from utilitarian, he was an acute critic of the notion of utility, of the view of human nature as self-interested and motivated by pleasure and pain, and of consequentialist normative ethics.
5. He advocated unlimited freedom of opinion for both believers and unbelievers. He argued that nobody is the owner of the truth and that there are several sets of beliefs which reasonable persons may adopt, and he also argued that even those who adopt mistaken beliefs cannot change them at will.
6. For the same reasons as Kant, he believed not only that theodicy is impossible, but also that such impossibility is no argument for unbelief.
7. He sided with the poor, believing that poverty is a social evil to be cancelled, and rejected the idea that any greater good justifies it as suggested by Malthus and Sumner's *theodicy* and Bentham's and Mill's *anthropodicy*. He was, however, cautious about practical measures out of awareness of the additional misery that any significant change could carry.

References

Unpublished

Ricardo Correspondence and Papers. Miscellaneous Private, Cambridge University Library. GB 12 MS.ADD.7510

Published

Bayle, P. 1682a, Pensées diverses sur la comète, vol. 1; edn used: A Prat (ed.), Droz, Paris, 1939.
Bayle, P. 1682b, Pensées diverses sur la comète, vol. 2; edn used: A Prat (ed.), Droz, Paris, 1939.
Bayle, P. 1697a, *Dictionnaire historique et critique*, vol. 1, edn used: Brunel, Amsterdam, 1740.
Bayle, P. 1697b, *Dictionnaire historique et critique*, vol. 2, edn used: Brunel, Amsterdam, 1740.
Belsham, T 1801, *Elements of the Philosophy of the Mind, and of Moral Philosophy. To Which Is Prefixed a Compendium of Logic*, Johnson, London.
Belsham, T 1814, *Prospect of Perpetual and Universal Peace, A Thanksgiving Sermon*, Johnson & Eaton, London.
Belsham, T 1827, *Discourses, Doctrinal and Practical*, vol. 2, Hunter, London.

Bentham, J 1776, 'A Fragment on Government', in *A Comment on the Commentaries and A Fragment on Government*, JH Burns & HLA Hart (eds), The Collected Works of Jeremy Bentham, Clarendon Press, Oxford, 1977, pp. 393–551.

Bentham, J 1789, *An Introduction to the Principles of Morals and Legislation*, JH Burns & HLA Hart (eds), Introduction by F Rosen, The Collected Works of Jeremy Bentham, Clarendon Press, Oxford, 1996.

Bentham, J 1817, *Plan of Parliamentary Reform, in the Form of a Catechism*, Hunter, London.

Bentham, J 1822, 'Securities Against Misrule', in J Bentham (ed.), *Securities Against Misrule and other Constitutional Writings for Tripoli and Greece*, TP Schofield (ed.), The Collected Works of Jeremy Bentham, Clarendon Press, Oxford, 1990, pp. 23–73.

Bonner, J 1995, *Economic Efficiency and Social Justice, The Development of Utilitarian Ideas in Economics from Bentham to Edgeworth*, Elgar, Aldershot.

Brougham, H 1839, 'Sketch of Ricardo In Parliament', in *Works*, vol. 5, pp. xxxii–xxxiv.

Burke, E 1770, 'Thoughts on the Present Discontents', in E Burke (ed.), *The Writings and Speeches*, vol. 2, P Langford & WB Todd (eds), Clarendon Press, Oxford, 1981, pp. 241–323.

Christian Reformer 1823a, 'Intelligence. The Christians' Petition against the Prosecution of Unbelievers', *The Christian Reformer, or, New Evangelical Miscellany*, June 1823, vol. 9, no. 102, June, pp. 221–224.

Christian Reformer 1823b, 'Christians' Petition to Parliament against the Prosecution of Unbelievers', *The Christian Reformer, or, New Evangelical Miscellany*, vol. 9, no. 103, July, p. 254 (Reprinted in the Appendix of this book).

Cookson, JE 1982, *The Friends of Peace: Anti-War Liberalism in England, 1793–1815*, Cambridge University Press, Cambridge. DOI: 10.1017/CBO9780511896422.

Cremaschi, S & Dascal, M 1998, 'Malthus and Ricardo: Two Styles for Economic Theory', *Science in Context*, vol. 11, no. 2, pp. 229–254. DOI: 10.1017/S0269889700003008.

Cremaschi, S 2014, *Utilitarianism and Malthus's Virtue Ethics. Respectable, Virtuous and Happy*, Routledge, London. DOI: 10.4324/9781315819235.

Cremaschi, S. 2020, 'The Italian Enlightenment and the Rehabilitation of Moral and Political Philosophy', *The European Legacy*, vol. 25, no. 7–8, pp. 743–759. DOI: 10.1080/10848770.2020.1758411.

Crimmins, JE 1994, 'Bentham's Political Radicalism Reexamined', *Journal of the History of Ideas*, vol. 55, no. 2, pp. 259–281. DOI: 10.2307/2709899.

Depoortère, C 2002, 'On Ricardo's method: The Unitarian Influence Examined', *History of Political Economy*, vol. 34, no. 2, pp. 499–504. DOI:10.1215/00182702-34-2-499.

Edgeworth, M 1971, *Letters from England 1813–1844*, C Colvin (ed.), Clarendon Press, Oxford.

Fenn, RA 1987, *James Mill's Political Thought*, Garland, New York.

Gentlemen's Magazine 1823, 'David Ricardo, Esq. M.P.', *The Gentlemen's Magazine*, vol. 93 (July–December), October, 1823, p. 376.

Hartwell, RM 1971, 'Introduction', in D Ricardo, *The Principles of Political Economy and Taxation*, Penguin, Harmondsworth, Middlesex, pp. 7–47.

Henderson JP 1997, *The Life and Economics of David Ricardo. With Additional Chapters by J.B. Davis*, WJ Samuels & GB Davis (eds), Kluwer, Dordrecht.

Hume, D. 1757, *A Dissertation on the Passions. The Natural History of Religion*, TL Beauchamp (ed.), Clarendon Hume Edition Series, Clarendon, Oxford, 2007. DOI: 10.1093/actrade/9780199575749.book.1.

Jensen, HE 1999, 'The development of T.R. Malthus's Institutionalist Approach to the Cure of Poverty: From Punishment of the Poor to Investment in Their Human Capital', *Review of Social Economy*, vol. 57, no. 4, pp. 450–465. DOI: 10.1080/00346769900000016.

Johnson, JT 1981, *Just War Tradition and the Restraint of War. A Moral and Historical Inquiry*, Princeton University Press, Princeton, NJ.

Jortin, J 1771, 'Sermon III. Matt. 5.44 But I Say Unto You. Love Your Enemies', in J Jortin (ed.), *Sermons on Different Subjects*, vol. 2, White, London, pp. 43–62.

King, JE 2013, *David Ricardo*, Palgrave Macmillan, Houndsmills, Basingstoke. DOI: 10.1057/9781137315953_1.

La Vergata, A 1990, *Nonostante Malthus. Fecondità, popolazioni e armonia della natura. 1700–1900*, Bollati Boringhieri, Torino.

Lees, LH 1998, *The Solidarities of Strangers: The English Poor Laws and the People, 1700–1948*, Cambridge University Press, Cambridge.

Locke, J 1695, *The Reasonableness of Christianity*, edn used: JC Higgins-Biddle (ed.), Clarendon Edition of the Works of John Locke, Clarendon, Oxford 1999.

Malthus, TR 1798, *An Essay on the Principle of Population*, EA Wrigley & D Souden (eds), The Works of Thomas Robert Malthus 1, Pickering, London, 1986.

Malthus, TR 1803a, *An Essay on the Principle of Population*, vol. 1, P James (ed.), Cambridge University Press, Cambridge, 1989.

Malthus, TR 1803b, *An Essay on the Principle of Population*, vol. 2, P James (ed.), Cambridge University Press, Cambridge, 1989.

Malthus, TR 1820, *Principles of Political Economy*, vol. 1, J Pullen (ed.), Cambridge University Press, Cambridge, 1989.

Manzoni, A. 1855, *Osservazioni sulla morale cattolica*, edn used: R Amerio (ed.), Ricciardi, Milano, 1965.

Marx, K 1987, *Marx/Engels: Briefwechsel, Januar bis August 1852/Text*, Marx/Engels Gesamtausgabe, III. Abteilung: Briefwechsel 5, Internationale Marx/Engels Stiftung (ed.), Dietz, Berlin.

Marx, K. 1910, *Theorien über den Mehrwert*, vol. 2, K. Kautsky (ed.), Karl Marx and Friedrich Engels Werke 26, Dietz, Berlin, 1972.

Middleton, C 1750, *An Examination of the Bishop of London's Discourse Concerning Prophecy*, Manby & Cox, London.

McCulloch, JMR 1846, 'Sketch of the Life and Writings of Mr. Ricardo', in *The Works of David Ricardo*, JMR McCulloch (ed.), Murray, London, 1888, pp. xv–xxxiii.

Milgate, M & Stimson, SC 1991, *Ricardian Politics*, Princeton University Press, Princeton, NJ.

Mill JS 1873, *Autobiography and Literary Essays,* JM Robson & J Stillinger (eds), The Collected Works of John Stuart Mill 1, Routledge, London, 1981.

Mill, J 1817, *The History of British India*, vol. 1, 3rd edn, Baldwin, London, 1826.

Mill, J 1820, 'An Essay on Government', in *Essays on Government, Jurisprudence, Liberty of the Press and Law of Nations*, pp. 1–32, The Collected Works of James Mill 2, Routledge/Thoemmes, London & Kinokuniya, Tokyo, 1992.

Mill, J 1821a, 'Liberty of the Press', in *Essays on Government, Jurisprudence, Liberty of the Press and Law of Nations*, pp. 1–34, The Collected Works of James Mill 2, Routledge/Thoemmes, London & Kinokuniya, Tokyo, 1992.

Mill J 1821b, *Elements of Political Economy*, The Collected Works of James Mill 6, Routledge/Thoemmes, London & Kinokuniya, Tokyo.

Monthly Repository 1815, 'Benjamin Travers "The Sinfulness of War"', *The Monthly Repository*, vol. 10, no. 112, April, p. 250.

Monthly Repository 1823a, 'The Christians' Petition to Parliament against the Prosecution of Unbelievers', *The Monthly Repository*, vol. 18, no. 210, pp. 362–364.

Monthly Repository 1823b, 'Parliamentary. Christians' Petition against the Prosecution of Unbelievers', *The Monthly Repository*, vol. 18, no. 212, August 1823, pp. 485–494 (Reprinted in the Appendix of this book).

Monthly Repository 1823c, 'David Ricardo', *The Monthly Repository*, vol. 18, no. 213, September 1823, p. 551 (Reprinted in the Appendix of this book).

Opocher, A 2015, 'Population', in H Kurz & N Salvadori (eds), *The Elgar Companion to Ricardo*, Edward Elgar, Aldershot, pp. 409–414. DOI: 10.4337/9781784715489.

Paley, W 1785, *The Principles of Moral and Political Philosophy*, DL LeMahieu (ed.), Liberty Fund, Indianapolis, IN, 2002.

Paley, W 1802, *Natural Theology*, edn Used: Gregg, Farnborough, 1970.

Parys, W 2020, 'David Ricardo, the Stock Exchange, and the Battle of Waterloo: Samuelsonian Legends Lack Historical Evidence', University of Antwerp, Department of Economics, Research Paper 220–009, Available at https://repository.uantwerpen.be › docstore › d:irua:3740 (Accessed 1 February 2021).

Parys, W. 2021, 'Some additions and corrections for Sraffa on Ricardo in Business', *Cambridge Journal of Economics*, pp. 1-17, viewed 31 March 2021. DOI: 10.1093/cje/beab003

Peach, T 1993, 'Milgate and Stimson, "Ricardian Politics"', *The Economic Journal*, 103, no. 420, pp. 1337–1339. DOI: 10.2307/2234272.

Peach, T 1997, 'The age of the universal consumer: a reconsideration of Ricardo's politics', *The European Journal of the History of Economic Thought*, vol. 4, no.2, pp. 217–236. DOI: 10.1080/10427719700000037.

Poynter, JR 1969, *Society and Pauperism, English Ideas on Poor Relief 1795–1834*, Routledge, London.

Ricardo, D 1815, An *Essay on the Influence of the Low Price of Corn on the Profits of Stock*, in *Works* 4, pp. 1–42.

Ricardo, D 1817, *The Principles of Political Economy and Taxation*, in *Works* 1.

Ricardo, D 1821, 'Notes on Mill's Elements of Political Economy', in *Works* 9, pp. 126–133.

Ricardo, D 1824a, 'Observations on Parliamentary Reform', in *Works* 5, pp. 495–503.

Ricardo, D 1824b, 'Defence of the Plan of Voting by Ballot', in *Works* 5, pp. 504–512.

Ricardo, D 1928, 'Notes on Malthus', in *Works* 2.

Ricardo, M 1824, 'A Memoir of David Ricardo', in *Works* 10, pp. 3–15.

Siméon, O 2017, *Robert Owen's Experiment at New Lanark. From Paternalism to Socialism*, Palgrave MacMillan, London. DOI: 10.1007/978-3-319-64227-7.

Smith A 1759, *The Theory of Moral Sentiments*, DD Raphael & AL Macfie (eds.), The Glasgow Edition of the Works and Correspondence of Adam Smith 1, Oxford University Press, Oxford, 1976.

Sraffa, P 1952, 'Introductory Notes to the Correspondence', in *Works* 6, pp. xiii-xli.

Sraffa, P 1955a, 'Addenda to the Memoir of Ricardo', in *Works* 10, pp. 16–64.

Sraffa, P 1955b, 'Ricardo in Business', in *Works* 10, pp. 65–106.

Sraffa 1955c, 'Appendix (C) 'Commonplace Books', in *Works* 10, pp. 393–398.

Sraffa 1955d, 'Appendix (D) Ricardo's Library', in *Works* 10, pp. 389–402.

Stephen, L 1900, *The English Utilitarians*, vol. 2, Duckworth, London.

Sumner, JB 1816, *A Treatise on the Records of the Creation and on the Moral Attributes of the Creator*, vol. 2, Hatchard, London.

Sunday Times 1823, 'David Ricardo', *The Sunday Times*, September 14, 3rd edn, p. 1 (Reprint in the Appendix).

Travers, B 1814, *The Sinfulness of War*, Skelton, Southampton.

Tribe, K 1992, 'Review of M Milgate & SC Stimson "Ricardian Politics"', *Sociology*, vol. 26, no. 4, pp. 722–723. DOI: 10.1177/0038038592026004023.

Trower, H 1813, *Christianity in India. – Letters between Laicus and an East India Proprietor as They Appeared in the Times Newspaper in the Months of August, September and October, 1813*, Rivington, London.

Watson, R 1776, *An Apology for Christianity*, Merrill, Cambridge.

Watson. R 1796, *An Apology for the Bible*, edn Used: Evans. London, 1796.

Weatherall, D 1976, *David Ricardo. A Biography*, Nijhoff, The Hague.

Weber, M 1915, 'Religious Rejections of the World and Their Directions', in M Gerth & C Wright (eds.), *From Max Weber: Essays in Sociology*, Oxford University Press, New York, 1975, pp. 323–359.

Whewell, W 1852, *Lectures on the History of Moral Philosophy in England*, Thoemmes, Bristol, 1990.

Winch, D 1983, 'The Cause of Good Government: Philosophic Whigs versus Philosophic Radicals', in S Collini, D Winch & J Burrow (eds), *That Noble Science of Politics, A Study in Nineteenth Century Intellectual History*, Cambridge University Press, Cambridge. DOI: 10.1017/CBO9780511559365.

Winch, D 1996, *Riches and Poverty, an Intellectual History of Political Economy in Britain 1790–1834*, Cambridge University Press, Cambridge.

Young, BW 2004, 'Jortin, John (1698–1770)', in HCG Matthew, & B Harrison (eds), *Oxford Dictionary of National Biography*, vol. 30, Oxford University Press, Oxford, pp. 710–713.

Conclusions

A man from another planet

This book, while reconstructing contexts and conducting a solid reading of texts, has examined chapters of Ricardo's intellectual history. Every time the historical Ricardo seemed to be vanishing from sight, the context could at least show what he might have thought and done, as well as what was inconceivable for him to have thought or done. Every time one source says something that may support a particular interpretation of Ricardo's work, a reading of the sources as utterances intended by somebody for a specific addressee and aimed at achieving a given communicative end – with the added intention of producing specific effects on the addressee – may prove the interpretation either plausible or a gross misunderstanding. We have avoided both anachronism, that is reading terms in their present meaning, and teleology, that is, reconstructing what sources say while assessing how much they *anticipate* later, more *advanced* ideas. Let us summarise what we may have gained from the attempt.

In Ricardo's biography there is evidence of successive membership of or proximity to three different religious communities. Against a current unwitting tendency to underestimate the weight of religion in modern history by backdating the twentieth-century's widespread secularisation to earlier ones, the first three chapters have tried to take extant evidence of Ricardo's religious affiliations at face value. They have drawn attention to the fact that being a Jew in the eighteenth century did not mean simply adhering to one religious denomination among others, but growing up in an ethnic, cultural and linguistic community of immigrants with its own institutions, educational system and laws. Attention has been drawn to the fact that adherence to Unitarianism in the early decades of the nineteenth century was not a choice of convenience that one could make so as to have a patent of respectability while paying the cheapest entrance fee. Instead, it was adherence to the most radically 'progressive' community of the time, when religious faith was the driving force behind the commitment to such campaigns as women's emancipation, unlimited freedom of opinion, and the abolition of slavery.

The fourth chapter has reconstructed Ricardo's intellectual training, so utterly different from that of the Anglican elite though not unique in the English landscape and similar to that of many who did not belong to the

DOI: 10.4324/9781003162100-8

majority. One can point to John Bowring, Bentham's editor and example of an intellectual who had attended school until the age of 14, then started to work while continuing some form of part-time education over the next few years. In Ricardo's case the university he attended was the London Geological Society, which represented the spearhead of intellectual progress in that it focused on the frontier science that was still excluded from universities and at the crossroads of the clash between progress and conservation in the battle of ideas. Bearing in mind that we are talking about 200 years ago, we will not be surprised that Geological Society members had more intellectual interests than one would meet today in an Earth Sciences department. Kirwan, its father figure, was an author of philosophical works and Francis Horner was the author of reviews and essays on economic subjects.

Partly through the Geological Society, and partly through the Unitarian congregations, Ricardo made friends with some of the best-known philosophers of the day: authors of works on logic, ethics and politics, some of whom were venturing into the discipline of political economy, a subject no less recent and no less central to the battle of ideas than geology was. Ricardo moved on from the study of the newborn science, geology, to the other cutting-edge science of the time, political economy – a choice that was encouraged not only by his experience in finance but also by the civic commitment that found inspiration in his contacts with Quakers and Unitarians. His earliest writings dealt with the Bullion Controversy, an issue that was being debated in Parliament at the time. The writings took the usual form of contributions by well-informed citizens to the discussion of public choices as a contribution to better legislation. The 'methodological' inspiration of these writings also reflects the jargon of the Bullion controversy, inherited from the debate on the French Revolution and centred on the opposition between principles and facts, or 'philosophy' and practical experience.

Yet, from the *Essay on Profits* onwards, there is a change in his way of proceeding. Ricardo now opts for simplified representations, drawing practical consequences from connections between their elements. In the *Principles*, the attempt is the same: to consider a few phenomena, assumed to be universal while leaving others aside, believed to be nothing more than appearance, the effect of occasional causes. Ricardo professes loyalty to Adam Smith and declares that he only wants to modify some of his claims. Apart from a different way of writing and preference for the most simplified picture possible, leaving out historical reconstructions, Ricardo's method does not deviate from analysis and synthesis. We may describe it as proceeding from many, discordant phenomena to a few general principles, and from these to the prediction of the main phenomena observed – the 'Newtonian' procedure that contemporaries believed Adam Smith had followed.

After the *Principles*, Ricardo's discussion with Malthus takes a more decisive turn in the direction of meta-scientific reflection. The themes are multicausality, the realism of hypotheses and the heuristic function of hypothetical cases, the possibility of causal explanation, and general laws. Gradually, a

Ricardian logic emerges, a constellation of theoretical positions on specific themes in which Ricardo's claims distinguish themselves from those of Malthus and exhibit a certain coherence, an attitude we may describe as 'limited scepticism'. This attitude is compatible with distinct traditions of thought: Bayle's scepticism, Priestley's and Belsham's epistemological anti-realism, Adam Smith's post-scepticism, Kirwan's and Greenough's meta-scientific theses. On the other hand, it is incompatible with Cartesianism, Scottish common-sense realism, and Bentham's Lockean associationism.

Despite the apparent rift between moral philosopher Adam Smith, who would moralise even when talking about the economy, and hard scientist Ricardo, who was stoic and objective, their views on 'ethics and economics' are closer than commentators believed. Although Ricardo did not publish anything on ethics or politics, his readings and conversations have left sufficient traces for anyone wishing to look into them. His views on human nature and the foundation of morality are incompatible with Bentham but close enough to Adam Smith and – strangely enough – to Kant, an author he certainly never read. His view of economic laws and social justice are at once sharply separated and mutually complementary. In his view, economic theory goes no further than *descriptive laws* and never formulates *prescriptive laws*. It does not dictate policies but fixes boundaries within which policies can go. On its part, ethics dictates the ends to pursue, namely the elimination of poverty so that the workers can have what is due to them as a right and not as an act of beneficence.

Appendix

The Christian Reformer: text of the Christians' Petition

'Intelligence. The Christians' Petition against the Prosecution of Unbelievers', *The Christian Reformer, or, New Evangelical Miscellany*, June 1823, vol. 9, no. 102, pp. 221–224.

To the Right Honourable the Lords Spiritual and Temporal in Parliament assembled:

To the Honourable the Commons of the United Kingdom of Great Britain and Ireland, in Parliament assembled:

The Humble Petition of the undersigned Ministers and Members of Christian Congregations, SHEWETH,

That your Petitioners are sincere believers in the Christian Revelation from personal conviction on examination of the Evidences on its behalf; and are thankful to Almighty God for the unspeakable blessing of the Gospel, which they regard as the most sacred sanction, the best safeguard, and the most powerful motive, of morality, as the firmest support and most effectual relief amidst the afflictions and troubles of this state of humanity, and as the surest foundation of the hope of a life to come, which hope they consider to be in the highest degree conducive to the dignity, purity and happiness of society.

That with these views and feelings, your Petitioners beg leave to state to your [Right] Honourable House, that they behold with sorrow and shame the prosecutions against persons who have printed or published books which are, or are presumed to be hostile to the Christian Religion, from the full persuasion that such prosecutions are inconsistent with, and contrary to, both the spirit and the letter of the Gospel, and, moreover, that they are more favourable to the spread of Infidelity, which they are intended to check, than to the support of the Christian Faith, which they are professedly undertaken to uphold.

Your Petitioners cannot but consider all Christians bound by their religious profession to bow with reverence and submission to the precepts of the Great Founder of our faith; and nothing appears to them plainer in the Gospel than that it forbids all violent measures for its propagation, and all vindictive measures for its justification and defence. The Author and Finisher of Christianity has declared, that his kingdom is not of this world; and, as in his own example he shewed a perfect pattern of compassion towards them that are ignorant and out of the way of truth, of forbearance towards objectors, and of forgiveness of wilful enemies, so in his moral laws he has prohibited the spirit that would attempt to root up speculative error with the arm of flesh, or that would call down fire from heaven to consume the unbelieving, and has commanded the exercise of meekness, tenderness and brotherly love towards all mankind, as the best and only means of promoting his cause upon earth, and the most acceptable way of glorifying the Great Father of mercies, who is kind even to the unthankful and the evil.

By these reasonable, charitable and peaceful means, the Christian Religion was not only established originally, but also supported for the three first centuries of the Christian era, during which it triumphed over the most fierce and potent opposition, unaided by temporal power: and your Petitioners humbly submit to your Right Honourable House, that herein consists one of the brightest evidences of the truth of the Christian Religion; and that they are utterly at a Loss to conceive how that which is universally accounted to have been the glory of the Gospel in its beginnings, should now cease to be Recounted its glory, or how it should at this day he less the maxim of Christianity, and less the rule of the conduct of Christians, than in the days of those that are usually denominated the Fathers of the Church — that it is no part of religion to compel religion, which must be received, not by force, but of free choice.

Your Petitioners would earnestly represent to your Right Honourable House, that our holy religion has gone uninjured every test that reason and learning have applied to it, and that its divine origin, its purity, its excellence, and its title to universal acceptance, have been made more manifest by every new examination and discussion of its nature, pretensions and claims. Left to Itself, under the Divine blessing, the reasonableness and innate excellence of Christianity will infallibly promote its influence over the understandings and hearts of mankind; but when the angry passions are suffered to rise in its professed defence, these provoke the like passions in hostility to it; and the question is no longer one of pure truth, but of power on the one side, and of the capacity of endurance on the Other.

It appears to your Petitioners that it is altogether unnecessary and impolitic to recur to penal Laws in aid of Christianity. The judgment and feelings of human nature, testified by the history of man in all ages and nations, incline mankind to religion, and it is only when they erringly associate religion with fraud and injustice that they can be brought in so large number to bear the evils of scepticism and unbelief, Your Petitioners acknowledge and lament the wide diffusion amongst the people of sentiments unfriendly to the Christian faith: but they cannot refrain from stating to your Honourable House their conviction that this unexampled state of the public mind is mainly owing to the prosecution of the holders and propagators of infidel opinions. Objections to Christianity have thus become familiar to the readers of the weekly and daily journals, curiosity has been stimulated with regard to the publications prohibited, and adventitious, unnatural and dangerous importance has been given to sceptical arguments, a suspicion has been excited in the minds of the multitude that the Christian religion can be upheld only by pains and penalties, and sympathy has been raised on behalf of the sufferers, whom the uninformed and unwise regard with the reverence and confidence that belong to the character of martyrs to the truth, Your Petitioners would remind your [Right] Honourable House, that all history testifies the futility of ail prosecutions for mere opinions, unless such prosecutions proceed the length of exterminating the holders of the opinion prosecuted – an extreme from which the liberal spirit and the humanity of the present times revolt.

The very same maxims and principles that are pleaded to justify the punishment of Unbelievers would authorize Christians of different denominations to vex and harass each other on the alleged ground of want of faith, and likewise form an apology for Heathen persecutions against Christians, whether the persecutions that were anciently carried on against the divinely taught preachers of our religion, or those that may now be instituted by the ruling party in Pagan countries, where Christian missionaries are so laudably employed, in endeavouring to expose the absurdity, folly and mischievous influence of idolatry.

Your Petitioners would entreat your [Right] Honourable House to consider that belief does not in all cases depend upon the will, and that inquiry into the truth of Christianity will be wholly prevented if persons are rendered punishable for any given result of inquiry, Firmly attached as your Petitioners are to the religion of the Bible, they cannot but consider the liberty of rejecting, to be implied in that of embracing it, The unbeliever may, indeed, be silenced by bis fears, but it is scarcely conceivable that any real friend to Christianity, or any one who is solicitous for the improvement of the human mind, the diffusion of knowledge and the establishment of truth, should wish to reduce any portion of mankind to the necessity of concealing their honest judgment upon moral and theological questions, and of making an outward profession that shall be inconsistent with their inward persuasion.

Your Petitioners are not ignorant that a distinction is commonly made between those unbelievers that argue the question of the truth of Christianity calmly and dispassionately, and those that treat the sacred subject with levity and ridicule; but although they feel the strongest disgust at every mode of discussion which approaches to 'indecency and profaneness, they cannot help thinking that it is neither wise nor safe to constitute the manner and temper of writing' an object of legal visitation; inasmuch as it is impossible to define where argument 'ends and evil speaking begins. The reviler of Christianity appears to your Petitioners to be the less formidable of it

seems; because his scoffs can rarely fail of arousing against him public opinion than which nothing more is wanted to defeat his end. Between freedom
of discussion and absolute persecution there is no assignable medium, And
nothing seems to your Petitioners more impolitic than to single out the
intemperate publications of modern unbelievers for legal reprobation, and
thus by implication to give a licence to the grave reasonings of those that
preceded them in the course of open hostility to the Christian Religion,
which reasonings are much more likely to make a dangerous impression
upon the minds of their readers.

But independently of considerations of expediency and policy, your Petitioners cannot forbear recording their humble protest against the principle
implied in the prosecutions alluded to, that a religion proceeding from Infinite Wisdom and protected by Almighty Power, depends upon human patronage for its perpetuity and influence. Wherefore they pray your [Right]
Honourable House, to take into consideration the prosecutions carrying on
and the punishments already inflicted upon unbelievers, in order to exon-
erate Christianity from the opprobrium and scandal so unjustly cast upon it
of being a system that countenances intolerance and persecution.

And your Petitioners will ever pray, & c.

The Christian Reformer & The Monthly Repository: presentation of the Christians' Petition in the House of Commons and the House of the Lords

'Christians' Petition to Parliament against the Prosecution of Unbelievers',
The Christian Reformer, or, New Evangelical Miscellany, vol. 9, no. 103, July
1823, p. 254; *The Monthly Repository*, vol. 18, no. 210, June 1823, pp. 362–364.

This Petition, inserted in the last Number, (pp. 221–224) was presented to
the house of Commons by Mr. Hume on the 1st instant, who followed up
with corresponding motion. The motion was negatived without a division
but the debate was important.

Christians' Petition to Parliament against the prosecution of Unbelievers

The mover vindicated the cause of free discussion with much ability and
discretion, and was powerfully supported by Mr. Ricardo. He received a
faint and qualified support from Mr. W. Smith. The opposers were Mr. But-
terworth, (the Wesleyan leader,) Mr. Wilberforce (who spoke as a member
of the busy Society for the Suppression of Vice,) Mr Horace Twiss, Mr. T.
Wilson, Mr. Money and Mr. Peel, It is not difficult to decide on which
hand the weight of argument lies. We expected that some other distinguished
Members of the House would have given their countenance to the cause of
Christianity on this occasion; but we have every reason to be satisfied with
the debate. Had there not been a word said, the entry of the Petition on the
Journals would have been of itself cause of congratulation to the lovers of the
Christian religion for its own sake. – The signature of the Petition would

have been much more numerous but for the remissness of some persons in various parts of the country, to whose care it was entrusted. By an accident, one sheet was not set up in time, which of peculiar value on account of its containing the signature of the learned Dr. Samuel Park, one of the most distinguished members and ministers of the Church of England.

The Petition was presented in the House of Lords on the 4th instant, by the Marquis of Landsown, who declared himself friendly to free religious discussion, though he was not prepared to go the full length of the Petitioners. We understand that the venerable Bishop of Norwich has expressed his approbation of the Petition, which would have been put into his hands to present, if he had been in town.

The Sunday Times: **Daniel Whittle Harvey's obituary**

'David Ricardo', *The Sunday Times*, no. 48, September 15, 1823, 3d edn, p. 1.

Just as we had written that name, and were to join with it the name of William Huskisson, for the purpose of laying before our readers a parliamentary sketch and contrast, which they could contemplate with fewer 'ifs and exceptions' than any other which we could trace for them, the melancholy news reached us that DAVID RICARDO was no more; thus our delineation of a living and active patriot must give place to an obituary notice, and boast that England possessed a man so able and so honest, must be changed to sorrow that she now possesses only his memory. It is, however, a memory which will long be cherished: and, unlike the memories of many Statesmen, the more it is studied the brighter it will appear. Men of more talents, and more school-information, we might have lost; but, for liberality of sentiment, acuteness of penetration, soundness of judgment, manliness of character, and fair and unsullied political honesty, Ricardo has left no superior, – we cannot, at this moment, name an equal in the House of Commons. At the same time, his worth in private life needs no eulogy, and can receive no amplification. Ricardo was a man to whom all parties looked up; and the greatest men upon the other side of the House were animated when they felt they had his approbation, and depressed and embarrassed when they found him opposed to them. Not the least part of his merit consisted in his being originally of the people, in his acquiring a splendid fortune by the application of his own talents, by his coming through the dangerous ground of the money-changers without a stain, or a whisper of accusation, and by his preserving the same modesty and the same firmness in every circumstance of life. His moral worth, his scientific acquirements, and his senatorial influence, placed him at the very head of British Commoners: and yet while he had the best reason to be proud, he was the mildest man in England. He was the very man whom, in the beginning of a system of liberal policy his country, could the least spare; but he was the man whose house was the best in order, and whose epitaph was the most complete. Over the bier of such a man it is impossible to speak as we ought, and yet it is painful to be silent. As the wounds in Caesar's body stirred up the Roman soldiers to revenge, so may the virtues of Ricardo stir up our Senators to imitation.

The first thing that struck us when we heard the news, was – a 'how very quickly great men die:' Horner had barely carried the torch of science into the intricacies of our finance, when Horner and the torch were extinct together: Romilly had but put his hand upon the disorderly mass of our criminal laws, when Romilly was looked for by ten thousand eyes, but looked for in vain: Ricardo had snatched up the torch which was extinguished by Horner's fall; he was again trimming it into lustre; – and now – Where is Ricardo? The man is enshrined in the hearts of his friends, the philosopher has taken his place in the library, the memorial of the patriot has gone forth over the whole land. By all, all will be cherished; and they will be as loath to change the pure and unsophisticated recollections as we were to strike out the two simple words 'DAVID RICARDO,' which we had written for a very different purpose, and substitute any thing more sounding in their place. Still he will be sought for. Into the parlour of Gatcombe Park we dare not look – the sorrow of the amiable ones there, who were so endearing and so endeared is too full and too holy for the most admiring stranger; but when that sorrow finds utterance its first feeble and panting cry will be 'Where is Ricardo?' When the great and good men of the land assemble for the securing of their own liberties, or of the liberties of the world: and when they look around for the wanted solution of a difficulty, or support of a truth which many wish, but few dare to speak, sadness will come over them, and they will ask, 'Where is Ricardo?' In St. Stephens, we shall miss the little plain man with the acute features and the keen eye, who sat by the pillar, and to whom every financial difficulty was referred as to an umpire. – Robinson, and Huskisson, and Wallace will rise as before, and as before they will not address the Speaker: but where now will they look for that all-eloquent glance where now which is to applaud them, when right, or check them hen wrong?

Their eyes will range from bench to bench – there will be the blankness of unfeigned regret upon their faces – they will turn to each other, and the whisper will be 'Where is Ricardo;' – Who can dwell upon the thought that the answer to all those inquiries must come in the hollow echo of the grave!

Ricardo's father and family were of the Jewish persuasion; blameless according to the Decalogue, and uncommonly strict in all the peculiarities of the Mosaic ritual. In the same faith he was himself initiated; and he, being we believe the eldest of a large family, at a very early age assisted his father in the profession of a stock-broker, in which the elder Ricardo had been pretty successful; and when the younger was judged old enough he was taken into the firm as a regular partner. The father's residence was at Bow, not far from that of an eminent surgeon of the name of Wilkinson. Ricardo formed an honourable attachment to one of the daughters of this gentleman; she was beautiful, accomplished, and amiable; but she was not of the seed of Jacob, and perhaps had not the inheritance of Rachel. The old man forbade his son's union with a Christian; and upon his persevering, deprived him of his share of the business. Ricardo was, however, firm in his attachment, which the event proves to have been made with that judgment which was the leading-feature of his character; and so he married the lady, and became a Christian, attaching himself to the Unitarian Chapel, in Essex-street, where he and his family have regularly attended the instructions of Mr. Belsham. Renounced and disinherited, Ricardo was not without friends. An eminent banking-house in the city, (Lubbocks and Forster, we believe) knowing his character, and hearing how he had been used, sent for him, told him that, as they had every confidence in him, he need be at no loss for money; for if he continued prudent, 'they would honour any check which he pleased to draw upon them.' This support and his own talents were quite enough for Ricardo, he immediately began business and in the course of a very few years was a richer man than the father.

Finding his son prospering, preferring a rich Christian to a poor Jew, or, perhaps, rather from the *storge* of nature, the father was the first to seek a reconciliation and we have never heard that Ricardo harboured the least resentment for the harsh measure which had been dealt him. The firm of 'Ricardo, brothers,' soon rose to great eminence in the moneyed world. Ricardo was always a great shareholder, and very often the original contractor in those numerous loans which marked the destructive policy of Pitt, fettered Europe, and hung a mill-stone round the neck of this country; but while he did this in the way of business, he was no advocate for the system, and no man could attach to his principles, or his conduct, a single stigma. While but too many of those who engaged in that traffic became obsequious admirers and unreasoning followers of Pitt, Ricardo passed through the ordeal without an imputation. It is no slender proof of the vigour of his mind, the steadiness of his principles, and the integrity of his conduct, that while all around him gave themselves unto the most prostituted and clamorous worship of the 'great Statesman,' Ricardo held fast his integrity, and silently followed those admirable chains of reasoning, which enabled him to bring true science into the counting-house, and elevate the character of a British merchant to a rank which it never before occupied. We well remember, that when the breach of the peace of Amiens made all the tribe of the bear-garden in the Alley toss up their caps, and astound the neighbourhood with their yell, it was Ricardo who gave them the manly rebuke for rejoicing at gains, which were to be made by the dissolution of kingdoms and the misery of mankind. Ricardo's success in business was so complete as his means of seeking it were honourable. Upon a single occasion, that of the battle of Waterloo, he is said to have netted upwards of a million sterling. His success enabled him to become proprietor of Gatcombe Park, in Gloucestershire; and the superiority of his mind, and admirable candour of his manners, soon overcame the pride and poverty of the aristocracy, and made his society to be courted by all. Ricardo was first known as an able political economist by his pamphlets on Finance Questions in 1810 and 1811; then by his essay in 1818; and by the assistance which he gave to the Bullion Committee; and latterly, by his more matured system, and by his speeches in Parliament. He was returned for Portarlington, to the proprietor of which he lent a large sum upon very honourable terms; and no man by so short a Parliamentary career (Horner perhaps excepted), ever gained so much influence in the House, or gained it upon grounds so honourable and so lasting. Ricardo died of an inflammation of the brain, brought on by an abscess. He was in the vigour of his age, being only in his 53d year; he left a widow, one married son, and two unmarried daughters, to weep for him as a model of husbands and fathers, – and the country to deplore him as one of its best and brightest ornaments.

In his person Ricardo was under the middle size; slender, but active; the air of his head was very acute, but at the same time very benevolent; and the expression of his face was candour itself. No man could look at Ricardo, without being pleased with him, – no man could hear him speack without feeling that every word which he said was not only his own fixed and deliberate opinion, but absolutely true in itself. As a philosopher he was extremely cute, and if he has not added much to the theory of political economy, he has greatly extended the practical knowledge of it. In the House of Commons he was always listened to with the most profound attention, as well for the importance of what he said, as for the manner in which he said it. He was at once the boldest and the most modest man in the House. Always upon the liberal side, he could not be said to belong to any party. On the principles of reform, he fairly out-ran the Whigs, and upon some questions (religious toleration for instance) where they felt the check-string, he spoke out; but he went not along with them in merely personal attacks. His death had left a blank upon the liberal side, which the present House cannot, and the present age may not supply. He was the real power which produced so complete an investigation of all matters of revenue and expenditure. Hume was, no doubt, the guerrilla, but it was Ricardo who supplied the materiel, and directed the master-movements; ay, and who saved the other when his own temerity had brought him within the enemy's lines, and exposed him to the bushfiring of such light troops as Croker. Upon the whole, no man had the will or the power of doing more good to his country than Ricardo; and there is not a man whom that country could so ill have spared.

The Morning Chronicle: Mill's Letter to the Editor

'Mr. Ricardo', *The Morning Chronicle*, Monday September 15, p. 1.

The following tribute to the attainments and virtues of Mr. Ricardo, is from the pen of one of the first names in English Literature: –

To the Editor of *The Morning Chronicle*.

Sir – Permit me to pay a tribute, in the name of my country, to the memory of one of the most valuable men, whose loss she has ever had to deplore. Perhaps no man was ever taken from his friends, having in their minds a mora unmixed sensation of having been deprived of one of the greatest blessings which it was possible for them to possess. His gentleness united with firmness, his indulgence tempered with prudence rendered him an object of affection and confidence to all connected with him, beyond what those who have not witnessed an equally perfect character can easily conceive.

The history of Mr. Ricardo holds out a bright and inspiring example. Mr. Ricardo had every thing to da for himself: and he did every thing. Let not the generous youth, whose aspirations are higher than his circumstances, despair of attaining either the highest intellectual excellence, ore the highest influence on the welfare of his species, when he recollects in what circumstances Mr. Ricardo opened, and in what he closed his memorable life. He had his fortune to make, he had his mind to form, he had even his education to commence and to conduct. In a field of the most intense competition, he realized a large fortune, with the universal esteem and affection of those which could best judge of the honour and purity of his acts. Amid this scene of active exertion and practical detail, he cultivated and he acquired habits of intense and patient and comprehensive thinking, such as have been rarely equalled, and never excelled.

The lights which Mr. Ricardo shed upon the science of political economy may be compared, either for difficulty or for importance, with those which have given renown to the very greatest names in the history of moral and political science.

A new field of exertion was opened to him in the house of Commons; and when one reflects on what he has done, and on what he was capable of doing, to accelerate the progress of enlightened legislation, it is difficult to point out another life the loss of which could be regarded as such an evil to his country.

It is universally known how signal a change has taken place in the tone in the house of Commons, on subjects of political economy, during his short Parliamentary career; and though he had the advantage of a Ministry, some of whom were sufficiently enlightened to be warm in the same beneficial course, yet they will not be among the most backward to acknowledge how much his clam and clear exposition of principles, his acute detection of sophistry, and unwearied industry, contributed to the general result; and they will not be among those who will be the most insensible to his loss.

Mr. Ricardo had given indication that his mind was not confined to the department of Political Economy, but embraced the Science of Legislation in its most extensive sense. When one reflects on the decisive exposition he had made of what he has essentially demanded as security of a good government; on his intrepid and ever memorable declaration in favour of unlimited freedom of thought, and freedom of speech, on subjects of religion; on the perseverance with which he pursued his objects; on the growing influence inseparable from his intellectual and moral character; on his total exemption from the vulgar trammels of party, and from all those weaknesses by which so many men of considerable parts render themselves the voluntary slaves of the interests and prejudices of the great, it is impossible to estimate the amount of obligation under which we might have been laid to that truly great man, had his life been prolonged some years for our service.

By affording insertion to this simple statement, you will gratify the feelings of one, who, in the death of Mr. Ricardo, has sustained a loss which can never be repaired, and who will cherish the recollection of this friendship, while sense and memory remain.

The Monthly Repository: obituary

'David Ricardo', *The Monthly Repository*, vol. 18, no. 213, September 1823, p. 551.

Sept. 10, after a few day's illness, at his seat, *Gatcomb Park, Gloucestershire,* DAVID RICARDO, Esq., Member of Parliament for Portarlington. The death of this gentleman, in the midst of days and of fame, has occasioned an indescribable shock to his family and friends. An abscess in the ear, a constitutional complaint, which extended to the brain, put an end to his valuable life. He was the head, and in one sense the founder of a large family, who looked up to him with affection and reverence. His sound mind, sterling integrity, nice honour and amiable manners, made him universally respected and beloved. By his talents he had acquired in the money-market a princely fortune, which was gained honourably and used generously. He is known to the English public, and to the literary and scientific men of Europe by his works on Political Economy, which evince an uncommon reach and peculiar acuteness of mind. He was regarded as the leading political economist in the House of Commons, where all parties agreed to show deference to his opinions. This universal respect is the more decisive proof of his great mental powers, as he was scarcely eloquent in the Parliamentary sense of the term, and as he maintained political principles to which the majority of the House of Commons are strongly opposed. With extraordinary talents he united great simplicity of character and urbanity of manner, and hence he was everywhere a favourite. On all great public questions he was with the people, and the reader will turn back with new interest to his admirable speech given in our last number, pp. 490–492, in support of the 'Christians' Petition against the Prosecution of Unbelievers,' – a speech the more manly and virtuous on account of the suspicions and opprobrium to which he knew himself to be subject from his origin among the Jewish people.

The Gentlemen's Magazine: obituary

'David Ricardo, Esq. M.P.', *The Gentlemen's Magazine*, vol. 93, July–December 1823, October, 1823, p. 376.

Sept. 11. At his seat, G P, co. Gloucester aged 51, DR, sq., M.P. for Portarlington. His death was occasioned by an abscess in the head, which, after causing as much torture as it was possible for the human frame to bear, broke, and is supposed to have produced a suffusion on the brain, followed very quickly by death.

He was a gentleman of distinguished abilities; and, as a political economist, had the faculty of discussing the intricate principles of that science with singular acuteness and perspicuity: his writings upon those subjects, indeed, constituted almost as marked an aera as the celebrated work of Adam Smith. In the H C, his opinions on subjects of a commercial and financial nature, were always received with the most respectful attention, as well from the general opinion of his profound knowledge of all the mysteries of commerce, as from his amiable disposition and conciliating manners. His loss will not be more regretted as a public man than as a private character: his exemplary benevolence to the poor – the enduring qualities of an affectionate husband and parent – and the generosity of a liberal and kind friend, combine to render his death a calamity universally deplored.

To him the country is indebted for the original plan by which the resumption of Cash Payments by the Bank of England was affected without danger.

Mr. Ricardo is supposed to have died worth 700,000*l*. He has left three sons. The eldest, Osman, has the estates of Bromeberrow, the White-leafed Oak estate, &c. To his second son, David, he has bequeathed Gatcomb Park. To the third, Mortimer, who is now at Eton School, Hadlow Place and Berrow, Kent. Five daughters have also liberal fortunes.

On the 18th, his remains were removed from Gatcomb Park, and interred in a vault in the parish church of Huish, about one mile and a half from Chippenham. The church is situated in the park of Mr. Clutterbuck, the son-in-law of Mr. Ricardo. The funeral was conducted in the most private manner, but nevertheless excited great interest in the town of Minchinampton, Tetbury, and Malmesbury, through which it had to pass. The attendants on the funeral were chiefly relatives – the three sons of Mr. Ricardo, Osman, David, and Mortimer, his six brothers, his three brothers-in-law, three sons-in-law, and some of his nephews. The Rev. Mr. Cockin, the Rector of Minchinampton, and Mr. Hume, M.P. intimate friends at Gatcomb, were the only mourner not related to the deceased. The coffin was plain, with the inscription – 'David Ricardo, died at Gatcomb, on Thursday, Sept. 11, aged 51.'

Among his financial and commercial works are the following: -the High Price of Bullion a Proof of the Depreciation of Bank Notes, 8vo, 1810. -A Reply to Mr. Bosanquet's Observations on the Report of the Bullion Committee, 8vo, 1810.-An Appendix to his work on the high Price of Bullion, 8vo, 1811.-Essay on the Influence of a Low Price of Corn on the Profits of Stock, 8vo, 1815.

An excellent mezzotinto portrait of Mr. Ricardo has lately been published, scraped by Hodgetts, from a painting by T. Phillips, esq. R.A.

The Penny Cyclopaedia: George Porter's entry

'Ricardo, David', *The Penny Cyclopaedia of the Society for the Diffusion of Useful Knowledge*, vol. 19, pp. 507–508, Knight, London, 1841.

Ricardo, David. To whom the science of political economics perhaps more indebted than to any other man of our day, was born in London on the 19th April, 1772. His father, a native of Holland, has then been for several years a member of the Stock Exchange in London; and designing his third son, David, for the same occupation, gave him a good but plain commercial education. For this purpose he was sent, when eleven years of age, to a school in Holland, where he remained for about two years. Soon after his return to England he was taken into his father's office as a clerk, and, when of age, was associated with him in business. In 1793 he formed a matrimonial alliance displeasing to his father, by reason of his religious scruples, the elder Mr. Ricardo having been born of Jewish parents, and continuing to profess their faith until his death. This breach between the father and son, which was afterwards entirely healed, necessarily caused their separation as regarded business, and threw the subject of this notice altogether upon his own efforts, seconded however, in manner highly honourable to all parties, by many of the leading members of the stock exchange. Mr Ricardo continued to be a member of the Stock Exchange until 1818, and was eminently successful in taking for many years a leading part in its business, and realising a princely fortune by conduct which gained for him universal respect.

During the years in which Mr. Ricardo was most actively engaged in business, he continued to devote much time to study and to scientific pursuits. He was of the original promoters of the Geological society of London, and for some years a member of its council; he also acquired a considerable knowledge of chemistry, as well as an acquaintance with mathematics. Of late years, the powers of his mind were almost wholly devoted to the elucidation of questions connected with political economy, a study which was at once best suited to the peculiar quality of his mind and most in unison with his daily pursuits in business, and by his attainments in which he was enabled to take his place among the deepest and most original thinkers of his day.

In the beginning of 1819, Mr. Ricardo was returned to parliament by the Irish borough of Portarlington, which place he continued to represent until his death.

The reputation which Mr. Ricardo had previously acquired by his writings ensured to him the attention of the House on all occasions when he spoke, and not unfrequently induced the members present to call upon him for his opinion when the subject-matter of the debate was such as might receive light from his extensive knowledge. Although he confined himself in his parliamentary speeches almost entirely to subjects of finance, and such as fell strictly within the line of economical science, his reported speeches are numerous; and although, form the nature of the subject which he handled, and with which the newspaper reporters could not be familiarly acquainted, it could hardly be expected that justice could be done to his reasonings, these reports yet furnish a full justification of the desire so constantly evinced by the House, and a more reason for the respectful attention which he always experienced. During each of the five sessions in which he sat in parliament, his name constantly appears as a speaker; and in the latest two years of the series (1822 and 1823) his addresses were very frequent. Although his voice was not good, and his utterance was rapid, it was yet so distinct, that he could be heard without an effort by every member present. His manner was wholly unpretending, and his argumentative style was relieved by any oratorical effort; he endeavoured to convince by reason, and to influence only by truth and justice. Those persons who had most narrowly watched the progress of his public career, felt justified in predicting for him a future of the highest usefulness; and had his life been spared, it is reasonable to think that their predictions would have been fulfilled. At the close of the session of 1823, he retired to his estate at Gatcomb Park in Gloucestershire, and, after a very few days' illness, died on the 11th September, of an inflammation of the brain, in the fifty-second year of his age. In private life, Mr. Ricardo was extremely amiable; his temper was mild and equable, and he enjoyed in the highest degree the respect and affection of every member of his family.

Mr. Ricardo first appeared as an author during the discussions that led to and accompanied the famous Bullion Committee in 1810. His pamphlet, which was entitled 'The High Price of Bullion a Proof of the Depreciation of bank Notes' (Ricardo 1810–1811) speedily passed through four editions, and occasioned the publication of several replies. His next publication was entitled 'A Reply to Mr. Bosanquet's Practical Observations on the report of the Bullion Committee;' and however much opinions may at that time have been divided upon the subject, it has long since been generally acknowledged that the victory rested with Mr. Ricardo. Although the peculiar interest which attended those discussions has long since passed away, Mr. Ricardo's pamphlet will be read with pleasure by all who delight in marking the case with which a man of superior intellect can trace and exhibit the constant and active operation of general principles through all the intricacies of practical detail.

In 1815 Mr. Ricardo published 'An Essay on the Influence of a Low Price of Corn on the Profits of Stock', in which he combated the justice of restrictions on the importation of corn; but the essay is chiefly remarkable for the doctrine which it propounds concerning rent.

The following year produced 'Proposals for an Economical and Secure Currency with Observations on the Profits of the Bank of England.' The principal recommendation put forth in this pamphlet was, that the Bank of England should be obliged to exchange its notes for gold ingots of a certain fineness, and not below a certain weight, at prices diminishing from time to time, until the price should be brought down from its then market rate to the Mint price of 77*s* 10 1/2*d*. per oz.

Mr. Ricardo great work, that upon which his lasting fame as an economist must rest, 'On the Principles of Political Economy and Taxation', was published in 1817, and was at once pronounced the most valuable contribution made to economical science since the days of Adam Smith.

In 1822 Mr. Ricardo again appeared as the author of a tract entitled 'On Protection to Agriculture,' in which he exposed certain fallacies and prejudices of the landed proprietors. The effect of legislative protection afforded to products of the soil upon wages, profits, public revenues, and non-agricultural branches of the national industry, are all discussed within the limits of eighty-seven pages, with a clearness and precision that may be said to exhaust the matter, and which prove the author to have been perfect master of the whole subject.

The only remaining work of Mr. Ricardo was found among his papers after his death, having been the latest matter of a public character that occupied his attention. This was his pamphlet in recommendation of a national bank, which was soon afterwards published by his family, in the exact state on which he left it probably only a few days before his death.

Index

agriculture 59–61; experimental farming 59–61, 122
Allen, William 56
Amsterdam 2–3, 7; and Ricardo's education 7–9; and Ricardo's family network 2, 11–12
anti–Semitism 1–2, 6
art and science 54–55, 120, 122–124
Aspland, Robert, Unitarian Minister 25–27, 31–34, 36, 116, 141–144
atheism: and morality 38, 131; Ricardo's hidden atheism 32, 41, 85, 130; and theodicy 159–160

Bagehot, Walter 166
Barclay, Robert 19–20, 26
Bayle, Pierre 75, 112, 125, 131–132, 158–159
Beccaria, Cesare 143
Belsham, Thomas 13, 30, 34–38, 45, 72–73, 80–81, 83–86, 106–107, 116, 141, 162
Bentham, Jeremy 46, 69–71, 73, 77, 112, 115–116, 136–137, 148–149, 152–153, 174
Bevis Marks Synagogue 1–6
Bosanquet, Ch. 69, 95–99
Bowring, J 40, 70, 173
Boyle, R 51
Brougham, Henry Lord 42, 88, 121, 143

Cambridge philosophy 76–78
Capadose, Avraham, Ricardo's relative 11
Capadose, Immanuel, Ricardo's relative 11
Carlile, Mary Ann, radical activist 144
Caroline of Brunswick, wife of King George IV 142–143

causality 103–109; causes and laws 80, 85, 115, 120; effects and causes 47, 58, 80–81, 86–87, 123, 156, 165, 173; multi-causality 105; temporary or accidental causes 104–105, 107–111
chemistry 26, 46–52, 56, 59–62
Corn Laws 61, 79, 105, 123–124

Davy, Humphrey, Professor of Chemistry 57, 59
definitions 52–55, 57–58, 79, 85, 98–103, 137; see also logic
Delvalle Lowry, Rebecca, Ricardo's aunt 12, 48–49
Delvalle Ricardo, Abigail, Ricardo's mother 2, 23
Descartes, René 96, 106
Destutt de Tracy, Antoine-Louis-Claude 100

Edgeworth, Maria 2, 5, 9, 22, 40, 133, 136–138, 153
Edinburgh Review 61, 66–70, 118, 121, 144
Enlightenment 5, 11–12, 29; see also Haskalah, Scottish Enlightenment
epistemology see logic
essences vs. phenomena 35, 67, 81, 85, 101–102, 106–107, 109, 115
ethics 83–84, 72–73, 76–78, 130–136; beneficence 72, 154, 174; Cambridge consequentialist voluntarism 76–78; Hartley and Priestley's ethics 81–84; moral impressions 130; natural morality vs. revealed morality 130–132; rational pursuit of happiness 139; utilitarianism 69–70, 73, 84, 135–138; see also lying; penal law; private morality; war

evil *see* theodicy
experience *see* facts; logic; theory

facts *vs.* laws and general principles 67–69, 78, 80, 86–87, 95–96, 99–100, 106, 131; *see also* logic
Fleck, Ludwik 121
Foster, Thomas, leader of a Quaker secession 26–27
Foucault, Michel 121

Geological Society of London 53–61
geology 26, 46–63, 103, 122, 173
Godwin, Richard 84
Goldsmit, Isaac Lyon, financier, Britain's first Jewish baronet 144
gravity, law of 104, 106
greatest happiness principle *see* utilitarianism: utility
Greenough, George Bellas, chairman of the Geological Society 57–58

Haldimand Marcet, Jane 49
Halévy, Élie 69, 106, 112, 120–121
happiness: and desire of approbation 147–148; and family life; and cultivation of the intellect 134; and felicific calculus 137; fragility of 116, 134, 138–139; rational pursuit of 139; and wealth 133–134; *see also* human nature
Harris, John 102
Hartley, David 79–82
Haskalah 5
Hollander, Samuel 11, 89, 119
Horne Tooke, John 103
Horner, Francis 61, 66–69, 96, 118
Horner, Leonard 61
Horton, Wilmot, MP 158
human nature 134, 147; desire of approbation 134–135, 147–148; indolence 138; love of distinction 138; self-deception 132–133; *see also* happiness; self-interest
Hume, David 66, 96, 107, 132, 160
Hume, Joseph, MP 32, 144, 160–161,
Hutton, James, chemist and geologist 52–54
hypotheses 52, 54, 76, 80, 96, 98, 115, 119; realism of 98, 107, 110, 120, 173

interest *see* self-interest

Jeffrey, Francis 68–69, 70, 79
Judaism 1–14; *see also* Haskalah

Kant, Immanuel 29, 36, 107, 124, 158–159
Kirwan, Richard 52–56; *see also* Geological Society; Hutton
Kuhn, Thomas 97–98, 118–119

language, theories of 98–103; questions of 136; scientific 98–99, 102–103; *see also* definitions; logic
Lavoisier, Antoine–Laurent de 51–53, 59
laws of nature 36, 77
laws or principles 36, 66–68, 74–75, 77–78, 80–81, 85–87, 95–97, 100, 103–111, 120, 145, 163–165, 173–174, 188; *see also* logic
Lindsay, James 38–40, 144
Locke, John 38, 83, 132; on language 101–103, 116; on toleration 30, 33–34, 37–38
logic 94–124; limits to knowledge 38, 83, 85, 105, 138, 163; *see also* causality; definitions; essences; hypotheses; strong cases
London Institution 50–51
Lowry, Wilson, Ricardo's acquired uncle 48–49
Lowry Varley, Delvalle, Ricardo's cousin 49–50
lying 133

Mallet, John Lewis, Secretary of Audit Office 1, 163
Malthus, Thomas Robert 76–79, 85, 96–101, 103–111, 114–124
Marcet, Jane *see* Haldimand Marcet, Jane
Martineau, Harriet, essayist and philosopher 29–31
Marx, Karl 109, 144, 166
McCloskey, Donald 98
McCulloch, John 9, 75, 94, 104, 153, 157
metaphysics 38–39, 48, 55, 79, 162–163; *vs.* science 66–67, 107
method (methodology) *see* logic
Mill, James 71–76, 96, 107, 112, 115, 122, 135–137, 147–152, 156–157, 159–161, 165

natural order 109
natural price/value 97, 100, 108–109, 155
Newton, Isaac 58, 61, 67–68, 72–73, 76–78, 80–81, 96, 106–107, 115
Nieto, David, London's Sephardic Chief Rabbi 4–5, 11

optimism *see* theodicy
Oriel School 94
Owen, Robert 85, 156, 163

Paley, William 77, 84, 133–134, 139, 144, 146, 161
permanent states and causes 58, 62, 98, 105, 107–111, 124
philanthropy 153–154
Philosophic Radicals 69, 71
phlogiston 51–53
Place, Francis 70, 136, 157
political economy, definition of 100
politics: art of government 67; extension of the suffrage 146–151; good government 67, 146–152; public opinion 147–151, 178; science of legislation/of politics 74–75, 85, 146–148; secret vote 148, 150–151; *see also* self–interest
Poor Laws *see* poverty
population, principle of 75, 104, 109, 114, 154–156, 161, 164
Porter, George, statistician, Ricardo's brother-in-law 9, 24, 47
Porter, Sarah *see* Ricardo Porter, Sarah
poverty 53, 114, 133, 154–158
Pownall, Robert 68
price *see* natural price
Priestley, Joseph 29, 31, 36–37, 51–52, 59, 66, 72, 80, 82–83, 102, 106–107, 116
principles *see* laws
private morality and penal law 142–143
Providence 4, 36–37, 162–164
public happiness 81, 86, 138, 164–165

Quakers 18–27, 30–31, 50, 140, 143

realism of hypotheses *see* hypotheses
reform *see* politics
religion: faith as a practical attitude 35; Hindu religion 160–161; and morality 130–132; rational belief 35, 83, 162; *see also* Judaism; Quakers; theodicy; theology; toleration; Unitarians
rent 71, 79, 97, 99, 103–104, 107, 122, 154, 162–163
rhetoric 94–98
Ricardo, Abraham Israel, Ricardo's father 2, 5–6, 9–10, 22–25
Ricardo, Moses, Ricardo's brother, medical doctor 7, 50
Ricardo, Samson, Ricardo's brother, MP 7

Ricardo Porter, Sarah, Ricardo's sister, novelist and essayist 7, 50
rights, innate/natural 34, 136

savings banks 153, 155
Say, Jean–Baptiste 86–88, 97, 100, 112–113
scepticism *see* limits to knowledge; logic
Schopenhauer, Arthur 118
Schumpeter, Joseph Alois 88, 94, 124
science *see* art and science; logic; laws; strong cases
science of legislation *see* politics
Scottish Enlightenment 54
Scottish Philosophy 39, 66–69, 71–76; *see also* Stewart; Dugald
self-interest 72, 77, 81–84, 86, 116; and benevolence 84; and sympathy/desire of approval 148
self-love *see* self-interest
Senior, Nassau William 94, 117–118, 166
Sismondi, Jean Charles Léonard Sismonde de 13, 97
slavery 56, 143
Smith, Adam 25, 41, 61, 66, 68, 97, 112, 119, 134, 143, 160, 163,
Smith, Thomas, Unitarian friend 32–33, 40–41, 133–134
Sraffa, Piero 7, 31, 38, 46–47, 58–59, 74, 89, 130
state of nature 97–98
Stephen, Leslie 166
Stewart, Dugald 55, 66–67, 69, 72–73, 75, 96, 102–103, 106–107
strong cases 109–112, 121–122, 141
Stuart, James 97
style, scientific 98; *see also* Fleck, Ludwik
Sumner, John Bird 158, 161–162, 164
sympathy 81–82, 134–135, 148

tendencies 103–104
Tennant, Smithson 60
theodicy 37, 158–166
theology 29–30, 76, 162; lack of objective criteria in theological matters 34–35, 162; natural 56; rejection of 20, 162; revealed 56
theory: practical men 46, 95, 99; pure 94–96, 119; questions of theory and questions of fact 111; simplicity 52, 57; theory and experience 94–96; *see also* logic
Thornton, Henry 50–51

toleration and unbounded freedom of
  opinion 19, 22, 32–33, 37–40, 83,
  143–146; Dr. Lindsay's principle 40,
  144; Unitarians on 30
Trower, Hutches 109, 130–131, 138, 146
Turgot, Anne-Robert-Jacques Turgot 97

Unitarians 29–45; Essex Street Chapel
  29, 32, 34, 38; New Gravel Pit Chapel
  31–34; *see also* Belsham, Thomas;
  Hartley, David; Lindsay, James; Priestley,
  Joseph
Utilitarianism 69–76, 82, 84, 135–138,
  151–152
utility: principle of 98, 137–138, 149;
  Ricardo's objections to the 'doctrine of
  utility' 135–138; and value 112–117

value 97, 111, 122; labour theory of 75,
  79, 97; measure of 79, 99–100; natural
  79; and utility 70, 87, 100, 112–117;
  and wealth 100
Verri, Pietro 143

wage *see* natural price
Wakefield, Edward, Ricardo's land
  agent 61
Wakefield, Gilbert 30
war: just war 140–142; Napoleonic
  wars 70; Quakers on 19–21;
  Ricardo's volunteer
  service 142
Watson, Richard 132, 159,
Watts, Isaac 13, 59, 78, 94,
  96, 101
wealth (riches) 87, 104–105, 113, 117,
  133–134; and value 100
Weber, Max 166
West, Edward 97
Whately, Richard 104
Whittle Harvey, Daniel, *Sunday Times*
  editor 23, 179–183
Wilkinson Ricardo, Priscilla, Ricardo's
  wife 21–27, 33, 116,
  134, 153
working classes 138, 156,
  157–158

Printed in Great Britain
by Amazon

23863856R00117